D1737172

Transformation Through Global Value Chains

TRANSFORMATION THROUGH GLOBAL VALUE CHAINS

Taking Advantage of Business Synergies in the United States and China

Behnam N. Tabrizi
and
Mitchell M. Tseng

STANFORD BUSINESS BOOKS
An Imprint of Stanford University Press
Stanford, California 2007

Stanford University Press
Stanford, California

Library of Congress Cataloging-in-Publication Data

Tabrizi, Behnam N.
  Transformation through global value chains : taking advantage of
business synergies in the United States and China / Behnam N. Tabrizi
and Mitchell M. Tseng.
    p. cm.
  "Stanford Business Books."
  Includes bibliographical references and index.
  ISBN 978-0-8047-5482-8 (cloth : alk. paper)
    1. International business enterprises—China—Management—Case studies.
2. International business enterprises—United States—Management—Case
studies. 3. Business strategy—China—Case studies. 4. Business strategy—
United States—Case studies. I. Tseng, Mitchell M. II. Title.

HD2910.T33 2007
658'.049—dc22   2007012197

Typeset by James P. Brommer in 10/13.5 Sabon

Contents

Preface

The rapid rise of manufacturing capability in China is turning that country into a dominant player in the world economy. In the meantime, the largest homogeneous market on Earth is emerging. Few businesspeople can afford to ignore a new market of more than 1.3 billion individuals with one common language, a similar cultural background, and rapidly increasing living standards. These and other critical but less visible forces are significantly changing the landscape of global competition. They affect not only the way businesses operate from day to day but also the very models on which businesses are based. It is difficult to find a major U.S. company that does not have a presence in China. At the same time, almost every major Chinese company has a growing presence around the world. Companies worldwide are all facing complex challenges in their global value chain spanning from strategy to design, production, logistics, supply chain, information technology, sales, and marketing. It is clear that we need a new cadre of business professionals to help companies thrive in this new economic order.

Since 1994, both Stanford University and Hong Kong University of Science and Technology have recognized the necessity for education programs to address this need by partnering with businesses. We, the authors of this book, along with our esteemed colleague Hau Lee of the Stanford Graduate School of Business, foresaw China's rapid economic rise as well and, also since 1994, have been working with industries on various projects and interacting with students of various levels. We have developed a revolutionary project-based course based on the following specific objectives:

- To articulate a global vision, with emphasis on synergies between the United States and China
- To serve as a bridge between the needs of industry and the skills and experience of academics with extensive industry background
- To facilitate global value chain problem solving for companies' stakeholders
- To learn to work with people of different cultures

This book is a collection of solutions for various companies' global value chain challenges. We have written it with assistance from teams of graduate students from both Stanford University and Hong Kong University of Science and Technology. The companies profiled here were selected on the basis of their needs and the issues they were facing. Our diverse global industry and consulting experience, together with Hau Lee's credibility in supply chain management, opened up many challenging and exciting projects for us. The graduate students who participated in our global project coordination program were chosen through a highly selective and rigorous process in which their research expertise, relevant work experience, and analytical skills played a key role. These factors were also considered in placing them on a particular project team. All of the cases presented articulate detailed solutions to our global clients' real-world problems. In a few cases, as per the client's request, the actual name of the firm is not revealed.

The cases are organized into chapters that deal with a particular facet of the firms' value-chains, thus highlighting the comprehensive breadth of the work that has been accomplished. From waste management issues in an apparel production company to suggestions for strategic expansion of a niche player in supply chain management, we first clearly identified the problems and then provided thorough suggestions and solutions to address the issues. In this way the cases are exceptional in their clarity in stating the problem and demonstrating appropriate solutions. In addition, much of the material presented reflects on the growing industrial might of China. Each case involves a firm that does business with China or with Chinese firms, demonstrating how China has emerged as a major outsourcing location for electronics and apparel production and manufacturing. Conversely, the book also presents an unbiased and realistic picture of the business environment in China and will help readers become aware of the challenges in outsourcing to China, such as communication and language barriers, lack of transparency in transactions, and transportation issues (applicable mostly to inland regions). In some of the cases, such challenges have had enough impact to influence the firm to outsource somewhere besides China. The book also illustrates the growing sophistication of business processes in many Chinese firms and, more surprisingly, an increasing trend among Chinese manufacturers to address and respond to the demands of the sophisticated North American market.

Chapter Organization

Taking a top-down approach to a firm's value chain, the book starts by discussing strategy. Chapter 1 looks at the strategy as a part of the value chain. To garner long-term growth while maintaining profitability in the short term, firms need to have clearly defined short-term and long-term goals as well as specific plans of action to accomplish these goals. This chapter presents two cases with focused suggestions on expansion strategies appropriate for two competitive companies operating in different industries, both doing business with China: PCH International, an outsource supplier of computers and consumer electronics; and Lil Lawton, a manufacturer of children's garments.

Chapter 2 is concerned with sales and marketing operations. Sales and marketing are the functions most closely related to a company's realized cash flows and they are the operations most visible to the outside world. The supporting case explores how HKS Products strives to reach customers by using a new tool, providing an example of how innovative, technology-driven solutions can aid the sales and marketing process.

Globalization of operations has allowed many firms to benefit fully from the competitive advantages that exist among countries. However, spreading operations across the world and sourcing component supplies thousands of miles away have introduced a whole new set of problems for today's global firm and have exposed its operations to complicated risk factors. Logistics and supply chain issues can have dire impacts on a business's bottom line. Late arrival of an order in a seasonal industry, for example, translates into lost customers, reduction of the firm's market share, and deprivation in the firm's current and future cash flows. An inefficient supply chain for parts and components can have serious ramifications for the firm's production capacity. The cases in Chapter 3 focus on companies that deal with logistics issues and supply chains. The first case analyzes the value added to a fast-growing supply chain management company by deploying radio frequency identification (RFID) across its supply chains to provide for better service and increased efficiency. The second case provides an in-depth look at the necessary strategic decisions and risk analysis in designing the supply chain. In this case, the firm chooses to source its production in a higher-cost region because of reduced risk.

In Chapter 4, the focus changes to information technology (IT) system capabilities. IT is a crucial part of the value chain because of its role in supporting crucial business processes. Managing the growth of the IT organization through optimal allocation of resources and by creating IT applications that have clear business targets (such as aligning IT with business processes) is of great importance to any firm that plans to leverage IT to enhance its operations and derive value from the technology. These two points are the underlying themes of the cases presented in this chapter. In the case of GTP America, the firm was dealing with governance issues in growing and aligning its IT organization. The case provides concrete suggestions that address these issues. The second case, about a region in China that is seeking to utilize a Web-based IT platform to assist non-Chinese companies that are planning to invest, depicts the crucial role of IT applications in providing mission-critical services to clients. The case analyzes the impact of such a comprehensive IT platform and provides a detailed functional analysis of such a system.

The final chapter deals with the most fundamental value-generation step in a manufacturing firm's value chain: the production process. Production has a pronounced impact on a company's underlying profitability because of its close association with value creation; however, most of the fixed and variable costs are incurred during the production process as well. As a result, minimizing waste, implementing industry best practices to create efficient processes, and introducing innovative methodologies that leverage advances in technology are of utmost importance for a manufacturing firm. This chapter presents three cases. The first two involve Esquel Group, a world leader in garment manufacturing. The first case analyzes applications of RFID in the company's spinning mills and provides suggestions for process reengineering across the entire value chain as a result of deploying RFID. The second Esquel case involves cost minimization through waste management. The case looks in detail at Esquel's production process and carries out statistical analysis to clarify sources of wastage. The third case focuses on Sterling Products Ltd., an apparel manufacturer, and examines how it can improve its processes to shorten production prototype lead time.

The Intended Audience

Instructors who would like to inject real-world practice into educating future managers and decision makers will find this collection of chapters a helpful guide to the scope of problems that are reasonable to tackle in a twelve-week period. Furthermore, the cases presented can provide benchmarks or examples to follow for ongoing efforts by student teams. This book may prove to be the perfect educational tool, especially in a graduate engineering curriculum, for making students realize the underlying nature of business problems in an increasingly global environment.

Industry practitioners will find the cases offered here to be of high quality and a great source of many analytical tools and best practices. In some cases, our team of experts applied their own research expertise to the solution of problems, adding depth and innovation in creating tools to solve business problems.

Behnam N. Tabrizi
Stanford, California

Mitchell M. Tseng
Clear Water Bay,
Kowloon, Hong Kong

Acknowledgments

We are indebted to the Management Science and Engineering Department at Stanford University, and the Industrial Engineering and Engineering Management Department at Hong Kong University of Science and Technology (HKUST) for their unwavering support over the last decade.

Professor Hau Lee of Stanford Graduate School of Business not only served as cofounder of this innovative global course, but also has been an impetus behind several projects in this volume. We appreciate his continued support and strongly feel that we could not have sustained this course without his unassuming support and inspiration.

Our administrative assistants, Isabel Cossio of Stanford University and Rebecca Tsang of HKUST, have been the backbone of this program throughout the years; they have always met the unforeseen challenges with grace and compassionate poise.

We would not have succeeded without the initial contribution and encouragement of Lynn Fritz from Fritz Institute, and the support of our sponsoring companies, including Bernhardt Furniture, Dow Chemical, Esquel Group, General Motors, Gymboree, PCH International, HKS Products, Nokia, Nortel, Novell, Sterling, Cisco Systems, Lucent, Lexibook, and Wyse. We are truly indebted to all of them.

Three of our students played key roles in the completion of this book. We first would like to thank Cyrous Jamé for his passion and intellect in assisting us in the selection, integration, and categorization of the chapters, and for serving as a window to our demanding editor. Next, we acknowledge the effort of Rami Bitar for his meticulous assistance in creating a workable template for each case, and for ensuring standardization, clarity, and coherency across the cases. We would also like to thank Rohit Acharya for his contributions to the final stages of ensuring the accuracy of the manuscript.

Above all, we thank our excellent students for their contributions to the cases in this book. Stanford students Maria Gonzales, Vaibhav Gupta, Junrae Kim, and Florence Thng and HKUST students Deanna Ding, Ho Keng San, Janet Kou, and Howard Lam worked on the PCH expansion strategy case in Chapter 1. Among the contributors to the HKS Products Ltd. case in Chapter 2 were Daryl Chen, Judy Chen, Jay Preston, and Jason Shore from Stanford University and Dionne Lam, Victor Li, Ricky Tong, and Sheldon Wang from HKUST. Stanford students Kelly Bayer, Anne Robinson, Patrick Sagisi, and Yancey Smith and HKUST students Au Yim Lee, Chan Kwun Kiu, Wong Siu Hang, and Zhang Xiaoke contributed to the Garment Retailer case in Chapter 3. Stanford students Vaihbav Jain, Cyrous Jamé, and Oliver Wai and HKUST students Jacky Chow, Eric Wang, Kelly Sze, and Heidi Yip contributed to the PCH RFID logistics tracking system case in Chapter 3. In Chapter 4, the GTP case received contributions from Maher Aoun, Rami Bitar, Sri Harsha Kolar, and Adrian Mak from Stanford and Jennifer Ji, Ivy Lin, Jason Ma, and Ricky Tang from HKUST. Stanford students Jackie Chang, Christian Nassif, and Victoria X. Wu, and HKUST students worked on the ABC case. Stanford students Shyam Jankar, Roma Jhaveri, and Kenneth Cheung and HKUST students Kevin Zhang, Rosita Au, Chris Wong, and Gali Lee contributed to the Esquel RFID in spinning mill production planning case in Chapter 5. Stanford students Zoe Chu, Tiffany Hinton, and Angel Kong and HKUST students Anna Chan, Angela Cheng, Michael Chui, and Kaibo Wang worked on the Esquel production waste forecasting case, also in Chapter 5. We especially thank the members of our original class, who were also contributors to the Lil Lawton case in Chapter 1 and the Sterling case in Chapter 5: James Ahn, Lyndell Asbenson, Eric Bannasch, Patrick Chan, Judy Chen, Christine Fair, Tzu-tsen Kuo, Trevor Loy, Jason Moen, Jack Poon, Diogo Rau, and Balaji Sundararajan from Stanford and Jiao Jian Xin, Wong Hoi Ming, Lin Yu Fu, Au Mun Shan, Yien Tsang Sum, and Lin Fu Hua from HKUST.

Finally, we thank all the students who took our class in the past decade. It is they who provide the inspiration for us to continue bridging the gap between global companies and academia, and to provide creative solutions to intricate global value chain challenges.

1 Strategy

This chapter introduces cases that highlight strategy as an integral part of the value-creating process. Strategy is an appropriate starter because it glues together underlying value-creating processes ranging from production to sales and marketing. Strategy provides an overall direction to these processes and harmonizes their integration into a solid value chain. Although at each stage tactics are used in daily operations to overcome and smoothen issues, strategy contributes to a top-down plan for the entire value chain. A key point about strategy is that it is dynamic. Although a firm may be successful in executing its adopted strategies, even successful firms must constantly reevaluate their approach in light of continual market changes. In today's global economic environment, where economic barriers are constantly falling, constant change is a given. Firms move into each other's market space, constantly revamp their product lines, merge, or engage in hostile or friendly takeovers. Whatever the means, the purpose is to realize synergies, to achieve even higher levels of efficiency, and to maximize profits and shareholder value. In these ever-changing conditions, a successful approach to strategy calls for constant evaluation and adjustment of strategic positions on the basis of feedback on past and present operations and future market projections. The speed at which a firm can execute necessary changes in strategy is important and plays a central role in the overall success of the company.

Two cases are studied here. The first case focuses on PCH China, a firm that is discussed further in Chapter 3 (on supply chain management and logistics). In this chapter, PCH is experiencing rapid growth and has adopted an expansion strategy to catapult itself into the position of primary outsource supplier of computers and consumer electronics. As a result of this strategy, the consulting team has been asked to recommend organizational structures and requirements that would best align with such an expansion and to suggest a marketing strategy and business flow model to support the growth. The consulting team begins with SWOT (Strength, Weakness, Opportunity, and Threat) and Porter's Five Forces analysis and then carries out detailed analysis of each of PCH's four divisions to gauge each division's value and requirements as part of the greater strategic goal of the company. As a part of suggesting a marketing strategy, the team first segments the potential audience of PCH's sales team and comments on how to approach each segment. Further, the importance of brand equity and a marketing communication plan are discussed. Finally, the team provides a three-phase implementation plan for the needed changes. Its success depends on how quickly the changes can be implemented.

The second case illustrates a competitive player in the children's clothing market. The company, dubbed Lil Lawton (a pseudonym used at the request of the client), is a retailer facing a slowdown in growth and a fierce competitive environment in its primary market, the United States. In pursuit of a strategy to foster sustained growth, the firm is looking into entering other markets. The firm feels that East Asian markets could provide such an opportunity. In line with this strategic goal, the consulting team carries out market research on current market size, the nature of the competition, and growth potentials for Asian markets. Two markets in particular, China and Hong Kong, have been of special interest, and the researchers carry out detailed quantitative analysis on these two markets. On the basis of that analysis, the team suggests immediate entry into the Hong Kong market followed by a limited presence in the Chinese market. The team feels that an initial presence in China would provide the firm with a relatively risk-free test bed for its future buildup in the potentially huge Chinese market.

Case 1: PCH China

Market Segmentation and Analysis

Global supply chain management is our business. Working in partnership with our customers, we cater to their needs of competitive pricing, quality, and on-time delivery, as well as ethical sourcing.

—Mission Statement, Li & Fung, Inc.

This quote is the mission statement of the world's current largest sourcing company in the fashion and apparel industry, Li and Fung.[1] Today, PCH is referred to as the Li and Fung of the computer and consumer electronics industry. As companies globally are increasingly outsourcing consumer electronics manufacturing to China, the world's fastest growing nation in terms of gross domestic product, PCH is witnessing an exponential rise in year-over-year sales volume. The company is experiencing growing pains as it rapidly scales up its capacity to handle increases in customer transactions and build an employee base.

PCH has requested the services of a research team to recommend a new organizational structure that is in line with its expansion strategy and to develop a business flow and marketing strategy to support PCH's goal of becoming the world's largest outsource supplier in the computer and consumer electronics industry.

Background

Company Information

PCH was established in Ireland, United Kingdom, in 1996. Today its major operations are based in China. PCH provides supply chain solutions for global computer and consumer electronics companies. After China entered the World Trade Organization in 2001, companies around the world had increased access to sourcing opportunities in China. To capitalize on this trend, PCH positioned itself to become the "Pacific Coast highway" that would connect Western businesses and entrepreneurs to low-cost Eastern manufacturers of commodity goods.

Today PCH has relations with more than fifty Asian manufacturers who deliver quality products at competitive prices to customers worldwide, and thus serves as an important link in the global value chain. The company also provides services to reduce lead product manufacturing times and improve supply chain efficiencies.

Project Definition

PCH offers its supply chain management (SCM) services through its four subsidiaries: Engineering Design Solutions (EDS), Quality Assurance Solutions (QAS), Enterprise Software Solutions (ESS), and China Turn-key Solutions (CTS). Each of these subsidiaries has a unique mission and capabilities and is responsible for the various services that PCH offers.

To maximize the potential of PCH and its subsidiaries, the research team was charged with identifying the infrastructure requirements, assessing the value proposition, and segmenting the market for each of PCH's services. (Figure 1.1 summarizes the parameters of the team's project.)

Analysis

SWOT Analysis

The SWOT analysis provided useful insight into the main strengths and weaknesses of PCH.

Strengths. As a company based in Mainland China, PCH has developed intimate knowledge of the region that translates into a core competency. PCH takes responsibility for the proprietary title of the products it manages; thus it offers a convenient and attractive risk management solution to its customers. Moreover, PCH has an open-book policy about its transparency to its clients. Because PCH has virtual offices in many countries (Hungary, Mexico, the United States, Ireland, and China), the sun never sets on PCH, thus providing an attractive service benefit to customers. Customer service is highly valued at PCH, and the company has not lost a customer since its inception. Finally, PCH offers a one-stop solution that is highly valued in the industry.

Weaknesses. PCH lacks a clear execution strategy for growth and expansion. Internal and external communications are not optimal. PCH's CTS subsidiary began operating in March 2004 and therefore has to overcome the learning curve fast in order to maximize its benefits and

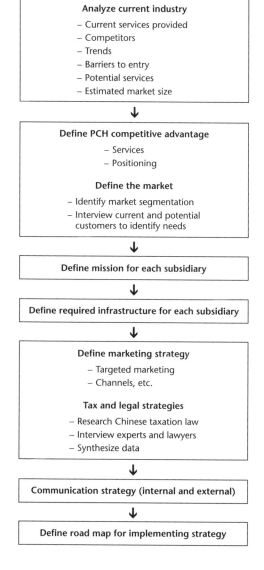

Figure 1.1   PCH research project methodology

capitalize quickly. Historically, PCH has not been proactive in capturing new opportunities.

Opportunities. PCH has identified several growth and expansion opportunities. First, it can expand its offerings to include local contract manufacturing in Mainland China. PCH can leverage its rapid raw material sourcing ability to capture a lead-time advantage from the competition. Second, the computer and electronics aftermarket may provide growth opportunities for PCH in Asia, Europe, and the Americas thanks to less stringent regulations. As another alternative, PCH can also conduct business with the consumer electronics retail channel. Finally, PCH can explore opportunities in the computer and electronics industry's growing reverse logistics market.

Threats. The global consumer source manufacturing market is a dynamic, fast-paced environment. PCH relies on established relations with key people at its client organizations, which may not represent a sustainable advantage, because there is also a need to build new relations. PCH must continue to understand the changing regulations in Mainland China.

Competitive Environment

An analysis of the competitive environment using Porter's Five Forces model (see Figure 1.2) provides an industry overview of the environment and highlights the drivers of the business.

Barriers to Entry. The barriers to entry are moderate, for the following reasons:

- Entering the SCM industry requires low capital investment.
- Switching costs for standard components are low (because they are perceived as commodities).
- It is difficult to develop a reliable supplier network.
- Monitoring government regulations is challenging because such regulations are constantly changing.

Suppliers' Bargaining Power. The bargaining power of suppliers is low, for the following reasons:

- Currently, suppliers are not consolidated; they are generally small and fragmented.

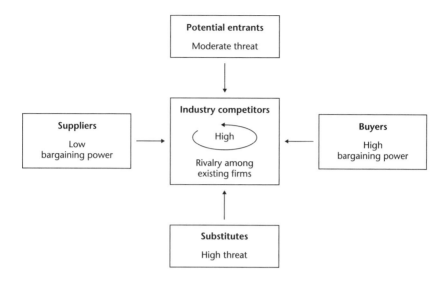

Figure 1.2   Porter's Five Forces

- Suppliers do not have resources for direct selling; sometimes they lack the necessary client network and suffer from language barriers.
- There is no threat of forward integration.
- The products managed are mainly commodities.

Currently, many suppliers within the region are not consolidated within a group or organization. This allows PCH to gain competitive pricing agreements from manufacturers that allow PCH to consolidate its list of vendors. Manufacturers who do not sell directly rely on PCH to source their business.

Buyers' Bargaining Power. The bargaining power of buyers is high for the following reasons:

- Buyers generally purchase in large volume.
- There are few switching costs because they are dealing with standard products.
- There is a credible threat of backward integration.

Because PCH provides high-volume, low-cost, low-technology products, large-volume purchasers, such as brokers and traders, compete in the region to serve foreign companies. The low level of switching costs for those standard products might decrease PCH's bargaining power with its customers. At the same time, many buyers have their own resources for comparing prices within the region. PCH must have a very strong bond with its customers in order to maintain its business.

Substitutes. Pressure from substitutes is also high, for the following reasons:

- There are many traditional traders and brokers and this damages PCH's reputation because PCH can be perceived as a middleman who does not add value to the value chain.
- Few small and medium-sized Chinese manufacturers sell directly to Western organizations.
- There are not credible electronic exchanges (Web marketplaces) where companies can trade products.

Rivalry Intensity. The intensity of rivalry is high for the following reasons:

- Because PCH's products are regarded mainly as commodities, there is strong competition over price.
- Currently there are only a small number of players.
- There is also a lack of differentiation among the current players. It is very difficult to differentiate PCH's business from that of similar competitors in Mainland China. Because they are selling almost exactly the same products, PCH must find a way to stand out from other companies, perhaps by changing from a product to a service orientation in which the product managed is not the main focus.

Industry Trends

It is important to estimate the size of the market where PCH can offer its SCM services. As mentioned earlier, PCH has been called the Li & Fung of the computer electronics industry; the market should therefore be analyzed relative to this industry.

It is first necessary to understand the making of the present network of orders and supply chains (see Figure 1.3). Original equipment manu-

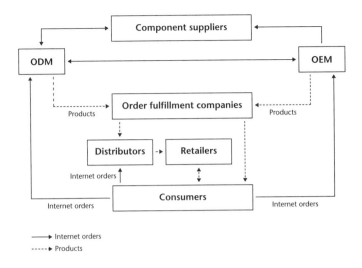

Figure 1.3   Industry network

facturers (OEMs) are gradually becoming merely brand owners. More-over, original design manufacturers (ODMs) are developing their own brands, which in the future may compete with those of the OEMs. In this arena, PCH fits into the order fulfillment role by providing services to every player in the game. Finally, the trend is that ODMs will out-source more of their low-value-added functions, and this will be a good opportunity for PCH to grow.

Other market trends are also important to PCH's business model. Among them is the customer preference for establishing a relationship with a service provider that offers one-stop solutions. This preference is a matter of convenience, because the costs (time and resources) associ-ated with managing the relationship decrease as the number of vendors decreases through consolidation. Moreover, the Sarbanes-Oxley Act of 2002, established to regulate corporate financial practice and gover-nance in order to protect investors, demands the increasing transparency of financial information, thus requiring managers to reduce inventory costs. Also, tier 1 freight carriers are moving into specialized logistic and supply chain services, which represents a clear threat to PCH because these freight carriers have the infrastructure advantage and expertise in logistics.

Recommendations to PCH and Its Subsidiaries

Engineering Design Solutions

Description. Engineering Design Solutions (EDS) provides services related to industrial and electrical design. It helps organizations to materialize concepts and ideas. It also provides design and redesign services. The customers of EDS include OEMs. Competitors include ODMs and design houses that focus on providing design services, such as IDEO and Titoma.

Value Proposition. EDS's mission is to provide product-design services to the computer and electronics industry. Its value proposition should focus on designing for manufacturability in China along with offering a vertically integrated service, from design to vendor sourcing to turnkey solutions. Thus EDS's bottom line should be to help companies reduce the time to market for design products and to reduce the costs associated with design and vertically integrated service.

Required Infrastructure. EDS should quote prices via an account manager from PCH. When a new design comes out, EDS should have in place the operation processes required to apply for intellectual property (IP) rights. EDS could register an office in Nansha Park of Science and Technology in Guangzhou because of its proximity to major government and corporate offices and its convenience for recruiting designers and engineers.

At the back end, EDS could also prototype and test the new design, splitting up the parts sourcing among multiple vendors approved by EDS's sister subsidiary QAS to learn and continuously train and update the skills and collaboration tools. As EDS gradually grows it can form an IP team to do IP database checking, IP protection, and IP registration, and a research and development (R&D) team for product development.

The holding cost for EDS to provide design services is minimal and EDS can position itself to design products (industrial design) that can be manufactured in China or to design manufacturing processes, such as R&D deployment. To ensure that a customer's design will not be used for other purposes, EDS can post a "Statement of Position Regarding Intellectual Property," as Flextronics does,[2] to gain trust from its customers. When EDS designs, it should consider the regulations issued and enforced by the Occupational Safety and Health Administration (OSHA) and the Environmental Protection Agency (EPA).

Enterprise Software Solutions

Enterprise Software Solutions (ESS) offers Web-enabled software solutions, including StatusFlo, which helps companies that purchase products from China track and monitor their orders; QuoteFlo, a quotation management solution; and FreightFlo, which calculates freight charges. ESS is currently developing other supply chain software functionalities, including forecasting software, decision support tools, and inventory cost control mechanisms for ensuring Sarbanes-Oxley compliance. ESS's customers include all PCH clients (who will use the software to track orders managed by PCH) and small and medium-sized U.S. businesses that outsource from China. ESS's competitors include, among others, companies that offer supply chain management solutions, supplier relationship management solutions, product lifecycle management solutions, and e-procurement suites.

Value Proposition. ESS's mission is to provide Web-based supply chain software solutions for managing outsourcing. Because its value proposition is to offer customized supply chain software solutions for outsourcing, it must also offer software solutions that provide an intuitive and relevant experience for the user and that allow faster decision making within the organization. ESS's bottom line is to provide software solutions related to SCM that allow companies to increase efficiency and maintain low costs.

Required Infrastructure. ESS has already registered as a company in Ireland, United Kingdom. It could also target small and medium-sized businesses in Mainland China and provide excellent and relatively cheaper software to them, as well as customer service and after-sale maintenance. Meanwhile, ESS is taking a role in maintaining Web-based CTS and its vendors' inventories as well as maintaining subsidiaries' databases, including the IP database, which will be used by both EDS and CTS. ESS should also implement radio frequency identification technology in CTS's factory because many customers are adopting this technology.

At the back end, ESS should be responsible for improving PCH's hardware infrastructure and ensuring the security of the system as well as for performing self-maintenance and product development.

ESS has two software development options: one is to outsource it, which would incorporate the costs of both the software and training; the other is to self-develop the software, which would incorporate R&D and maintenance costs and the need to consider IP rights, income tax, and value-added tax.

Quality Assurance Solutions

Description. QAS offers factory audit and evaluation services along with quality certification, work-in-progress audit, final product and packaging inspection, and loading supervision. Its customers include any company that sources from China and wants to verify the quality of the products manufactured there without establishing a presence in China, and Chinese vendors who want an external party to certify the quality of their product. QAS's competitors include full-service testing and certification companies based in Asia and focused on quality assurance services, such as Intertek-ETL Semko; supply chain solutions based in China, such as Vision Asia; and quality inspection specialists that offer their services in China.

Value Proposition. QAS's mission is to provide quality assurance services for computer and electronic products manufactured in China. Its value proposition should be to offer credibility to its customers regarding quality services for products manufactured in China. Moreover, it should leverage the knowledge it has of the region and provide a full range of quality services from factory auditing to product inspection. QAS's bottom line should be to offer services that reduce risk to its customers and increase the reliability of Chinese suppliers.

Required Infrastructure. On its front end, QAS requires an account manager who is deeply knowledgeable about the services it can offer and who can develop pricing according to the company's policies. Moreover, it needs customer-reporting software by which clients and the audited facilities can access relevant information. Finally, it must have access to dispute resolution resources to support customer service.

On its back end, QAS needs certified auditors, International Standards Organization licenses and all the government permits required to operate in China, and the certified facilities and resources to perform testing and auditing services. Finally, QAS will require the customer-reporting software mentioned in the front-end requirements.

China Turnkey Solutions

Description. CTS offers services such as cross docking (an inventory management system that eliminates warehousing costs by having all vendors deliver to a single location where products are aggregated and shipped out immediately), kitting (a pick-and-pack service for localizing or customizing products made up of different components), export documentation, and provision of localization and postponement. CTS's customers include OEMs based in the United States and China, contract manufacturers, small and medium-sized businesses that outsource to China, and distributors and retailers. Finally, its competitors are SCM providers with global presence (such as Modus and Saleslink), third-party electronic fulfillment service providers, and top-tier freight providers such as UPS and FedEx.

Value proposition. CTS's mission is to provide kitting and assembly services for the computer and electronics industry. Its value proposition enables postponement and reduces the excess and obsolescence inventory by providing flexible manufacturing services. Moreover, PCH provides logistical integration services. The bottom line of this subsidiary should be to increase the flexibility and reduce the response time associated with products that companies outsource to China and to reduce the costs of manufacturing in general.

Market Segmentation. CTS should focus on products that are manufactured in China; that are high-volume and small; that require, first, low-skilled labor for the cross-docking and kitting solutions, and second, low capital investment; and that are labor intensive. The objective is to add value through the Chinese manufacturing location.

On the basis of the service the product requires, the market is divided into two groups of products: standard and localization (see Figure 1.4). Localization products require customization according to country or

	Standard market segment *example: CD cases*	**Localization market segment** *example: power supply, frequency*
Attractiveness	Large volume	More value added
Switching costs	Low	Medium-high
Potential customers	Watches (Timex)	Apple, cell phone company

Figure 1.4   Market segments

type of product; for example, power-supply products have to meet different standards in European countries than elsewhere.

Required Infrastructure. At the front end, CTS will quote prices to both customers and vendors through the PCH account manager. Then it will acquire components from vendors to kit and pack. In addition, CTS should have a customer service strategy and develop its import and export expertise to handle all the required documentation. ESS tracking software is also an important requirement for CTS operation.

At the back end, Long Hua, where CTS is located, has a relatively inexpensive labor force and a spacious environment, and it is near the Hong Kong and Yan Tian ports, which handle both imports and exports. CTS needs to take care of reverse logistics or rework products. It should also make sure that parts are always ready to enable postponement. To better meet market demand, CTS must perform statistical analysis to forecast that demand.

PCH Solutions

PCH operates as a single point of contact for its clients, offering demand-driven supply chain services, design (through EDS), quality inspection (through QAS), inventory management (through ESS), and cross-docking and turnkey solutions (through CTS). It also offers vendor inventory management. Its clients include, among others, all those mentioned for each of the subsidiaries—OEMs based in the United States and China, contract manufacturers, small and medium-sized businesses that outsource to China, distributors and retailers, and Chinese vendors. Its competitors include Linmark, contract manufacturers, and brokers and traders (see Figure 1.5).

Value Proposition. For PCH to achieve its goal of becoming the Li & Fung of the computer and consumer electronics industry, its value proposition should focus on providing a one-stop solution for its customers and in general to make it easier to do business in China. Moreover, it should maintain its knowledge of the region because this knowledge clearly provides PCH with an advantage over its competitors. The credibility that PCH has with its customers and suppliers is extremely important.

Market Segmentation. PCH should focus on providing a one-stop service solutions organization. Moreover, it should concentrate on products

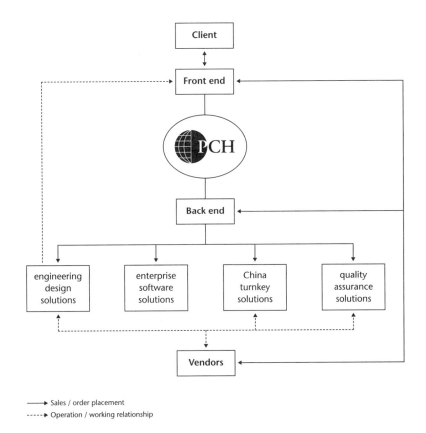

Figure 1.5   PCH supply chain

manufactured in China that are not high-tech. It should also prioritize establishing long-term relationships with its customers and suppliers.

The market segments for PCH are defined according to two variables. The first variable is the outsourcing experience of the client, who may have no previous exposure to outsourcing, some outsourcing experience but no experience outsourcing to China, or outsourcing experience in China. The other variable is PCH's familiarity with the type of products required. This familiarity can range from totally unfamiliar to highly experienced.

The most attractive market segments are, first, those potential clients with whose portfolio PCH is most familiar, because PCH knows this industry's behavior and trends and its suppliers' and customers' needs and thus can provide short-term responses; and, second, those potential clients who already have experience outsourcing to China, because PCH will have to make almost no marketing effort to convince these customers to value PCH's services. These potential clients are an attractive market niche because they represent an opportunity for PCH to expand its service offerings, and because these clients want to diversify in order to decrease their risk and will value the ease of doing business in China through PCH's solutions.

An example of the market segments appropriate for PCH to pursue (including the names of companies that were chosen for illustration purposes) is shown in Table 1.1.

Required Infrastructure. Finally, PCH requires at its back end the services that the four subsidiaries offer. It also requires corporate functions that are outsourced (such as human resources, accounting, and so on). A key element of PCH's infrastructure is its sales team, which will become a major component of its strategy and its success.

PCH has two front ends, one with customers and one with suppliers. For its customers, PCH must be physically present and have a business development function that manages its public relations. It is also necessary for PCH to define its strategy for holding and its strategies for the subsidiaries, including the pricing, customer service, and sales and marketing strategies. Finally, it is essential that PCH educate its clients about its business model.

For its suppliers, PCH must leverage its business development in China.

Table 1.1
Audience, concerns, key messages, and format for PCH marketing

Audience	Concerns	Key messages	Format
Sales people and account manager	Job security Sales revenue Client relationship Credibility	Market segmentation Pricing policies Compensation Defining boundaries Service metrics Industry and market trends	Internal Web site Customized e-mail newsletter Video conference Scheduled meetings
Supplier manager	Supplier relationship Quality Identify new suppliers	Supplier selection criteria Manufacturability capabilities Scope of the company Raw material sourcing	Socializing (local) Brown bag (case presentation: what they do within PCH) 360-degree evaluation (customer, supplier, sales, etc.)
Operations people	Information sharing Prioritization of resources Continuously update skill set	Flow of key operation processes Key responsibilities	
Management team and investors	Growing the company (revenue, market share, scope) Communicating with team (two-way) ROI Management team Risk (sustainability of the business model)	Performance of company Projections KPIs (key performance indicators)	
Everyone		Direction and vision of company Services range offered Communication protocol Key responsibilities	

It is also necessary that PCH have a strong presence in China, to recruit suppliers and to educate these suppliers about the PCH business model.

Sell-Focus Strategy

As has been said, the sales team is crucial for the success and sustainability of PCH's business model. Salespersons should engage in a proactive approach in which they identify the potential needs of PCH's customers and approach them with a preconceived solution. Moreover, they should be familiar with industry trends and, most important, with PCH's resources, limitations, and services. It is therefore necessary to develop a sales strategy specific to the potential client. Following are different sales messages suited to the value propositions most relevant to the intended audiences.

CFOs and Financial Controllers

Chief financial officers are concerned mainly with the financial performance of their organization. Moreover, the Sarbanes-Oxley Act requires that the accounting practices of companies that trade in any U.S. market must operate with a high degree of transparency. PCH should be able to provide its services in a way that enables the client company to reduce its inventory costs. Entitlement and transparency should be highlighted as ways of reducing the number of days of inventory.

Procurement Staff. A salesperson approaching a procurement executive should consider that these executives are concerned mainly with reducing the number of vendors from whom they purchase supplies and services. PCH should therefore stress its ability to offer a variety of products. (Because PCH is a service company, it can expand its range of products according to customer requirements.) Because PCH offers a one-stop solution, the procurement executive should prefer a relationship with PCH over relationships with many suppliers who do not have a global presence (in the United States and Europe) and who might lack customer and other value-added services that PCH offers. Also, PCH salespersons should emphasize PCH's ability to offer postponement as well as the right product at the right time at the right cost.

Engineers and Technical Staff. Finally, if the client contacts are engineers, PCH salespersons should draw attention to PCH's product flexibility and to the expertise its people offer regarding the products the engineers want to outsource.

Brand Equity

PCH currently has a well-established relationship with its existing clients, indicated by the high rate of repeat business and referrals. The main challenge in growing the PCH brand is to educate potential as well as current customers about the services PCH offers. This can be achieved with a public relations strategy that includes press releases and exposure in highly visible trade publications.

Additionally, PCH has to develop a proactive approach in which it seeks new services that clients require. We recommend that PCH hire a business development person to manage its public relations campaign and familiarize customers with the PCH business model and growth strategy.

Communication Strategy

To accomplish its mission, PCH should communicate with all its members using different formats and channels (see Figure 1.1).

Implementation Road Map

The implementation road map is divided into three phases. The first phase consists of quick hits that PCH can implement in less than three months. The second phase consists of short-term approaches that can be implemented in less than one year. Finally, the third phase consists of long-term recommendations that should be implemented in more than one year.

Quick-Hits Implementation. PCH should hire a business developer-manager to promote its services. This manager should be located in the United State to supervise the marketing strategy of PCH in the Western market. Moreover, PCH should rebrand itself as a unique service provider rather than as solely a cable supplier or broker. PCH should also increase its internal communication and communicate the new vision and services to the whole organization. For this reason it should establish adequate communication channels (suggested in the communication strategy presented earlier).

Regarding people management, PCH should define clear responsibilities and communication protocols (that do not become bureaucratic) to allow quick response time and effective business management.

To increase the effectiveness of its sales force, PCH should standardize the presentation format it uses to approach customers. Moreover, the management team should design the pricing strategy and policies for each of the services, the subsidiaries, and the holding offer. Finally, for IP purposes, PCH should establish EDS's presence in Guangzhou.

Short-Term Implementation. In less than one year, PCH should reorganize its sales force. It should analyze customer segmentation and design strategies for approaching each type of client. Regarding training, PCH's sales force should be constantly updated on the industries and on the technologies used by the companies so that customers perceive them as experts. PCH should also establish strategies to reorganize its sales team according to the type of customer, such as current clients or new clients. It should diversify its current portfolio of customers and build its image as a supply chain service provider in order to achieve its long-term mission of becoming the largest sourcing company in the computer and consumer electronics industry.

Finally, PCH should also build the required infrastructure to operate fully its subsidiaries and partial-stake holdings.

Long-Term Implementation. PCH should focus on becoming the computer and consumer electronics industry's Li & Fung, to which it has already been compared. It should continue to diversify its customer base. Finally, PCH should also consider divesting its subsidiaries in order to focus on its core business functions.

Discussion and Conclusions

The concept of strategic planning has become synonymous with the phrase "solution to business problems." In fact, the strategic plan appears to be most businesses' most vital product. To keep pace with today's highly competitive and fast-growing business environment, every company needs to learn the game plans of the "big guys," the top players in the field. Good strategic plans are essential tools for the success of any business, but they are not the ultimate goal in and of themselves.

As explained previously, a company needs to look first at the basics that will help position it strategically and aid its development in the direction in which it aims to go. One needs to understand the organization's goals, the industry trends, and the company's internal strengths and weaknesses (among numerous other things) before one can develop a clear growth strategy for the organization. Strategy is a road map that tells one where to head. All the actions one takes should align with the strategy. However, no strategy should be set in stone. It should be periodically revised in relation to changes in the industry.

Case 2: Lil Lawton and International Expansion

Charlene Brown, director of business development at the Lil Lawton Corporation,[3] looked at her watch. It was already past 7:00 P.M. and she was still in the office, poring over preliminary studies and database reports on the children's wear market in Taiwan, Hong Kong, and Mainland China. The decision for international expansion was weighing heavily on her mind, and she knew she would be asked at next week's meeting with CFO David Carey and CEO John Lawton to recommend whether or not Lil Lawton should take steps to move into a new overseas market.

U.S.-based Lil Lawton, a competitive player in the children's clothing market since the early 1960s, prided itself on being one of the leading retailers of durable, practical daily wear for children under the age of eight. Its high-quality products, brand image, and excellent customer service had made the company one of the top competitors in the domestic children's wear market.

With fierce competition and sluggish trends in the domestic children's clothing market, Lil Lawton anticipated that within the next five years it would reach saturation in the U.S. market. In a series of lengthy meetings over the course of several weeks, Brown, Carey, and Lawton discussed several strategic directions the company could take to continue to expand its business and increase its profitability. These directions included expanding its catalog business to supplement its stand-alone retail stores, expanding its current product lines, and venturing into completely new lines of products, such as clothing for adults. These options, however, did not seem like long-term solutions to the looming problem of domestic saturation. International expansion seemed to be a more promising next step for the company. The company had already decided to enter the Canadian market in the late summer or early fall of 1996 after an analysis of the market's size and potential. The company's products and business practices could be easily transferred to Canada, and typical barriers to international entry, such as duties, language problems, and distribution channels, were nonissues for Lil Lawton's entry into Canada.

The real potential market for children's clothing, however, was thought to lie not in North America but rather in the Far East. In countries such as Taiwan, Hong Kong, and China, where the combined population was on the order of billions, the natural growth rate was as high as 14.39 percent, manufacturing and labor costs were relatively low, and overseas brands were often highly valued, the potential market for children's clothing could be enormous. However, a number of issues remained to be resolved before Lil Lawton could decide to enter the market in any of these countries. What kind of information would Lil Lawton need to gather about the market before it could make a sound decision to enter it?

Brown's mind was swimming at the complexity of the decision. She knew that making the right call was crucial to Lil Lawton's future, and that if Lil Lawton decided to enter the market, execution would have to be efficient and accurately positioned. Poor positioning, early or late entry, or insensitivity to specific cultural expectations could cost the company millions of dollars.

Domestic Apparel Market

The U.S. apparel industry is quite large. In 1994, total sales at the wholesale level were $78.4 billion. Apparel retail sales were approximately $211 billion in 1994, about 4.3 percent of disposable personal income.

At the retail level, apparel is typically priced at one of four levels: popular, moderate, upper moderate, and upper. The domestic apparel market can also be divided into two tiers: (1) national brands, and (2) small brands and private labels.

National brands account for about 30 percent of all U.S. wholesale sales of apparel and are produced by one of twenty rather sizable firms. These manufacturers include publicly traded companies, divisions of publicly traded companies, and privately owned companies. Firms include Fruit of the Loom, OshKosh B'Gosh, Phillips-Van Heusen, and Levi Strauss.

Small brands and private-label establishments tend to be privately held. In 1992 there were approximately 23,048 firms involved in apparel manufacturing. These small units are either manufacturers, jobbers, or contractors. Manufacturers take care of the entire production process, from designing to finishing. Jobbers design their apparel, buy the materials, and arrange the details of selling the product, but they contract out most of their sewing and finishing. Contractors receive precut garments from jobbers and make them into finished products.[4]

The domestic apparel industry has always been highly labor-intensive, even with the advent of more modern technology such as highly automated manufacturing equipment and computer-aided design (CAD) systems. Wage costs and low profit margins continue to be a major factor in locating production facilities. Specifically, many clothing manufacturers seek low-wage developing countries to increase razor-thin margins. Some companies, such as Levi Strauss, have shifted much of their production overseas to take advantage of Tariff Item 807 of the U.S. tariff schedule. This tariff allows a U.S. company to do some of its production overseas and then import the partly finished products back to the United States, thus paying duties on only the value added part abroad.[5]

What Affects Apparel Sales?

Three primary factors drive apparel sales: developments in the economy as a whole, consumer attitudes and demographic trends, and fashion.[6]

1. Economy. Consumers generally spend more money on clothing when the economy is strong than when it is weak. For instance, from 1983 to 1990, the U.S. economy was growing and disposable income was rising at an annual rate of 7.2 percent. Apparel expenditures also increased at 6.8 percent annually during this time. However, in the early 1990s, growth in disposable income slowed and, correspondingly, apparel expenditures also dropped.

2. Consumer Attitudes and Demographic Trends. General attitude changes of the population affect the kinds of clothes people buy. For instance, in the 1980s, most people tended to buy clothes on the basis of image instead of cost because they wanted to be associated with a particular brand or designer. In the 1990s, however, this trend shifted and consumers began to focus more on price and value. Demographic trends have had a major impact on apparel sales as well, particularly in the children's wear segment. For instance, in the late 1980s and early 1990s, many children were born to parents who were, relative to parents in preceding decades, older, more highly educated, and more affluent and thus able to spend more money on their children's clothing.[7] This trend is certain to have an effect on the growth of this segment in the coming years.

3. Fashion. While fashion trends have typically been a driving factor in clothing sales, particularly in women's apparel, no strong trends developed in the 1990s.

Lil Lawton Today

Today Lil Lawton offers full lines of gender-specific basics and accessories. It prides itself on the quality of its products and its excellent customer service. Marketing director Alison Duback described why she believes Lil Lawton's clothes are superior to those of its competitors:

> Our 100 percent cotton clothing is comfortable and durable. We avoid the fleeting trendiness of many children's styles and popular cartoon characters, which tend to raise the price and quickly become outdated. Instead, we focus on simple, playful patterns and solid colors. Our clothes are machine washable, and colors do not fade no matter how often they are washed.

Ellen Payback, director of sales training, described Lil Lawton's philosophy on service:

> Our exclusive retail stores offer full lines of our products and all of our stores have the same floor layout to give our customers a sense of familiarity at any Lil Lawton store. We have a committed sales force dedicated to serving our customers and establishing customer loyalty. Our highly trained staff is eager to help the busy shopper quickly find the coordinates she needs and to offer creative ideas for outfits. Our sales staff is required to undergo a number of training sessions to understand the needs of younger children. Lil Lawton stores are well lit and childproof. Because we are interested in giving the customers what they want, we often call our regular customers to ask them what we can do to improve our service and what kinds of clothing attributes they are looking for before we enter a new season. We believe that Lil Lawton offers the best and most consistent quality service in the children's wear market anywhere.

Company History

Lil Lawton was founded in 1965 by John and Hillary Lawton, a Virginia couple who recognized the need for affordable, durable playclothes for children. Most of the children's wear available in the market at that time, Hillary discovered, was either overpriced or of poor quality. Hillary found that making clothes for her own children was an affordable alternative to control the style and durability of the clothing. The Lawton children's clothing elicited frequent inquiries and compliments from other parents with young children. The Lawtons' neighbors began ordering small numbers of their children's clothes from Hillary. Word spread and by 1966 the Lawtons found themselves managing a small business.

The Lawtons ran their business from home, taking orders by phone and allowing word-of-mouth to serve as their only form of advertising. In June 1968, order turnaround time was approximately three days. However, by January 1969, orders had more than doubled. As their staff grew, the Lawtons found it impossible to work out of their home. Armed with an entrepreneurial spirit and a $20 thousand investment of their own money, in March 1969 the couple opened their first Lil Lawton store in a major shopping mall in Arlington, Virginia. Hillary continued to oversee the general design of the clothing and John served as general manager of the store. Clothing production was sent to a contractor twenty miles north of Arlington.

The first Lil Lawton store was an instant success. By the end of the fiscal year, the company had achieved net sales of $21,477 and carried a line of mostly unisex playclothes and some gender-specific dressclothes. In 1970, Lil Lawton went public with an initial stock offering of $17. By the end of that fiscal year, shares were selling at $31.25. Between 1972 and 1984, Lil Lawton expanded its product line by introducing a full line of gender-specific children's apparel; accessories such as shoes, caps, socks, and belts; and high-quality bedding materials such as blankets and pillows. By the end of 1984 Lil Lawton had expanded to 125 stores in forty-eight states.

From the time of its inception in 1966 to 1984, the company focused on building brand equity and customer loyalty by offering the highest-quality products at a reasonable price. It targeted the middle- to upper-class family and sold exclusively through its own stand-alone retail stores. Because Lil Lawton wished to communicate its philosophy of great everyday value, it never promoted special sales or discount prices. It prided itself on quality products for which cost per wear was substantially lower than for competitors' poorer-quality products. Further, Lil Lawton relied on little external advertising and instead focused on word-of-mouth advertising and growing a loyal customer base through excellent customer service and a good product.

However, in the late 1980s, with a growing number of competitors and increasingly competitive prices in the market, Lil Lawton took on a new strategy, code-named Operation Baby. In an offensive move to grab market share and increase brand awareness in the domestic market, it launched a full-scale advertising campaign featuring full-page ads in all major parenting and home care magazines. In 1990 it expanded its distribution channels to include a catalog, which it sent to current customers and upper-middle-class homes with children under the age of eight. It began to sponsor a free monthly children's educational hour featuring puppet shows, storybook readings, and interactive games in public libraries, community centers, and schools. John Lawton, CEO for Lil Lawton in 1991, stated, "Lil Lawton's image for the 1990s is one of community. We wish not only to provide our customers with a wide variety of quality, affordable clothes, but also to communicate our commitment to the future of our community's children through our educational Lawton Learning programs."

In the early 1990s, Lil Lawton's net sales rose steadily at an average of 35 percent per year, from $92 million in 1990 to $342 million in 1996. The number of stores increased steadily, to a total of 320 stores in the United States by 1996. (See Table 1.2 for additional financial information on Lil Lawton.)

Examining the Asia Pacific Market

When growth of the domestic market slowed due to decreased consumer spending and fierce price competition from competitors, Lil Lawton estimated it would reach saturation of the U.S. market by 2001. Like many other U.S. manufacturers, Lil Lawton was targeting international markets as a vehicle for growth. Other leading U.S. manufacturers of clothing, such as Levi Strauss, Russell Corporation, and Fruit of the Loom, had already found their way into Europe. Children's clothing competitor OshKosh B'Gosh was already recognized internationally in Asia, Australia, Europe, and the Middle East.

Japan, the European Community countries, and Canada were the largest customers for U.S. apparel as of 1994. Although Lil Lawton was already planning to enter the Canadian market by late 1996, it recognized that the Asia Pacific market, particularly Taiwan, China, and Hong

Table 1.2
Lil Lawton Financial Data, 1992–1996

	1996	1995	1994	1993	1992
Operating results					
Net sales	342,822	263,709	181,868	143,203	103,771
Operating income	71,223	64,912	63,750	57,076	56,874
Net income	37,912	35,668	32,703	28,774	23,911
Net income per share	4.81	3.21	3.25	2.19	1.02
Weighted average shares outstanding	31,339	32,423	30,419	34,854	31,035
Balance sheet data					
Working capital	129,435	120,754	118,064	106,376	98,912
Total assets	210,437	202,845	182,302	142,993	119,649
Total stockholder equity	241,837	200,453	155,917	141,392	123,099
Operating data					
Number stores open at end of period	317	281	251	206	189
Net sales per average store	1,932,945	1,649,392	1,020,589	1,843,546	775,035
Net sales per average gross square foot	735	731	754	662	612

Kong, seemed to promise greater long-term potential for growth. U.S. manufacturers of clothing often had a reputation in the Asia Pacific for high quality and seemed to be associated with high status and popular Western styles.

Playing in the International Market: Things to Consider

The decision to expand into the Asia Pacific market was a complex one for Lil Lawton. As a relatively small player in the U.S. market, did the costs of expanding into the Asian market exceed the benefits? What costs of business needed to be considered? What were the shopping habits and customer preferences for children's clothes in the target markets? And how should Lil Lawton approach gathering information to answer these questions?

Charlene Brown tidied her desk and packed up her belongings to leave for the night. As she closed the door to her office, the words of John Lawton echoed through her mind: "Lil Lawton is at a critical stage in its thirty-one-year history. Our decision to expand into the Asia Pacific market is the most pivotal decision we have faced yet."

Hong Kong and Chinese Market Assessment

Charlene Brown along with David Carey and John Lawton began intensive research on the children's wear market in Hong Kong and China to ascertain Lil Lawton's market potential in the Asia Pacific region. Because a rapid but thorough decision-making process was necessary, Lil Lawton enlisted the aid of an international independent research group. The group was charged with ascertaining the potential market for children's wear in China and Hong Kong and with providing both quantitative and qualitative assessments of the market size and of competitors. The research group consisted of four members stationed in the United States and three members operating out of Hong Kong.

Over the course of three months, the research team attacked the problem from a number of angles. It gathered demographic data and information on buying behavior in the target countries to estimate the potential market size. It characterized the customer and product profiles to understand whether Lil Lawton's current products could meet market needs and wants. Finally, it conducted a quantitative and qualitative analysis of current competitors in China and Hong Kong.

Data and information were collected in one of four ways: through a written questionnaire distributed in the target countries, through a focus group of young parents with children in Hong Kong and China, through library and database research, and through walk-in interviews of employees and customers in competitors' retail stores.

The Asian Market

Hong Kong and China represent burgeoning potential markets for a number of industries. Large populations, lower labor rates, increasing consumer spending on clothing and footwear, and rapidly expanding markets all have served to entice U.S.-based apparel retailers into the Asian Pacific markets.

People's Republic of China

In terms of overall size, China is the second largest consumer market in Asia after Japan. Buoyed by rising household incomes, China's consumer market has been expanding rapidly during the past decade. Retail sales for consumer goods grew by 18 percent and 26 percent respectively in 1992 and 1993.

China's consumer market, marked by the presence of one-fifth of the world's total population, represents enormous sales and marketing opportunities for consumer goods manufacturers and distributors. With an average growth rate of 1.3 percent per annum, China's population is expected to rise from 1.186 billion to 1.3 billion by the year 2000.

China's expanding retail sales had been buoyed by substantial increases in people's income. In 1993, the country's total payroll rose by 21 percent to RMBY [renminbi yuan, currency of Mainland China] 477 billion. Annual per-capita living expenses by urban and rural residents were RMBY 2,377 (+28 percent) and RMBY 921 (+18 percent) respectively.

Reports such as these provided a positive outlook on China's market potential. Lil Lawton noted that in 1990, children below the age of nine constituted almost 20 percent of the country's population of 1 billion. Keri Davies, a lecturer in the Department of Marketing and Institute for Retail Studies at the University of Stirling, Scotland, stated, "Infant and child-oriented products are also big sellers. In Guangdong, the combination of China's single-child policy and relatively high discretionary incomes is creating a phenomenon known as the little emperor syndrome. In most homes in the province, no expense is spared in meeting the needs of the family's one child, and the market for disposable diapers, baby food, fashionable clothes, and toys is growing rapidly."[8]

Despite the growing market and perceived demand for children's apparel and accessories, Davies identified four areas of concern for foreign retailers in China: consumer demand (lower levels of disposable income and poor distribution channels), retail price inflation, currency movements (rapid devaluation of the renminbi), and smuggling and counterfeiting. Lil Lawton realized that entering the Chinese market would require looking beyond the positive evidence of market growth and into other complex issues.

Hong Kong

The total market in Hong Kong was US$7.64 billion in 1993 and was estimated to grow at an annual rate of 5 percent in the next three years. Imports from Japan, Europe, and the United States have generally dominated the children's wear segment, although in the mid-1990s, well-established local manufacturers were also beginning to compete successfully in the market. Italian, Japanese, and French products were the largest competitors in the mid- to high-end market that Lil Lawton would target, taking 2.6, 1.2, and 1.1 percent, respectively, of the total import market in 1993.

With children aged two to twelve making up 12.5 percent of the total population in Hong Kong in 1994, there was tremendous potential for U.S. exporters in the children's wear subsector. In addition, rapidly rising disposable income had made higher-priced, higher-quality clothing affordable to Hong Kong's people.

Besides the potential market, Hong Kong had long been considered China's window to the world—a strategic gateway to foreign business contacts, modern technology, and investment. More than half of China's exports are handled by Hong Kong, and Hong Kong is China's second largest trading partner, accounting for 18 percent of the country's total trade in 1994.[9] Despite labor rates comparable to those of the United States, and no import taxes, other business costs could be prohibitively high for small U.S. retailers. Land and property rental rates in some popular shopping areas, for instance, were as high as 800 percent of U.S. rates. Political changes were an additional concern in entering the Hong Kong market. At midnight on June 30, 1997, Great Britain would relinquish its governance of Hong Kong, and Hong Kong would become a special administrative region (SAR) of the People's Republic of China. The treaty between Great Britain and China that created the SAR of Hong Kong guarantees that Hong Kong will remain a capitalist enclave until at least 2047. However, companies interested in the Hong Kong market have been advised to watch the political and economic changes in China carefully because Hong Kong's economic life is directly tied to China's future.

Assessing Market Size

To estimate the total market size of cotton clothing for children under the age of eight, the research team explored a number of data sources from the World Bank, the Hong Kong Trade and Development Council, on-line databases, and articles.

A top-down approach was used to estimate the realistic potential market size for Hong Kong and for China. In each case, estimates began with the national expenditure on clothing and shoes for adults and chil-

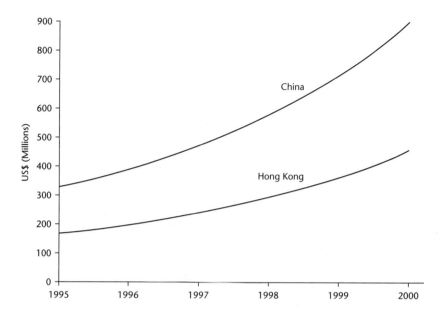

Figure 1.6   Five-year market projections for children's clothing

dren. Shoes, fabric, and noncotton clothing were excluded from the estimates. Estimates of the percentage of the population over eight years old were obtained from demographic data, and clothing expenditures within that population were excluded. Accounting for only urban markets further reduced the market size. Finally, the market size was reduced to include only the percentage of customers with the target household income levels. In the case of China, the market size was estimated for the three cities with the top clothing expenditures in the country: Shenzhen, Guangzhou, and Shanghai. Additionally, because of the proximity of Shenzhen and Guangzhou to Hong Kong, Lil Lawton could leverage Hong Kong advertisements.

The team estimated that the 1996 market size for children's cotton clothing for upper- and middle-class families in urban areas in Hong Kong was US$170 million, with an annual projected growth rate of 22 percent. The China market size was estimated to be US$321 million. In the three selected cities combined, the market size was estimated to be US$8.1 million, with an average growth rate of 22 percent. By 2000, the team estimated, Hong Kong's market size would be US$460 million, and China's would be almost US$900 million. (See Figure 1.6.)

Survey

Purpose. To better understand the customer profile and the buying behavior of the consumer, as well as general market sensitivity, in China and Hong Kong, the research team conducted a written survey in Hong Kong and in two target cities in China. Assessing the customer profile—such as the relative importance of price, quality, customer service, brand name, and durability—would help Lil Lawton determine whether it would need to alter its products to suit the market. Knowing the buying behavior of consumers would help the company target price and channels correctly. The survey would also give some indication of the sensitivity of the Asian market with respect to advertisements, U.S. brand names, manufacturing locations, and clothing attributes.

Design. The survey was divided into four main sections. Each section was designed to collect different information about the market. (See Table 1.3.)

- Demographics. The survey began with questions about demographics, such as household income, ages of the participant and spouse, and ages of their children. Demographic information would help to determine how representative the survey answers were of the population as a whole.
- Self-stated importance scale. This section of the questionnaire was designed to question the relative importance to customers of each major clothing attribute. The customers were asked to rank on a scale of one to five the importance of each of ten attributes: price, fashion, design, color, quality, customer service, brand name, pattern, durability, and softness.
- Multiple choice and fill-in-the-blank. A number of multiple choice and short-answer questions were asked to determine the buying habits of consumers.
- Kano questionnaire. The last section of the questionnaire was structured to help Lil Lawton understand the relationship between product characteristics (such as color and durability) and customer satisfaction. (See the appendix to this chapter for the theory behind the Kano method.)

The U.S.-based research team wrote the survey in English and then passed it on to the Hong Kong–based members for translation into Mandarin.

Table 1.3
Hong Kong and China children's clothing questionnaire

Section I

1. Please list gender and age of each child in your family.

	Child 1	Child 2	Child 3	Child 4	Child 5	Child 6	Child 7	Child 8
Gender								
Age								

2. Please circle the range of your and your spouse's combined annual household income. Convert to Hong Kong and China income range:

Under $30,000

Between $30,000 and $50,000

Between $50,000 and $75,000

Over $75,000

3. Please give us information about yourself and your spouse.

	Yourself	Your spouse
Gender		
Age		
Occupation		
Circle the highest education level you have completed.	1. Primary school	1. Primary School
	2. Secondary school	2. Secondary school
	3. University degree	3. University degree
	4. Postgraduate degree	4. Postgraduate degree

Section II (Please answer the following questions.)

My three favorite children's clothing brand names are:

1.

2.

3.

The three most important attributes I look for when buying clothes for my child/children are (please list the most important first):

1.

2.

3.

The top three attributes that I avoid when buying clothes for my child/children are (please list the worst attribute first):

1.

2.

3.

Estimate the amount you spent on clothing per child within the last year:

1. Under $250

2. Between $250 and $500

3. Between $500 and $1,000

4. Over $1,000

Estimate the amount you plan to spend on clothing per child in the coming year:

1. Under $250

2. Between $250 and $500

3. Between $500 and $1,000

4. Over $1,000

I found the place to shop for my child/children's clothing through

1. Word of mouth

2. Newspaper

3. Magazine

4. Television advertising

5. Street poster (flyers)

6. Walk-by

7. Other (please specify) _____

I buy most of my child's/children's clothes from

     1. Catalogs

     2. Discount stores

     3. Infants' / children's stores

     4. Department stores

     5. Hotel stores

     6. Other (please specify) _____

Section III (Please answer the following question.)

How important are the following attributes when you are buying clothes for your children?

	Not at all important	Somewhat important	Important	Very important	Extremely important
1. Fashion and design	1	2	3	4	5
2. Durability	1	2	3	4	5
3. Price	1	2	3	4	5
4. Color	1	2	3	4	5
5. Store location	1	2	3	4	5
6. Softness	1	2	3	4	5
7. Matching colors	1	2	3	4	5
8. Brand name	1	2	3	4	5
9. Pattern of clothing	1	2	3	4	5
10. Customer service	1	2	3	4	5

Section IV (Please circle one answer for each question.)

1. If your son wears vibrantly colored clothing, how do you feel? (If you do not have a son, what would you have chosen if you had a son?)

I like it that way	It must be that way	I am neutral	I can live with it that way	I dislike it that way
1	2	3	4	5

2. If your son wears pastel-colored clothing, how do you feel? (If you do not have a son, what would you have chosen if you had a son?)

I like it that way	It must be that way	I am neutral	I can live with it that way	I dislike it that way
1	2	3	4	5

3. If your daughter wears vibrantly colored clothing, how do you feel? (If you do not have a daughter, leave the answer blank.)

I like it that way	It must be that way	I am neutral	I can live with it that way	I dislike it that way
1	2	3	4	5

4. If your daughter wears pastel-colored clothing, how do you feel? (If you do not have a daughter, leave the answer blank.)

I like it that way	It must be that way	I am neutral	I can live with it that way	I dislike it that way
1	2	3	4	5

5. If your children wear clothing that has been advertised, how do you feel?

I like it that way	It must be that way	I am neutral	I can live with it that way	I dislike it that way
1	2	3	4	5

6. If your children wear clothing that has not been advertised, how do you feel?

I like it that way	It must be that way	I am neutral	I can live with it that way	I dislike it that way
1	2	3	4	5

---

7. If your children wear clothing that is made in China, how do you feel?

I like it that way	It must be that way	I am neutral	I can live with it that way	I dislike it that way
1	2	3	4	5

8. If your children wear clothing that is not made in China, how do you feel?

I like it that way	It must be that way	I am neutral	I can live with it that way	I dislike it that way
1	2	3	4	5

9. If your children's clothing is a U.S. brand, how do you feel?

I like it that way	It must be that way	I am neutral	I can live with it that way	I dislike it that way
1	2	3	4	5

10. If your children's clothing is not a U.S. brand, how do you feel?

I like it that way	It must be that way	I am neutral	I can live with it that way	I dislike it that way
1	2	3	4	5

After an accurate translation was obtained, the team tested the survey with a small sample of Chinese-literate volunteers to ensure that the meanings of the questions were clear and that the survey was not too long.

Survey Execution. The surveys were distributed in both Hong Kong and China. In Hong Kong, a total of 75 surveys were collected from a manufacturing factory and a piano classroom. In China, the surveys were passed out in a supermarket in the northern city of Tianjin and in a kindergarten in the southern city of Xinhui. A total of 156 survey forms were collected from China.

Results. Some survey results are summarized in Table 1.4.

Focus Group

Purpose. A focus group generally consists of a facilitator and five to nine volunteers who meet for the purpose of understanding the consumer's preferences, ideas, and desire for the products or services. There were a number of reasons for conducting an interactive focus group in addition to a written survey. Most important, the focus group format would allow a sample set of consumers to interact with Lil Lawton's products and its competitors' products and give direct feedback, something a survey format would not be able to accomplish. While a survey could collect more quantitative information, a focus group would employ a more qualitative market assessment approach. It was hoped that a focus group study would strengthen the market study's assumptions. Finally, the focus group had the potential to capture innovative ideas and missing pieces of information that might not be addressed by the survey.

Focus Group Execution. A total of four focus groups, each with five to seven members, were conducted over the span of two weeks. Two of the focus groups took place in Hong Kong, the other two in Guangzhou and Tianjin. Each focus group consisted of a mix of men and women who had children below the age of eight. A few of the participants were expecting children. Because Lil Lawton wanted to target the middle- to upper-class segments of the market, all invited participants were at that socioeconomic level.

Each focus group was run by a moderator, a logistics manager, and a transcriber. The interaction lasted for one and a half hours. The moderator was responsible for direct interaction with the participants. He first explained the purpose of the focus group to the participants and facilitated introductions of the participants to one another. For the remainder of the time, the moderator asked questions and directed discussion. He tried to encourage equal participation and spontaneous interchange. The logistics manager had several responsibilities, including keeping track of time, operating the video camera, working with the moderator to ensure that all questions that needed to be covered were being asked, and arranging clothing samples for participants to examine. The main responsibility of the transcriber was to capture the dialogue of the focus group members. In addition, the transcriber recorded the time in order to serve as a backup to the videotaping of the session.

Each focus group session was divided into three sections: introductions, product interaction, and general questions and answers (Q&A).

Introductions. The session began with the moderator introducing himself and explaining the purpose of the focus group. He then asked partic-

Table 1.4
Highlights of survey results

My three most favorite children's clothing brand names are (right-hand columns indicate the number of survey responses):

Xinhui		Tianjin		Hong Kong	
"Blank"	159	"Blank"	147	"Blank"	120
Any brand	69	Any brand	43	Any brand	38
Giordano	10	Croco Kid	3	Hippo Fant	22
Croco Kid	8	Small Red	3	Croco Kid	3
Bossini Kids	3			Oilily	3
U2	3			Cacharel	3
Other misc. brands	18			Pinco Pallino	3
				Snoopy	3
				Other misc. brands	30

The three most important attributes I look for when buying clothes for my child are:

Xinhui		Tianjin		Hong Kong	
Fashion and design	84	Fashion and design	54	Fashion and design	51
Color	45	Price	39	Price	27
Good price	30	Material	21	Material	18
Size	30	Quality	21	Durability	18
Quality	21	Durability	15	Color	15
Softness	21	Color	12	Quality	12
Durability	18	Size	3	Size	6
Matching colors	15	Country of origin	3	No response	84
No response	6	No response	30		

The top three attributes I avoid when buying clothes for my child are:

Xinhui		Tianjin		Hong Kong	
Bad quality	63	Poor design	54	Poor design	18
Nondurable	63	High price	30	High price	18
Poor design	51	Poor material	24	Poor material	12
Non-fitting size	24	Bad quality	9	Nondurable	9
High price	9	Non-fitting size	6	Non-fitting size	9
No brand	6	Nondurable	3	Bad quality	6
Color	6	Color	3	Color	6
No response	48	Other	6	Store location	1
		No response	63	No response	132

Table 1.4
Highlights of survey results (continued)

I buy most of my child's clothes from:

Xinhui		Tianjin		Hong Kong	
Infant/children's store	45	Infant/children's store	36	Infant/children's store	29
Discount store	36	Department store	24	Department store	26
Department store	9	Discount store	6	Discount store	26
Catalog	0	Catalog	0	Catalog	0
Hotel store	0	Hotel store	0	Hotel store	0
Other	0	Other	0	Other	0

I found the place to shop for my child's clothing through::

Xinhui		Tianjin		Hong Kong	
Walk-by	57	Walk-by	36	Walk-by	49
Word of mouth	18	Magazine	13	Word of mouth	10
Magazine	6	Word of mouth	11	Magazine	4
TV advertising	0	Street poster	6	Street poster	4
Newspaper	0	TV advertising	3	Newspaper	4
Street poster	0	Newspaper	0	TV advertising	0
Other	4	Other	0	No response	4

ipants to introduce themselves by stating their name, their city of residence, the number of children they had, and their children's ages.

Product Interaction. In the next section, samples of Lil Lawton's and its competitors' products were brought out and participants were encouraged to examine the clothing and comment on their relative attributes. They were also asked to compare the overall quality of one brand to that of another. All brand labels were concealed to eliminate brand bias, and clothing of the same brand was grouped only by numbered labels. The competitors' products included children's clothing from popular children's stores in Hong Kong, such as Naf Naf, Mothercare, and Oilily. This direct product interaction was a valuable means of capturing the participants' comments about Lil Lawton's and its competitors' products.

Q&A. The focus group session ended with a question and answer section. Most of the questions were similar to those found on the written survey and were meant to capture the spontaneous responses of participants. The team hoped that answers to the questions would confirm the survey results. Additional free-answer, open-ended questions were asked that were better suited for a focus group environment than for a survey.

Results. The results of the Hong Kong and China focus groups were largely similar. All participants expressed a generally favorable opinion of the Lil Lawton products. Lil Lawton's clothing was considered superior to that of its competitors in terms of softness, color, style, and taste. Some participants stated that, in general, price was more important than durability, because they preferred to purchase new clothes for each child instead of passing hand-me-downs from one child to the next. One hundred percent cotton material was seen as a plus because it was comfortable for the children and easy for the parents to wash. Most parents preferred that the clothes have few buttons or strings as decoration because these often fell off during washing and also posed a possible safety hazard for their children.

Participants revealed a number of interesting market preferences. They stated that, in general, clothing that was manufactured outside of China or Hong Kong was considered better than clothing manufactured in their home countries. However, for their children's clothing, brand names were not important. Mass media advertising of children's clothing was not prevalent in either Hong Kong or China. Most advertising was in the form of street posters and flyers. Promotions and sales at children's clothing stores were common and attractive to parents. In both Hong Kong and China, the decision maker and purchaser of the clothes was usually the mother and sometimes the grandparents.

The focus groups also revealed differences between the market in Hong Kong and the market in China. In Hong Kong, clothing with popular television cartoon characters, such as Sailor Moon, appealed to many children, whereas the China focus groups expressed no strong preference for clothing with cartoon characters. Price preferences differed dramatically between participants in Hong Kong and those in China. An acceptable price for Chinese parents was about one-third the price of most Lil Lawton products. The Hong Kong groups found the Lil Lawton prices to be slightly more expensive than most of the clothes they currently bought, but not outside of their price range. In terms of distribution channels, Hong Kong participants stated that they bought their children's clothing from both department stores in malls and stand-alone stores. In China, no one was accustomed to buying their clothing in stand-alone children's clothing stores; all children's clothing was bought in mall department stores. In terms of brand recognition, Chinese participants said they could not think of any particularly dominant brands. In Hong Kong, brands such as Oilily and CrocoKids were salient in participants' minds. In Hong Kong, however, parents had little brand loyalty and looked more at price and product attributes.

Another interesting point that Lil Lawton discovered from the focus groups was that parents in China valued different product attributes for their children who were less than three years old than for their children who were over three. For children under three, material and quality (such as soft, 100 percent cotton material) were of paramount importance in deciding what clothing to buy. For children over three, color, taste, and pattern became more important attributes than material.

Competitive Analysis

The research team took a two-pronged approach to the competitive analysis of the market in Hong Kong and China. One prong was quantitative, consisting of an eight-point comparison of each competitor and a pricing strategy comparison. The qualitative portion examined competitors' core competencies that might pose threats to Lil Lawton's success in the market.

Both quantitative and qualitative competitive analysis began with thorough searches of CD-ROMs and databases such as CARL, Lexis-Nexis, EDGAR, and Delphi, as well as library research using current periodicals and reference books. Studies from marketing research companies such as Robertson Stephens provided further insights into competitor strategies and products. The research team contacted the Hong Kong and China embassies for statistical information and lists of children's clothing retailers currently operating in their countries. Web sites and mailing lists also served as valuable sources of information on competitor profiles. Textile organizations, such as the Federation of Hong Kong Garment Manufacturers and the Textile Council of Hong Kong Limited, provided information on textile market trends, suppliers, and customers. The Society of Competitive Intelligence Professionals offered competitive international information about various industries.

Eleven major brand-name competitors were identified in Hong Kong. Competitor information within China was difficult to attain. Most competitors in China were thought to be privately owned retail outlets that sold generic brands at low cost.

In Hong Kong, hundreds of children's clothing retailers line the streets in fierce competition for customers. Paring down the hundreds of stores to eleven of the closest competitors for analysis involved careful study of competitors' product lines, pricing strategies, and salient clothing attributes. Learning more about the profiles of each company's product enabled the research team to determine whether or not Lil Lawton was in direct competition with a company. For instance, one local store specialized in relatively expensive children's wear for formal occasions such as weddings. Customers were usually one-time visitors to the stores, and the clothes were used for special occasions only. Thus Lil Lawton would not consider itself as a direct competitor to this store, because Lil Lawton products were intended for daily wear, targeted a lower price range, and actively built a loyal customer base. Eleven children's clothing retailers were identified as possible brand-name competitors: Miki House, Oilily, Bossini Kids, Walt Disney, Hipo Fant, Guess Kids, CrocoKids, Naf Naf, Barocco, OshKosh B'Gosh, and Mothercare.

Quantitative Analysis

The quantitative approach taken by the research team was twofold. First, the team conducted a walk-in eight-point audit of Lil Lawton and eleven of its current competitors in Hong Kong (see Table 1.5). This audit involved identifying eight of the most important children's clothing and store attributes, according to Lil Lawton (fashion and design, price, color, store location, softness, matching colors, clothing pattern, and customer service), and systematically performing a relative comparison in which each of the eleven competitors and Lil Lawton were rated on a scale of 1 to 5 on how well they satisfied each of these attributes. A score of 1 indicated that the company had a poor-quality attribute (bad store location, poor customer service, and so on) and 5 signified that the company had a high-quality attribute (low price, great color variety, and so forth). The auditors performed a walk-in audit of each store, which allowed them to experience customer service firsthand, examine store location, and inspect

Table 1.5
Results of eight-point audit

	Miki House	Oilily	Walt Disney	Guess Kids	Barocco	Oshkosh B'Gosh	Bossini Kids	Hipo Fant	CrocoKids	Mothercare	Naf Naf	Lil Lawton
Fashion and design	5	5	5	3	4	3	3	2	4	3	3	4
Price	1	1.5	1	3	2	1	5	3.5	4.5	4	3.5	2
Color	4	5	4	2	3	2	3	3	4	3	4	5
Store location	4	3	3	3	2	2	2	3	4	3	3	4
Softness	3	3	3	4	3	3	3	5	3	5	3	5
Matching colors	5	5	5	4	3	3	3	2	3	2	4	5
Pattern of clothing	4	5	3	2	2	2	3	2	3	2	4	4
Customer service	4	3	3	4	3	3	4	3	3	3	4	4

Note: 5 = more, 1 = less

a wide variety of clothes. The same set of auditors conducted the study for each of the eleven companies to ensure consistency.

Price ranges for competitors' products were obtained during the eight-point audit (see Table 1.6). This information allowed Lil Lawton to better understand the competitors' pricing strategies and how it could price its products competitively.

Qualitative Analysis

In addition to the quantitative analysis, a qualitative analysis of competitors' established core competencies was performed.[10] Four brand-name competitors—CrocoKids, Mothercare, Oilily, and Disney Stores—seemed particularly strong in core competencies.

CrocoKids. CrocoKids and Mothercare were both low-priced, established players in the market. In early 1996, CrocoKids had sixty stand-alone stores in Hong Kong. Its brand equity was established with the popular crocodile emblem, although counterfeiters around the world took advantage of the brand recognition by sewing their own little crocodiles onto clothes and selling them in night markets at lower costs. Nev-

Table 1.6
Competitors' pricing strategy

Brand	Country of origin	Blouse or pants (HK$)	Jacket or coat (HK$)
Miki House	France	$600–$1,000	$1,000–$2,000
Walt Disney	USA	$700–$900	N/A
Oilily	Holland	$300–$800	$1,000–$2,000
Guess Kids	USA	$200–$400	N/A
Hipo Fant	Hong Kong	$200–$300	$300–$400
Naf Naf	France	$200–$300	$600–$700
Mothercare	London	$150–$250	$300–$500
CrocoKids	Hong Kong	$100–$200	$200–$300
Bossini Kids	Hong Kong	$80–$120	$180–$250
Chicco		N/A	N/A
Ciunga		N/A	N/A
Oshkosh B' Gosh	USA	N/A	N/A
Barocco		N/A	N/A

ertheless, CrocoKids' market share was high relative to other brand-name players in the market.

Mothercare. Mothercare boasted excellent customer service. Simon Hughes, logistics director, stated that a priority for the company was to ensure that the sales staff were "emotionally involved" in their jobs and in the Mothercare brand. In 1994, Mothercare began a complete conversion of its stores to a new design and an overhaul of its supply chain in order to increase buying power and cut costs. By April 1996, 60 percent of its 1.2 million square feet of store space around the world had been refitted with the new design.

Oilily. Oilily had product attributes similar to those of Lil Lawton, including durability, pricing, and style. A Dutch-based company, Oilily's European brand name appealed to customers in Asia. Oilily's distribution channels included not only specialty shops and exclusive stores, but also direct ordering from the World Wide Web.

Disney Stores. There was no question that Disney had the advantage of deep pockets, strong brand recognition, and worldwide brand equity. Its image allowed it to compete more easily in an international market, and little direct advertising was necessary. In December 1994 there were 335 Disney stores in eight countries, and Disney planned to increase that number to six hundred within the following few years. Disney stores offered children's clothing as well as a number of home textile products, toys, gifts and stationery, and bedding.

No-name Competitors and Other Intangible Problems

In both Hong Kong and China, survey results showed that brand name was not a major factor in buying children's clothing. Most survey participants were unable to recall any particular brand names they preferred. The research team's assessment of competitors revealed that although a number of large name-brand retailers existed, a greater barrier to entry may have been the hundreds of small, no-name-brand retailers that attracted customers with relatively inexpensive, satisfactory-quality clothing. Unquantifiable, the competition that these retailers posed and the know-how they possessed of operating in their home environment added complexity to Lil Lawton's ability to ascertain the real competition it might face.

An additional problem that many brand-name apparel manufacturers struggle with is widespread counterfeiting in Asian markets. Would Lil Lawton remain profitable using the same brand equity strategy it employed in the United States?

The costs of doing business, including human labor, taxes, and rent, for the United States, Hong Kong, and China are shown in Table 1.7.

Table 1.7
Costs of doing business with Hong Kong, China, and the United States

	Hong Kong	China	United States
Labor (weekly wages)	$250	$8	$375
Rent (per sq. ft. per yr.)	$125	$20–$30	$50
Taxes	17.5%	30%	40%

Note: Other costs include design, manufacturing, transportation, distribution, utilities, advertisement, and government. All monetary amounts are in U.S. dollars.

Team Recommendations to Lil Lawton

The team concluded its three-month investigation of the China and Hong Kong markets in March 1996. On the basis of the information collected, the team recommended that Lil Lawton enter the Hong Kong market immediately because of this market's substantial size. Despite the heavy competition in Hong Kong, the team believed that Lil Lawton would do well if it priced in the medium-to-high range relative to competitors, advertised on par with other competitors, and located its stores in popular shopping areas such as Pacific Place or Ocean Terminals. Although stand-alone stores would be an effective distribution channel in Hong Kong, high rental rates were pointed out as a caveat to this avenue.

With regard to China, the research team believed that the market had enormous potential because of the large population and few established brand-name players. However, it recommended that Lil Lawton enter the China market in three cities (Guangzhou, Shenzhen, and Shanghai) to learn about the market and test its products. Pricing in China should be slightly lower than in Hong Kong, although not substantially lower, because then Hong Kong residents might be tempted to travel across the border to buy Lil Lawton clothing in China. Distribution in China should begin in department stores to minimize risk. Promotions should leverage on Hong Kong's brand awareness. With these initial moves into China, the team believed, Lil Lawton would be able to expand its presence more easily in the future.

The research team recognized that its research was far from comprehensive. It recommended that before a final decision was made, future investigations should take place in a number of areas, such as evaluation of a joint venture possibility; assessment of governmental factors such as regulations, quotas, and tariffs; investigation into avenues of advertising to increase market penetration; improvement of the eight-point audit to include other product attributes such as cartoon exhibits and materials; and a detailed analysis of the cost structure to determine profitability.

Appendix: The Kano Method

Nonaki Kano, professor and head of the Department of Management Science at the University of Tokyo, is an advocate of a concept called attractive quality.[11] Kano explains that expected product characteristics should be distinguished from those that make the product truly outstanding. Specifically, product characteristics can be grouped into three categories: dissatisfiers, satisfiers, and delighters (see Figure 1.7).

Dissatisfiers (also known as must be, basic, or expected characteristics) are characteristics the customer tends to expect in a product. The absence of dissatisfier characteristics is a strike against the product in the mind of the customer, but the presence of the characteristic is taken for granted. For instance, a scratched mirror or a bike that is missing pedals dissatisfies the customer, but a blemishless mirror or a bike with all of the basic parts gives the product no additional advantage over competitors' products.

Satisfiers (also called one-dimensional or straight-line characteristics) are characteristics that customers want in their products and usually re-

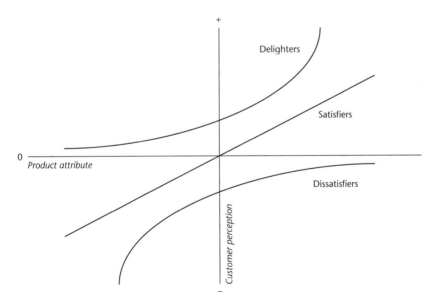

Figure 1.7   Categories of product characteristics

quest. In addition, the more of the satisfier there is present in the product, the happier the customer becomes. Examples of satisfiers are speed, volume, and low price.

Delighters (also referred to as attractive or exciting characteristics) are those qualities of a product that are a pleasant surprise to customers. Customers generally do not notice their absence and cannot even request them because they do not expect them. Delighters meet customers' hidden needs. An example of a delighter is the 3M Post-it, a product that filled a customer need that had not been adequately satisfied before.

The Kano method is often used in consumer questionnaires. It involves identifying customer needs and then asking two questions, one positive and one negative, for each need. For instance, if the user's need is for his or her children's clothing to have cartoon characters, the positive question would state, "If your child's clothes do have cartoon characters, how do you feel?" and the negative question would read, "If your child's clothes do not have cartoon characters, how do you feel?" For each question, the respondent can choose one of the following five answers: "I like it that way," "It must be that way," "I am neutral," "I can live with it that way," or "I dislike it that way." The responses are tabulated and analyzed using a two-dimensional table that measures customer perception (dissatisfied to satisfied) on the Y-axis and product or service attribute (insufficient to sufficient) along the X-axis. Delighters are found in the upper right-hand quadrant (satisfied or sufficient).

2   Sales and Marketing

Marketing and sales are what drive the value-creation process by directly contributing to cash inflows. This chapter deals with these two important components of a firm's value chain. No matter how efficient a firm is in production and logistics, if it is unable to execute production and logistics, finalize sales, and turn the product into a revenue stream, it has not created any actual value. In finance theory, a firm's value is the present worth of its expected free cash flows generated at the discount rate corresponding to the weighted average cost of its capital. The process that is most central to generating the cash flows is the firm's sales mechanism. Marketing, conversely, is responsible for creating the optimal level of demand for the firm's product by suggesting appropriate prices, increasing awareness, and creating a brand image, all of which lead to efficient sales execution. Marketing, furthermore, acts as a bridge between the firm's production process and its market. The product development and marketing functions carry out market research to enable the firm to understand what consumers want and what kind of competitors exist, and to help the firm design and engineer products and services that reflect features needed by consumers.

In this chapter, the reader will learn about HKS Products Limited, a manufacturer of children's apparel with operations in Hong Kong and manufacturing in low-cost South Asian countries and Mainland China. The focus of the case is HKS's North American division and its North American market, which constitutes the company's main body of customers. The interesting point about this case is that HKS, a manufacturing firm, is looking for growth opportunities on the retail side. This book's introduction mentioned that China- and Hong Kong–based companies are seriously engaging the U.S. market directly. This case is an example of that trend. In fact, HKS is looking into developing an outlet kiosk as a point-of-access and sales device. The kiosk is not only a powerful marketing tool, because it allows for bidirectional communication with potential customers and thus makes it possible to conduct customized marketing, but also functions as an automatic point-of-sale device, contributing to actual sales. The consulting team is given the task of creating the conceptual design for such a kiosk. The team starts with trying to understand what customers need. In this case, the customers are primarily young couples with children below age five. To achieve this understanding, the consulting team conducts a survey of this demographic group. It then analyzes the results and makes recommendations based on the replies. Furthermore, the consulting team builds a financial model that allows for return on investment (ROI) and net present value (NPV) calculations, and develops its capabilities to conduct sensitivity analysis.

Case: HKS Products Limited U.S.A.

It was the late 1990s and Dr. Lui, director of HKS Products Limited U.S.A., was considering the problems facing his clients and his business. HKS was a manufacturer of children's apparel, and its customers— young couples and business professionals—were increasingly less interested in spending time in stores and more interested in engaging in other activities. "What new technologies exist today that might help bridge this gap?" Dr. Lui contemplated. He thought for a moment about the fundamental shopping experience: being attracted to a particular item, trying it on for size, and then perhaps purchasing it. "What if a machine existed that could facilitate this entire process? Not only would this aid parents in their hectic lifestyles, but this machine could potentially increase profit margins for HKS." Dr. Lui decided to recruit a group of research consultants to develop his vision. Their mission was to design a kiosk for use in the North American market.

Company Overview

HKS Products Limited manufactures clothing for children, ages three months to twelve years. It sells under the brand labels Jet Set, Mickey and Co., Looney Tunes, and Riders for Kids. HKS also manufactures children's wear for specialty stores and private-label merchandise. Currently the United States is the core market for HKS clientele.

HKS operations are centered in Hong Kong, while manufacturing is done in lower-wage East Asian countries, such as Mainland China. Additional manufacturing facilities are located in Sri Lanka, El Salvador, Mexico, and the Philippines. A technical center and sample room, located in Dongguan, China, performs design and specification activities related to ever-changing consumer tastes. Sales issues are handled by HKS's partner, Mamiye Brothers, located in New York City.

HKS's Hong Kong headquarters presents several advantages as well as potential risks. Hong Kong is a strategic service center within the Southeast Asia region. In fact, Hong Kong is second (only to Italy) in exporting textiles and garments. Moreover, when exports are added, Hong Kong is the leading supplier of garments to the entire world market.

Unfortunately, inflation and increased costs have hampered Hong

Kong's advantage as a competitive manufacturing center. However, through product differentiation, process improvements, and increased production efficiency, Hong Kong has been able to maintain its edge in the world textile market. Recently, Hong Kong clothing manufacturers have begun to focus on niche markets, thereby allowing them to respond very quickly to market changes and the latest fashion trends. Also, the opening of the Chinese market has presented many opportunities for Hong Kong–based clothing manufacturers. For example, China represented a new retail market as well as a growth opportunity for design, planning, sales, and management activities. Yet the July 1, 1997, return of Hong Kong to the People's Republic of China posed myriad uncertainties to Hong Kong–based clothing manufacturers.

Competitive Environment

In today's tough, competitive climate and in the face of increasingly demanding retailers, it is difficult—but not impossible—for apparel manufacturers to generate growth. Strategies vary, but what they basically come down to is expanding product offerings through acquisitions, new brand creation, licensing, and brand name extension into new apparel categories; seeking wider and deeper distribution; and becoming more merchandise and technology oriented.

The intense competition that characterizes the apparel manufacturing industry is reflected in a slow rise in apparel prices vis-à-vis overall price inflation. Between 1988 and 1994, for example, the wholesale price of all apparel increased 10.1 percent, with women's wear prices rising 7.55 percent, men's wear prices 13 percent, and children's clothing prices 11 percent. For all commodities, wholesale prices increased 15 percent during this period. Competition in this industry is also demonstrated by its low profit margins. According to Internal Revenue Service data, after-tax profit margins for typical apparel firms were substantially below those for all manufacturing.

Video Kiosk System Research

Presently, North America (primarily the United States) constitutes HKS's main market. As a clothing manufacturer, HKS was searching for growth opportunities and for ways to enter the retail side of the business. The development of a video kiosk system appeared to be a unique way to accomplish these goals. In order to proceed, many questions had to be considered. Would potential customers be receptive to this newly proposed way of shopping? What features would be most useful to these potential customers? Can such a system be created at a cost that is justifiable? How should HKS approach gathering information to address these issues?

In January 1996, HKS had already been considering the concept of a video kiosk system internally and was seriously interested in pursuing the idea further. A joint team of graduate students from Stanford University and the Hong Kong University of Science and Technology was formed to analyze the key issues related to the introduction of such a system.

During the next three months, the team performed various research analyses and prototype development tasks related to the implementation of a video kiosk system. Initially the team distributed a survey to a sample of parents with children between the ages of three and five, the target market. The survey was designed to focus on several important factors that would influence the design of the kiosk system.

As mentioned earlier, the kiosk is a convenient point-of-access device designed to provide information, promote products or services, and enable customers to contact company representatives. Most kiosks are located in congested public places, such as retail outlets, malls, airports, and hotel lobbies, in order to increase customer traffic and use. In 1996 approximately twenty-one thousand kiosks were installed in the United States alone.

A kiosk consists of a touch-screen monitor, a computer processor, accessories, and sometimes a payment option for purchasing goods or services.

Touch-screen monitor. A touch-screen monitor allows users to interact with the kiosk by pointing to areas on the screen. In general the Kiosk application is a visually appealing, user-friendly interface.

Computer processor. The kiosk application's requirements determine the computer hardware requirements. In the late 1990s, kiosk computers began supporting video, digital audio, and even network connectivity, and thus required more demanding processing power.

Accessories. Kiosks also come equipped with several accessories for value-added functionality, such as the following:

- Video camera and telephone handset, which allow consumers to communicate with a representative displayed on the monitor
- Telephone, which enables users to connect directly to a company representative for customer service or technical support
- Web-browser, for providing online access to the Internet
- Speakers, to enable customers to preview music or information guides
- Privacy screen, to prevent others from viewing personal information
- Keyboard, which allows users to enter text information when a touch-screen monitor is not appropriate

Payment options. The kiosk often incorporates one or more of the following payment options:

- Magstripe card reader for processing credit card transactions
- Signature pad that allows users to complete a purchase transaction or authorize a credit card application
- Money acceptor for receiving bills and coins in order to dispense a product

On the basis of their functionality and application requirements, kiosks can be grouped into the following categories:

Product line extension. Product line extension kiosks allow retail stores to enable customers to purchase products that are offered by the company but not stocked by that particular store. These kiosks allow vendors to expand their storefront and increase profitability. Product line extension kiosks have the added benefit of minimizing the number of sales personnel required to service customers.

Informational. Informational kiosks are designed to address customers' questions about products or services or to provide other information. These kiosks often minimize the need for on-site personnel and reduce costly phone calls to the company. Additionally, point-of-information kiosks can dispense information twenty-four hours a day, seven days a week, minimizing the need for customer service personnel while increasing overall efficiency. The kiosks can provide answers to routine questions; the employees responsible for sales and customer service can then be used to respond to nonroutine customer requests.

Promotional. Kiosk technology can be used to encourage repeat store purchases by providing special offers, discount coupons, and advertisements to customers. Promotional kiosks have the added benefit of reducing the need for sales personnel and are sometimes referred to as independent in-store point-of-sale support. Retail stores often place promotional kiosk systems in outlets to increase awareness of their products and to provide cost incentives for consumers to purchase their products. These kiosks are also being used to collect customer information, which is valuable marketing data to companies.

Service. Service kiosks can be used to provide repeatable but custom services, such as bank loans, to customers who would otherwise be served by a representative. These kiosks can increase customer convenience and allow companies to save the costs of hiring personnel.

E-commerce. Manufacturers can implement e-commerce kiosks in their retail stores as part of a multichannel strategy. E-commerce kiosks provide Internet connectivity to allow consumers to access product information, purchase products, or complete a service transaction online through the corporate Web site. These kiosks also allow companies to combine global e-commerce sales with local in-store specials. By enabling Internet commerce through access to on-line shopping services, kiosks let retailers expand inventory without increasing floor space. The results are increased profits per square foot and enhanced customer satisfaction.

Recommendations and Conclusions

On the basis of the results of the surveys, the team chose to design a product line extension kiosk system that would provide measurable ROI. Given the proposed design, the team built a financial model to analyze the economic aspects of implementing such a system. On the basis of detailed assumptions regarding customer traffic for a given kiosk location, projected growth rates, and many other factors, the model can be used to calculate the NPV of cash flows for a shop's investment in a kiosk. Sensitivity analysis can be performed by simply changing the values of various input parameters and observing the resulting effect on the NPV. In this way, insight can be gained on an ongoing basis as better information is obtained, in order to understand more fully the key risks and value drivers of investing in such a venture.

HKS is an example of a company located in Asia that has been contributing to the global value chain at the manufacturing stage by providing low-cost apparel for children. The company needed to increase revenue and discovered that kiosks are an alternative to generating sales by promoting products or services, introducing product-line extensions, and providing enhanced customer support. Kiosks also enable retailers to have real-time access to customers, which in turn increases customer satisfaction and loyalty and helps foster long-term growth and profitability.

Kiosks experience great use in retail stores. By providing customers with access to an efficient and pleasant shopping experience, kiosks let retailers expand inventory without increasing floor space, and generate new sales leads. The results are increased profits per square foot and enhanced customer satisfaction. At HKS Limited U.S.A., kiosks that answer routine questions and handle routine transactions also enable the company to provide superior customer service. The team's recommendation has the potential to provide long-term, sustainable value to the company and its customers.

3   Supply Chain Management and Logistics

A supply chain is a network of facilities and distribution options that serve a company by procuring materials, transforming these materials into intermediate and finished products, and distributing these finished products to customers. Supply chains exist in both service and manufacturing organizations, although the complexity of the chain may vary greatly from industry to industry and firm to firm.

Supply chain operations provide the crucial link—the life support tube—that ensures timely arrival of products from source to destination. This statement is of course a supersimplification of the very complex process that spans such activities as demand forecasting, inventory management, order replenishment, logistics, and continuous monitoring. Another issue is to clarify what constitutes the source and the destination, the two ends of the supply chain. This book focuses on manufacturing sources in China, on retail or industrial clients in North America or the finished goods manufacturer in China and the party who delivers those goods to the client in the United States, or alternatively on the intermediary goods manufacturer in China and the client in the United States who turns the intermediary good into a finished good. It is not uncommon today for a relatively large firm to operate across different national boundaries to manage many supply chains, a task that is expensive and exposes the firm to major sources of risk. It is interesting to note that although firms first outsourced their manufacturing operations to parts of the world that are cheaper than the United States and thus gave rise to the phenomenon of supply chain management (SCM), many firms today have planned their manufacturing operations in such a way as to mitigate supply chain risks. It is not uncommon for manufacturing firms to have several manufacturing sources to ensure that even if there are supply chain disruptions from one source, other sources with enough capacity will make up for the loss of production. The same is true for the direct customers of the manufacturing firms, that is, they rely not on just one supplier but on multiple suppliers to hedge against the inherent risks associated with each supply chain. Buildups in ports in China and North America (some due to strikes or other labor-related issues) have forced firms to follow such strategies. The growing complexity of such operations has also attracted the attention of academia. An article published in the *Wall Street Journal* on March 1, 2004, titled "Globalization Creates Logistics Jobs in U.S.," explained that the increased attention of many top engineering and business schools to SCM and logistics issues has prompted some of these schools, including the Massachusetts Institute of Technology, to expand their academic programs and departments, even to devote them entirely to such issues. The importance of the efficient, well-run supply chain is very clear; a slight delay means lost sales and customers who are lost forever, both of which translate into lost revenue. At the same time, managing supply chains may not necessarily be among the core competencies or focuses of a firm. There has therefore been a flurry of outsourcing of SCM operations by firms that want timely delivery of input goods.

This chapter introduces two cases that focus on different aspects of SCM. The first case is unique in that it does not involve China. In fact, this case demonstrates a point made earlier, in the Introduction, that companies that are aware of potential issues in China have hedged against the supply chain risks of concentrating their entire production in China by distributing their production sites. The case focuses on a company we have called Garment Retailer, which has chosen to outsource its production to Mexico.[1] The case provides detailed analysis of Mexico's macroeconomic conditions and its manufacturing and garment production capabilities, and clarifies advantages that Mexico offers in comparison to other countries, in particular China, despite higher labor costs. The case discusses the North American Free Trade Agreement (NAFTA) in detail, and looks at transportation between the United States and Mexico and at some of the risks associated with various transportation methods. In particular, the consulting team suggests backhauling as the optimal and most cost-effective ground transportation program.

The second case in this chapter revisits PCH China, an SCM company introduced in Chapter 1, and elaborates on the company's decision to deploy radio frequency identification (RFID) technology across its widespread supply chains. As discussed in Chapter 1, PCH acts as intermediary between companies based in the

United States and Europe and manufacturers in China. PCH does not own a warehouse; however, it provides full services for the end customer by finding an appropriate manufacturer in China and by guaranteeing the timely arrival of the finished goods at the customer's door. The key to PCH's strategy is high-quality service and smooth transportation of goods to the customer to guarantee on-time arrival. Consequently, having in place an automated system for monitoring its supply chains is very important. However, considering the high capital investments that RFID has required since the first large-scale implementation of RFID in 2005, the decision to implement RFID should be made very carefully. The consulting team first explores the RFID technology and risks and then discusses an approach to assessing return on investment (ROI). The focus then turns to providing a set of technical guidelines to help PCH's management identify the supply chains that are most appropriate for RFID implementation, and to choosing a model for economic analysis of RFID's costs and benefits. The team also analyzes different options for integrating the RFID system into PCH's existing enterprise software system.

Case 1: Garment Retailer

Mexican Manufacturing and Operations

Mexico has increasingly become a strategic location for manufacturing and sourcing products intended for North American markets. Particularly since the 1994 signing of NAFTA, Mexico offers American manufacturers low-cost labor advantages, favorable currency exchange rates, and short cycle times. Additionally, in 2004, all tariffs between Mexico, the United States, and Canada were eliminated. This case evaluates the advantages and challenges of expanding Mexican sourcing opportunities for Garment Retailer.

Industry Overview

Mexico exported $8 billion worth of textiles to the United States in 1997 alone, an increase of close to 30 percent over 1996, which represents substantial growth. Several government-backed initiatives, a strong labor pool, and a stable economy have contributed enormously to this growth.

The Mexican government encourages FDI and will assist as far as possible with setup, infrastructure, and training costs. An example of this is the government's involvement in NuStart and Denim City, two textile clusters built around solid infrastructure and good training facilities that it has provided with low interest rates on loans. This project included both American and Mexican textile manufacturers.

The Mexican labor pool has become more skilled as the popularity of Mexico as a manufacturing location has increased. Currently, Mexico has a pool of 36 million unskilled and semi-skilled laborers who will work for competitive wages of around US$5/day. It is hard to get information on these wages. Going to different vendors and locales and doing a little digging is the only way to determine the real wages, although salary information is relatively confidential for most vendors. As more manufacturers enter Mexico, fewer workers are jobless and unemployment has dropped considerably. This could be a problem moving forward because labor prices may increase as demand rises and supply decreases.

Mexico's economy has been extremely stable in recent years. NAFTA has tied Mexico to America's markets, strengthening the stabilizing effect.

Also, Mexico's government has been very conscious of Mexico's economic standing in the world and has been working hard to forge trade agreements and treaties to increase foreign investment in Mexico. Brazil's 1999 currency crisis has also reminded Mexico how precarious its position is and is helping the business and government people in charge to remain focused on intelligent economic action.

One of the most underestimated aspects of companies' interest in Mexico is an understanding their culture. Personal contacts and good worker relations are crucial for successful operations. They require stringent attention to societal norms and cultural sensitivity. Hiring locals for middle management positions often alleviates this pressure. Many companies have tried to enter Mexico and ignored the culture, only to find it a costly and time-consuming process to fix the mistake.

A manufacturing facility's location needs to be well chosen. Water is the most critical component of textile manufacturing; it is needed for washing and to create consistent colors in dyeing. New technologies and heavy investment by large textile and apparel manufacturers are making water purifiers more prevalent. Roads and communication media are improving constantly, and there are opportunities for Garment Retailer to negotiate with local governments for additional support. The main transportation mechanisms from Mexico to the United States are trucking and shipping. The use of toll roads, convoys, safe havens for stopping and resting, and even escorts should be worked into any contract that Garment Retailer negotiates with its trucking companies.

In addition to its embrace of NAFTA, Mexico is pursuing other trade agreements, such as the Free Trade Area of the Americas (FTAA), and bilateral deals with other countries, such as the European Union (EU). These agreements will improve Mexico's competitiveness and will likely increase the demand for manufacturing facilities in Mexico. This demand could drive up labor and production costs as labor, raw materials, and production lines become scarce. Capacity will be the most likely constraint on unbridled growth for Garment Retailer in Mexico.

One outlet for future capacity would be the Caribbean Basin, which may achieve NAFTA parity rates for textiles and apparel if the Caribbean and Central America Relief and Economic Stabilization Act (HR 984) is ever passed. The Caribbean Basin offers low labor rates and a close proximity to the United States. Because of its existing advantages, even with tariffs on textiles, many manufacturers are establishing relationships with factories in the region. Should NAFTA-type parity be granted through the Caribbean Basin Initiative (CBI, discussed later in the chapter), an influx of American investment in the region would occur, causing the same capacity issues that Mexico now faces.

We also found in our investigations that Garment Retailer is not operating as efficiently as it could. Most of the information we uncovered came from the company's own employees in different business units. Some suggestions on what Garment Retailer should be looking for in terms of inefficiencies and how the current organization could be improved can be found in the concluding section of this case.

This investigation suggests that Garment Retailer should move some of its sourcing to Mexico in order to capitalize the cost advantages and to build relationships with vendors to secure future capacity. Garment Retailer should also consider joint sourcing of materials across business units to achieve greater bargaining power with vendors, and possible organizational enhancements and communications tools to ensure successful adoption of the new sourcing venues across all business units.

Garment Retailer

After surviving a somewhat rocky start and overcoming its sense of an uncertain future during its first few years of existence, Garment Retailer became one of the United States' top retail clothing companies. It placed seventeenth in a March 30, 1998, *Business Week* article covering the top performers of Standard & Poor's 500 Index.

As the success of its retail clothing outlets grew, Garment Retailer became one of America's top household brands, joining the ranks of such companies as Gillette, Coca-Cola, and Disney. Between 1983 and 1998, Garment Retailer went from 566 to 2,237 stores around the world (in Japan, the United Kingdom, Canada, France, and Germany). Its stock rose from $26 in August 1997, to $66.5 in January 1998. To maintain its rapid growth and ensure its continued success, Garment Retailer diversified its offerings. Business Unit 2 (BU2) was transformed from its former safari theme and repositioned as a seller of high-end clothes and housewares. At the low end, Garment Retailer formed Business Unit 1 (BU1) to target the discount retailers. One of the keys to Garment Re-

Table 3.1
Number of stores owned by each business unit

	July 1998	January 1999	% change
BU1	321	441	37.4%
BU2	269	304	13.0%
Garment Retailer	1,056	1,136	7.6%

tailer's exceptional performance was the amazing growth of BU1 (see Table 3.1), which managed to hit $1 billion in revenue in just four years (it took Garment Retailer eighteen years to reach a billion in sales).

Although Garment Retailer overall is able to maintain gross margins between 35 and 40 percent, BU1 is limited to around 25 percent. One of the biggest influences on this margin is the cost of goods sold (COGS). Buried in the COGS are the costs of materials, manufacturing, and shipping. Garment Retailer is trying to identify ways of reducing inventory and manufacturing costs while maintaining the high level of service for which its supermarket-like stores are known. Mickey Drexler, Garment Retailer's CEO, has said he never wants a customer not to be able to purchase an item because Garment Retailer does not carry her size. To reach all of these goals, Garment Retailer has turned its sights on Mexico as a new source of low-cost, high-quality, and geographically close labor.

Mexico

Over the past twenty years, Mexico has become a strategic location for manufacturing and sourcing products intended for North American markets. Facilitated by the 1994 signing of NAFTA, Mexico offers manufacturers tactical positioning in the North American marketplace, as well as low-cost labor advantages. Other benefits include Mexico's proximity to the United States and the numerous transportation links connecting the two countries. The peso's weak position, relative to the U.S. dollar, and the country's ample labor pool (35 million in a total population of 95 million) make Mexico a source of low-cost semiskilled labor. Additionally, since 2004, all tariffs between Mexico, the United States, and Canada have been eliminated as a result of NAFTA.

Realizing that their low-labor-cost advantage is likely to disappear due to dwindling labor supply, Mexican manufacturers have also been taking steps to improve quality, control costs, cut inventory, and reduce manufacturing lead times. They have also intensified their focus on worker training in an attempt to improve productivity.

Before NAFTA, a number of American companies set up subassembly plants just south of the U.S. border. This was a result of the National Border Program, instituted by the Mexican government in 1961, which fostered the establishment of manufacturing operations along the northern border of Mexico to stimulate economic growth, enhance the country's infrastructure, and encourage tourism in the area. Such manufacturing plants were called *maquiladoras*. The specially designated maquiladora region in Mexico could not extend more than a hundred kilometers below the U.S. border. Favorable tariff provisions allowed these plants to import materials free of duty so long as a certain proportion of the finished products or components were exported from Mexico. The final products could then be shipped across the border with a duty paid only on the value added during manufacture or assembly. This program, combined with an abundance of low-cost labor, made this region of Mexico very attractive to manufacturing firms.

Mexico's system of maquiladora plants is extensive. As of December 1998 there were close to three thousand plants employing approximately one million laborers. Tijuana has the largest number of plants, 666, employing 147,000 people, while Ciudad Juarez in the state of Chihuahua has the largest concentration of maquiladora workers, with 204,000 workers in 252 plants. Among the various industries, the textiles and apparel sector operates the largest number of plants, 820, employing 203,000 workers, and the electrical and electronic machinery and accessories sector employs the largest number of workers, 254,000 people spread across 469 plants.

The maquiladora region was commonly used as a "rescue" area for products that needed to be manufactured more cost effectively and subsequently sold to consumers for a more competitive price. This is now an outdated motivation for manufacturing in Mexico, which has become a strategic location for labor-intensive manufacturing. Although the traditional maquiladora region will be phased out over the next ten years, NAFTA now allows Canadian and American manufacturers to maintain maquiladora-like investment opportunities anywhere in Mexico. The trend is to move these manufacturing plants to inland Mexico to be closer to local markets and suppliers. This trend is supported by the fact that 62 percent of the Mexican population is located in the triangle of Monterrey, Mexico City, and Guadalajara. Growth of these investments in the maquiladora industry is expected to continue at 10 to 15 percent annually through the end of the decade.

Mexico is a federal republic and has been relatively stable politically in the past few decades. Mexico seems to have learned much from the 1994 currency crash and the 1995 recession, and despite Brazil's recent currency problems, Mexico is showing strong growth in its domestic output; 1997 gross domestic product (GDP) was $415 billion, a 7 percent growth over 1996. Mexico exports in excess of $110 billion in goods, 85 percent of which goes to the United States. The United States also happens to be Mexico's biggest source of imports (77 percent, or $71 billion).

Recently, Mexico has been increasing its textile manufacturing capabilities. In some people's minds, Mexico has produced a glut of excess capacity. This will soon change, however, because many U.S. companies are moving into Mexico and many companies that are already there are growing at an alarming rate.

Manufacturing in Mexico

North America is one of the leading garment vendors in the world. This is due primarily to the explosive growth of the apparel industry in Mexico. An article in the September 22, 1998, issue of *Women's Wear Daily,* "Cotton Summit: Big Surge for Mexico," stated that within two years exports from Mexico would leap 40 to 45 percent, with U.S. businesses sourcing from between fourteen thousand and fifteen thousand factories.[2] This is a drastic change considering that Mexico was considered a low-quality manufacturer of goods. Much of Mexico's success can be attributed to NAFTA: the number of factories has increased by 81 percent since its inception, and they are not low-tech, poor-quality operations.

Much of this growth has and will come from strategic alliances between American and Mexican companies. There will also be increasing European investment (through a pending trade agreement between Mexico and the EU) in Mexican industries, especially those whose low labor costs provide a significant strategic advantage. Because of this influx of cash, very large manufacturers that provide complete garment solutions are expected to increase in number between 15 and 20 percent.

NuStart

One example of an attempt to stem the flow of manufacturing to Asia was an initiative known as NuStart, a joint venture between one Mexican and three U.S. companies, specifically, Grupo Alfa, Guilford Mills, Burlington Mills, and DuPont. These companies aimed to help their customers set up shop south of the border.

They founded a city focused on the vertical integration of U.S. fiber, fabric, and apparel manufacturing. NuStart's premise was that the margin squeeze that the apparel industry faced was forcing the industry to move offshore to Asia and that the only way for U.S. companies truly to lower costs was to control the process themselves in a low-cost region such as Mexico.

One of the primary advantages to the NuStart city, located close to Temixco, Emiliano Zapata, and Xochitepec, is the large pool of inexpensive laborers. These four cities provided close to 400,000 potential workers, 25,000 of whom were women between the ages of seventeen and thirty-five. To prepare this labor force for the potential jobs, a training center for middle managers was set up in the area with aid from the Mexican state and federal government.

Investment in NuStart was a not-for-profit undertaking used by the Mexican government to jumpstart U.S. companies' confidence in Mexico as a quality locale for apparel manufacturing. To encourage local citizens to learn the necessary skills, NuStart sponsored programs such as the Integral Training Program for Women (to show female employees the integral part they would play in the company's success, thus overcoming a cultural barrier) and a ninety-day scholarship program offered by PROVECAT (Programa de Capacitación Técnica). Also recruited were the National School of Professional Education (the Colegio de Educación Profesiona Tecnica del Estado de Sonora, or CONALEP) and the secretary of public education, to support recruitment and personnel support for training programs. The training programs involved not only manufacturing skills but also included personal hygiene, family planning, building self-esteem, assertiveness, managing finances, and healthy eating.

A large part of NuStart's ability to proceed came from the support of the state of Morelos and the Mexican government. Morelos offered land at a nominal price and the Mexican government extended a four-year grace period on property taxes. On top of that, the state of Morelos did not collect payroll taxes. Morelos also committed to supplying electrical networks, potable water, wastewater treatment, and access roads connecting to the Sol Highway. This infrastructure gave companies locating in that area a head start on getting everything set up.

Guilford Mills

Companies establishing new manufacturing facilities in Mexico are looking to integrate the value chain. One company, Guilford Mills, built a factory on close to six hundred acres of land on Mexico's Gulf Coast. Located in Tampico-Altamira, the factory was designed to integrate the cutting and sewing processes at one location.

Guilford Mills's goal was to be a large source not only of textiles but also of apparel. Dyeing and finishing services would remain at one of Guilford's other companies. The primary reason for building this plant was to gain speed in the ever-changing apparel market. By having control over the entire plant, the company would be able to set priorities and try new and unique products and processes without having to deal with layers of approval.

Guilford also decided to take part in the NuStart initiative. While they did not have the wherewithal to operate new plants in Mexico, they were interested in building and leasing plants there. Their previous business model involved dealing with companies that had between $10 and $150 million of revenue per year—companies that could move in and set up shop, such as giant apparel manufacturers VF Corporation and Sara Lee.

Akra

Akra is a division of Alfa, the largest yarn producer in Mexico. Not only is its site enormous, spanning sixteen plants with thirty thousand square feet of production space per plant, but it also employs four to five thousand sewers.

Burlington Mills

Burlington has been operating plants in Mexico since 1994. It has used these plants to support the four major lines of its garment business: Burlington Menswear, Klopman Fabrics (synthetics), Burlington Denim, and Burlington Sportswear. Through plant expansion they hoped to add $225 million in annual sales.

Two new fabric plants became operational in 1999: a joint venture yarn plant and a joint venture denim processing plant. They also built four cutting and sewing facilities at NuStart in Morelos, in 1999. This three-year expansion required more than $80 million in investment.

In 1999, Burlington announced it would close seven, or 25 percent, of its apparel plants. Most of these plants handled operations such as dyeing and finishing and yarn dyeing and spinning. The closures were blamed on the Asian crisis and the lack of a near-term cure. The company felt that fabrics and garments were selling below cost and decided to reorganize the business according to three criteria:

1. To reduce capacity, using only the most modern facilities and running the U.S. facilities only on value-added fabrics
2. To make the reorganization as comprehensive as possible so that future reorganization would not be necessary
3. To become well positioned on a global basis by doing what it was presently doing and continuing to expand into Mexico

On the basis of these initiatives, Burlington decided to focus on growing its Mexican operations and modernizing its North American facilities.

Denim City

Similar to NuStart, Denim City, aka La Laguna Denim City, was from the beginning a fully vertical solution for denim vendors. There are more than three hundred factories in the municipalities of Coahuila and Durango employing more than forty thousand laborers with an average weekly production of three million garments. This region offers denim mills, cutting and sewing facilities, washing, finish labeling, and packaging. The ability to gain advantages in denim has attracted huge apparel manufacturers such as VF Corporation, Garment Retailer, Sears, and JCPenney.

Kentucky Lajat

Kentucky Lajat is an enormous U.S.-Mexico joint venture that focuses on jeans. The plant added capacity to Kentucky Apparel, LLP's three large facilities located around Tomkinsville, Kentucky. The machines for the plants were installed one year before the terms of NAFTA were scheduled to lift the duty on all apparel machinery (cutting included). The plant currently produces more then 500,000 pairs of jeans per week for Garment Retailer, Penney's, Liz Claiborne, DKNY Jeans, and others. More than a dozen contractors around the region added capacity to the company's large sewing plants.

Pafer Huichita S.A. de C.V.

Pafer is a midsized contractor for VF Corporation. Its factory in La Laguna has fourteen hundred employees and works in conjunction with offices in New York and El Paso, Texas (in a twenty-thousand-square-foot shipping center). It currently produces five-pocket fashion jeans and Casual Pants overalls. Pafer is planning to open another facility in Florida, a Mexican town approximately twenty minutes outside of Torreon. This will require another thousand workers. Pafer's current capacity is between 85,000 and 100,000 units per week. It currently works with long-term contractors that order between 5,000 and 49,000 units per week. The Florida facility should bring total weekly production to 165,000 units.

Industrias Papadopulos S.A. de C.V.

Industrias Papadopulos contracts for Polo for Boys. Its main customers are the Mexico education department, Garment Retailer, L.L. Bean, and Polo Ralph Lauren. Besides pants, shorts, jackets, and overalls, it also produces knitted shirts, pleated pants, and adult formal and casual clothing. The factory uses U.S. and Mexican cotton and U.S. woven polywool, polycotton, and cotton-rayon blends. The fabric for its knitwear comes from the company's own mill. The capacity is currently five thousand pairs of five-pocket jeans per week. However, there is significant slowdown when a new fashion product is introduced; production drops to four to five thousand pairs per week due to quality issues. The plant currently employs more than a thousand people.

Caribbean Basin Initiative

A region with high potential for garment sourcing is the group of countries that make up the Caribbean Basin Initiative. The CBI builds on the worldwide Generalized System of Preferences (GSP), under which the United States and other industrialized countries eliminate tariffs on most products from developing countries. The CBI was originally launched in 1983 to encourage growth in export-oriented industries in the smaller economies of the Caribbean and Central America, with the goal of helping to reduce the region's dependence on exports of traditional but price-volatile basic commodities and agricultural products. CBI's ultimate goal is to bring all member countries into parity with NAFTA in terms of tariff rates and regulations.

Imports of cotton and synthetics from Mexico and the Caribbean Basin region have increased 20.3 percent and 14.6 percent respectively. The import of knit fabrics from the Caribbean Basin increased more than 36 percent between 1996 and 1997. While El Salvador, Honduras, and the Dominican Republic offer superior economic incentives, there is currently no CBI parity with Mexico.

The CBI's centerpiece is the unilateral U.S. tariff exemption and tariff reduction program, the Caribbean Basin Economic Recovery Act (CBERA), which began on January 1, 1984, and was expanded in 1990. CBERA affords nonreciprocal tariff preferences to developing countries in the Caribbean Basin area to aid their economic development and to diversify and expand their production and exports. CBERA tariff reduction benefits apply to merchandise entered into or withdrawn from a warehouse for consumption on or after January 1, 1984.

CBI tariff exemptions and reductions cover more products than the GSP does, are permanent, and are not subject to annual reviews in which they can be suspended for certain reasons, as are those under the GSP. The twenty-four CBI participants comprise all of the Central American countries, all of the Caribbean island countries (except Cuba, Anguilla, the Cayman Islands, and the Turks and Caicos Islands), and Guyana. The beneficiaries cannot be graduated from the program because of increased per capita incomes, as under the GSP, although countries can be suspended for other reasons.

The CBI initially excluded apparel. However, a special program grants CBI countries liberal import quotas for apparel produced from fabric made and cut in the United States. Apparel is the region's most rapidly growing export to the United States. In 1996, apparel accounted for 42 percent of the value of total U.S. imports from the CBI-eligible countries. Generally more than 60 percent of the content of apparel imported from the CBI region is from the United States, compared to less than 10 percent for imports from Asia. What this means for the remaining mills based in the United States is that some portion of the output lost to the closure of domestic apparel vendor plants is being shifted to new vendors in CBI countries.

In 1996, of the $14.5 billion in goods imported to the United States from CBI countries, 18.9 percent entered duty free and another 0.3 percent entered with reduced tariffs under the CBI program. Costa Rica and the Dominican Republic provided about 57 percent of the total. These two countries are also the biggest Caribbean-region exporters to the United States. By 1997, the import figure had grown to $17.8 billion. Currently, 68 percent of imports from CBI countries enter the United States duty free under CBERA, but most textile and apparel products are still excluded from this program.

The development of CBI into a law is interesting. An effort was made to ratify it in July 1997, when the House of Representatives passed CBI provisions as part of an omnibus tax bill. However, these provisions were stripped from the final bill by the House and Senate Conference Committee that drafted the final version of the omnibus bill.

In November 1997 there was a move to enact the bill in conjunction with fast-track authority in the House of Representatives. Both the House Ways and Means and Senate Finance Committees favorably reported separate versions of the bill. A vote was taken on the CBI bill on November 4, 1997, and it was defeated 234 to 182.

Bill HR 984 attempted to use Hurricanes George and Mitch as reasons to pass legislation granting temporary NAFTA parity to CBI states for five years. The first congressional hearing in the House Ways and

Means Committee took place on Tuesday, March 23, 1999. Strong lobbying efforts were made by various labor and industry groups both for and against the bill. The purpose of the hearing was to gather public comment on and to examine the success of the CBI, the state of economic development in the region following Hurricanes George and Mitch, and the benefits and costs to U.S. national security interests and to U.S. firms and workers.

Enactment of the Caribbean Basin Trade Partnership Act (CBTPA) in 2000 marked an important expansion of these benefits, allowing duty-free and quota-free treatment for certain apparel assembled in qualified CBI countries, and applying reduced duties to certain other previously excluded products. Effective October 2, 2000, apparel manufactured in eligible CBI countries from U.S. yarns and fabrics would enter the United States free of quota and duty. Effectively, CBI beneficiary countries now enjoy NAFTA parity with respect to U.S. imports of applicable apparel produced in those countries. In mid-2000, the Administration conducted an extensive review of each of the twenty-four CBI beneficiary countries in connection with the process of considering their designation as beneficiaries under the CBTPA. Direct engagement with CBI country governments during that review helped bring about improvements, in some cases substantial, related to CBTPA criteria, including protection of internationally recognized worker rights, protection of intellectual property, and participation in the World Trade Organization and Free Trade Area of the Americas. In 2000, manufactured products, such as apparel and electrical and nonelectrical machinery, amounted to more than half of CBI exports to the United States.[3]

Opportunities

Passage of the CBI brought a host of benefits to Garment Retailer. First and foremost was the expansion of NAFTA-level tariff parity to the countries of the CBI region. CBI countries became a potential source of complementary production for current and future vendors already operating in Mexico and for those considering shifting production out of the United States. In essence, CBI expanded the available labor pool of textile workers. It also helped create the potential to bring more low-cost production capacity online in the Americas. This was especially important because most vendors expected capacity constraints to become an issue in Mexican sourcing in the early years of the new century as a direct result of the increased attractiveness of Mexico as a textile and manufacturing source location.

According to publicly available statistics from the Association of American Chambers of Commerce in Latin America (AACCLA) and the U.S. Bureau of Labor Statistics, CBI countries have cheaper labor rates than Mexico ($3.52 per day versus $3.95 plus). A secondary benefit is a potential reduction in cycle time for product shipments. Although there is a forty-eight-hour shipping time from most Caribbean ports to the United States, it is much easier to clear products through customs at the ports than it is to clear trucked products through customs at the U.S.-Mexico border. Garment Retailer should further explore the possibility of cycle time reduction by comparing sea shipments from CBI-based vendors to trucked shipments from Mexican vendors.

Challenges Encountered South of the Border

Even though there has been explosive growth in textile imports from Mexico and the Caribbean Basin countries, the growth of textile imports from Asia will continue to increase and will remain on top for a few years. Labor costs are currently dropping in the China and Bangladesh regions as Southeast Asia has had to deal with currency devaluations. Above-normal growth from Asia will continue.

The textile industry in Mexico seems to be a solid choice for future growth. There are many advantages to be gained from expanding Garment Retailer's operations and following the lead of other garment manufactures that have paved the way in Mexico.

National Incentives

Because of the government's need to bring in foreign investment, Mexico allows foreign investors to own 100 percent of companies incorporated in Mexico. The government also offers a corporate income tax rate of 34 percent, which is lower than that of the United States, Canada, the United Kingdom, Germany, Japan, Malaysia, and Thailand.

There is a minimum 2 percent tax on the average value in a year of a company's fixed and financial assets that is mandatory from the third taxable year after the start of operations. This is applied only when the amount exceeds the regular income tax due, in which case the corresponding difference is paid. The rate of the value-added tax is generally 15 percent. There are some major exceptions to these statutes for such items as exported goods and services and the sale of basic staples and drugs.

Businesses must also pay state and municipal taxes. In eighteen states a special tax is imposed on payrolls. This ranges from a minimum of 0.9 percent in Baja, California, to a maximum of 4.6 percent in Quintana Roo. Another significant state and municipal levy is the property tax imposed on the use of the soil, based on the property-appraised value. In this case, the annual rate for urban land varies between 0.001 and 0.04 new pesos per thousand.

During the first or second year of operation, companies may take the option of a one-time depreciation deduction of their fixed assets. Except for investments in industrial bays, this option excludes companies located in Mexico City and its surrounding areas, Guadalajara, and Monterrey. Purchased automobiles, other transportation, and office equipment, excepting computer equipment, are also excluded. The immediate depreciation rate for industrial bays is 62 percent. In the case of machinery and equipment, it varies from 62 to 95 percent, depending on the sector.

Banco Nacional de Comercio Exterior (Bancomext) and Nacional Financiera, Mexico's largest development banks, may participate on a temporary basis and with minority ownership as stockholders in the investment projects of foreign companies. Once the project is mature, the corresponding development bank withdraws from the partnership and sells its stock to the charter partners or to third parties at a price agreed upon in the initial contract. Bancomext may also contribute venture capital resources for projects generating foreign currency.

Companies choosing to set up business in Mexico may also take advantage of the following programs to help reduce import duties on raw materials and merchandise:

Maquiladora Program

- *Benefits.* Companies choosing this program may import raw materials, containers and packing materials, fuels, spare parts, and machinery and equipment without paying duties or value-added tax to manufacture their goods.

– *Requirements.* Goods produced are for export only.

Temporary Importation to Manufacture Export Goods (Programa de Importación Temporal para Producir Artículos de Exportación, or PITEX)

– *Benefits.* Raw materials, containers, packing materials, fuels, and machinery and equipment may be imported without paying tariffs or value-added tax.
– *Requirements*: (1) to be engaged in the manufacturing of non-oil goods; (2) to export no less than 10 percent of sales, or an amount equivalent to US$500,000 per year, in order to be able to import inputs used on the exported production, under the above terms; and (3) to benefit from tax exemption on imports for machinery and equipment by assigning to exports at least 10 percent of sales.

Import Duty Drawback

– *Benefits.* Refund for import duties paid on inputs used to produce goods to be sold abroad or required by the exporting companies.
– *Requirements.* Submit the corresponding application, one year at the latest after having imported the necessary inputs, and within not more than sixty working days after having exported the goods.

State Programs

To attract foreign investment, some federal and state governments, depending on the benefits of the project, grant reductions on the price of state land leased or sold to an investing foreign company.

Practically all Mexican state governments have a secretary for economic development who coordinates and oversees state incentive programs. Each state also has a state government Web site (usually parsed www.<state name>.gob.mx, as in www.jalisco.gob.mx) that lists resources available, including industrial parks, specific tax and tariff breaks, support organizations, the state's five-year development plan, and state government contact information. However, these sites generally have little hard information on the exact programs available. Foreign companies interested in investing should contact the state secretaries directly in order to negotiate terms.

For example, Aguascalientes, a state in central Mexico, has become one of the country's biggest success stories and a leading recipient of FDI due to an extensive support infrastructure it has created to attract and retain companies.

In December 1994 the peso experienced a sudden devaluation. Soon after, one of Siemens AG's subcontractors reneged on a shipment of electronics for a Siemens plant in Puebla. The local Siemens vice president was able to go to Aguascalientes' State Council on Economic Trade and Development for a quickly executed aid package that allowed Siemens to meet its shipping deadline. In rapid order, the council located two vacant buildings for a factory and arranged for the installation of electricity and eleven telephone lines, including fiber-optic data lines to Guadalajara and Mexico City. Within two days they accomplished tasks that can easily take up to twelve weeks in Mexico. The state government also rounded up three hundred local workers and offered, as they do for all new businesses, to pay minimum wage and social security for three months of training. In less than six weeks, the first delivery truck rolled out.

Aguascalientes' economic council wows visiting businessmen with bilingual computer graphic presentations, tours of the local vocational training school, and a full agenda of appointments with potential joint venture partners, real estate agents, lawyers, and accountants. Instead of feeling stymied by red-tape-loving bureaucrats, business owners in Aguascalientes regard the state government as a partner, an ally. The state government helps expedite permit and licensing procedures for foreign investors. It also diffuses reams of demand-related information to local exporters and potential exporters through its monthly bulletin, *Exportunidades,* which lists international companies needing anything from garlic to ladies' raincoats. In this manner, exporters can more easily find an outlet for their products.

Opportunities

The Mexican national and local governments endeavor to encourage foreign investment in Mexico. Garment Retailer will thus be able to negotiate favorable terms for investing in the Mexican textile sector.

Mexico is a member of the World Trade Organization (WTO) and has several other bilateral and multilateral trade agreements in place. The most important of these agreements is NAFTA. A few others are worth mentioning as well.

North American Free Trade Agreement

In 1994, NAFTA was signed by the United States, Canada, and Mexico, formalizing a trading alliance between the three nations. NAFTA's main objectives are to eliminate trade barriers and facilitate the cross-border movement of goods and services, to promote conditions of fair competition in the free trade area, and to increase investment opportunities in the three countries.

NAFTA was established to encourage a free market throughout North America while at the same time ensuring compliance with protectionist policies against goods from outside the region. NAFTA allows for special breaks on import duties and tariffs and taxes, and the eventual elimination of virtually all duties, tariffs, and quotas among the three member nations.

Mexican industry has benefited greatly from NAFTA-related benefits because it is difficult for Mexican manufacturers to compete with their Asian and other foreign counterparts on cost. Compared to their international competitors, Mexican firms are generally small and lack the modern quality and production controls that are common among many Asian vendors. This situation is changing as large U.S. and Asian firms move operations to Mexico, bringing with them their best practices.

NAFTA includes special provisions regarding textile and apparel trade between Mexico, Canada, and the United States. These provisions cover fibers, yarns, textiles, and apparel goods specifically identified by a harmonized code. In the event of inconsistency or conflict between member countries, the NAFTA provisions generally prevail over any other treaty such as the Uruguay Round of negotiations on the General Agreement on Tariffs and Trade and World Trade Organization (GATT-WTO).

Special rules regulate the region and country-of-origin determination process. A textile or apparel good may be required to meet two distinct origin determinations. First, a good can comply with the NAFTA rules of origin to qualify for preferential treatment within the NAFTA block, as explained in greater detail in the Mexico Direct brief *The Future of Rules of Origin in NAFTA Trade*. Second, a product can meet the country-of-origin marking rules to specify its treatment in binational trade.

Tariffs

Tariff elimination for textile and apparel goods is regulated separately from other goods through its own set of reduction regulations, NAFTA Annex 300-B. Each country has established its own schedule for phasing out the duties on imports in the NAFTA region on an item-by-item basis. Most duties on textiles and apparel goods were eliminated by January 1, 1999.

Import Duties

NAFTA calls for the progressive elimination of duties on textile and apparel products for goods fulfilling the rules of origin. By 1999, Mexico's tariffs on 89 percent of U.S. fabric exports were eliminated, as were 95 percent of U.S. duties on Mexican fabric exports.

Textile and apparel goods that do not originate from NAFTA countries will not benefit from these tariff preferences. The tariff elimination will make foreign fabrics and inputs very costly factors in apparel manufacturing processes.

Quotas

Textile products that qualify as NAFTA-originating are free of quota and visa requirements and are traded on the block for a special NAFTA tariff rate.

Rules of Origin

The NAFTA rules of origin establish the criteria for goods to qualify for preferential tariff rates and nontariff advantages. Goods that comply with any one of the general NAFTA rules of origin are considered to be NAFTA-originating. The three general rules of origin are as follows:

1. Wholly obtained or produced in the region
2. Made from materials totally obtained or produced in the region
3. Transformed significantly from incorporated foreign materials

Strict rules of origin for textile and apparel customs duties are eliminated immediately once rules of origin are met. Textiles and apparel must be cut and sewn in NAFTA countries from yarn made in the NAFTA countries (the yarn forward rule). Textiles and apparel spun from cotton and synthetic yarns must be cut and sewn in the NAFTA countries from fibers made in the NAFTA countries (the fiber forward rule).

These rules ensure that no more than a small fraction of the total volume is added in non-NAFTA countries. However, if more than 7 percent of the combined weight of the principal component is from yarn and fiber that originated in non-NAFTA countries, the product loses its NAFTA country origin. Certain apparel made from silk and other fabrics in short supply in North America and certain items of apparel such as brassieres are subject to rules of origin other than the yarn forward or fiber forward rules.

The Mexico Special Regimen

The Mexico Special Regimen is a specific in-bond program for textile and apparel manufacturing. Goods imported into the United States under the Mexico Special Regimen are not subject to quota or visa requirements and are completely duty free. The basic requirement for a textile or apparel good to be included in this program can be found under harmonized tariff code 9802.90000, summarized as follows:

1. The product must be assembled in Mexico.
2. The fabric must be wholly formed in the United States.
3. The fabric must be cut into components in the United States.

Marking Rules

Until 2008, marking rules may come into play for specific textile goods. For the binational textile trade, besides fulfilling labeling requirements, marking rules help determine exact tariff rates, material processing fees, quotas, and visas. Since Mexico, Canada, and the United States each maintain separate tariff phase-out schedules, the country of origin is necessary to levy the correct duty.

If NAFTA origin can be proved, however, the importance of country of origin is reduced, because it affects only tariff reduction schedules and merchandise processing fees (meaning that NAFTA-originating goods are free of quota and visa requirements). In fact, after 2008, country of origin will have no bearing for all textile goods for which NAFTA preferences can be claimed.

The compliance process for U.S. marking rules for textile and apparel goods is a step-by-step process that determines the specific country in which a good originated. Marking rules are applied sequentially and importers are free to apply those rules that most favor their international trade programs. In the case of sets and ensembles, special provisions have been defined for the determination of textile country of origin.

Standard Version of Country of Origin Rules for Textiles

The first marking rule, C1, Sourcing Goods, provides that goods that are wholly obtained or produced in a country must be marked as the product of that country. Similar to the definition of goods wholly obtained or produced for the purposes of NAFTA tariff preference, this marking rule is narrowly defined and the goods may not contain any foreign materials.

Under C2, Tariff Change or Other Change, the materials may have some foreign content; however, they must have undergone a specified change in tariff classification, or any other specified change, to assign them the same country of origin as the final product. The majority of marking rules require a change in tariff classification or other specific change, but none require calculation of regional value content.

C3, Country Where Knit to Shape or Country Where Wholly Assembled, states that if the apparel good was knit to shape, the country of origin is the single country in which the good was knit, and if the good was not knit to shape and was wholly assembled in a single country, the rule also applies. This rule lists a number of possible tariff shifts that would confer origin and make the rule inapplicable.

Under C4, or Country of Most Important Assembly or Manufacturing, when the country of origin of a textile or apparel product cannot be determined by the previous three rules, it can be defined as the place where the most important assembly or manufacturing process occurred. This rule involves some subjective analysis on the part of the customs agent as to which assembly process is most important.

C5, Country of Last Important Assembly or Manufacturing, states that if the most important assembly process cannot be determined, the last country where an important process took place is the country of origin.

Tariff Preference Levels

Apparel that is cut and sewn in a NAFTA country from non-NAFTA-country fabric will not meet the NAFTA rules of origin but nevertheless may qualify for NAFTA tariff reductions up to certain specific tariff preference levels (TPL). To obtain a tariff preference, a NAFTA country exporter applies to its government for a certificate of eligibility for tariff preference levels, which the exporter then sends to the NAFTA country importer. The importer presents the certificate of eligibility to its customs office to obtain the TPL duty reduction. Imports of apparel made from non-NAFTA-originating textiles beyond the TPLs qualify for Most Favored Nation (MFN) duty rates.

Emergency Action

Emergency tariff action can take effect only if serious damage to or actual threat toward the import country is about to occur. These actions include but are not limited to the following:

1. Limiting import volumes (for Mexico)
2. Suspending the duty reduction
3. Increasing duties to the lesser of the MFN rates

Trading Agreements with Other Countries

Regional Agreements

In recent years, free trade agreements have become a fundamental component of Mexico's trade policy. Mexico began developing agreements before the conclusion of the 1986-1993 Uruguay Round of GATT-WTO negotiations in order to enhance its economy's competitiveness and open up new markets. These agreements include the following:

1. *Economic Complementary Agreement with Chile* (1992). This agreement calls for a phased tariff elimination between the parties. It excludes many product categories such as agricultural commodities.

2. *North American Free Trade Agreement* with the United States and Canada (1994).

3. *Group of Three Free Trade Agreement* with Colombia and Venezuela (1995). The Group of Three Agreement calls for the total elimination of tariffs over a ten-year period, with some exceptions in the textile, petrochemical, and agricultural sectors. In addition, the arrangement includes agreements on services, intellectual property rights, government procurement, and investment.

4. *Mexico–Costa Rica Free Trade Agreement* (1995). This agreement is generally modeled on NAFTA but excludes many agriculture and energy products.

5. *Mexico-Bolivia Free Trade Agreement* (1995). This is similar to the Mexican agreement with Costa Rica.

These agreements include disciplines and commitments in the following areas: trade in goods, including agriculture; technical barriers to trade; government procurement; investment; trade in services; intellectual property; and institutional provisions, including dispute settlement.

Trading Agreement Negotiations in Progress

Mexico has continued to broaden and diversify its markets, particularly with the countries of North and South America and the EU. Mexico is negotiating free trade agreements with Guatemala, Honduras, and El Salvador. Bilateral negotiations are also under way for agreements with Nicaragua, Panama, Ecuador, and Peru, as well as for expanded agreements with Chile. Negotiations are continuing with Mercosur (a 1991 customs agreement among Argentina, Brazil, Venezuela, Paraguay, and Uruguay) for a transitional agreement to replace the existing agreements under the Latin American Integration Association, which will then serve as a basis for broader negotiations.

Mexico is participating with the other Western Hemisphere nations in negotiations for the progressive elimination of trade and investment barriers and the creation of a free trade area of the Americas; these negotiations were be completed by the end of 2005. Mexico has also signed cooperation agreements relating to trade and investment with such countries as the Republic of Korea, Australia, and New Zealand, and has set up ad hoc groups, committees, and binational commissions to administer trade relations.

Mexico participates as well in other regional initiatives such as Asia-Pacific Economic Cooperation (APEC), which has set the goal of achieving a free trade and investment regime by the year 2020.

WTO Agreement on Textiles and Clothing 1995–2005

From 1974 until the end of the Uruguay Round in 1993, the textile and clothing trade was governed by the Multifibre Arrangement (MFA), a framework for bilateral agreements or unilateral actions that has allowed signatories to place quotas on textile imports to prevent market disruption.

In 1995, the WTO's Agreement on Textiles and Clothing (ATC) took over from the MFA. Since 2005, the sector has been fully integrated into normal GATT-WTO rules. In particular, the quotas have come to an end, and importing countries are no longer able to discriminate between exporters. The ATC no longer exists: it is the only WTO agreement that had self-destruction built in. The primary goal for the phaseout was the expansion of textile trade through liberalization of world trade and reduction of trade barriers.

Integration: Returning Products Gradually to GATT 1994 Rules

Textiles and clothing products were returned to GATT rules over a ten-year period. This happened gradually, in four steps, to allow time for both importers and exporters to adjust to the new situation. Some of the products were previously under quotas. Any quotas that were in place on December 31, 1994, were carried over into the new agreement. For products that had quotas, the result of integration into GATT was the removal of these quotas.

The ATC agreement stated the percentage of products that had to be brought under GATT rules at each step. If any of these products came under quotas, the quotas had to be removed at the same time. The percentages were applied to the importing country's textile and clothing trade levels, using 1990 levels as the basis. The agreement also said that the quantities of imports permitted under the quotas were to grow annually and that the rate of expansion was to increase at each stage. The speed of that expansion was set out in a formula based on the growth rate that existed under the old MFA.

The actual formula for import growth under quotas is as follows: 0.16 x pre-1995 growth rate in the first step, 0.25 x Step 1 growth rate in the second step, and 0.27 x Step 2 growth rate in the third step.

Products brought under GATT rules at each of the first three stages had to cover the four main types of textiles and clothing: tops and yarns, fabrics, made-up textile products, and clothing. Any other restrictions that did not come under the MFA and did not conform to regular WTO agreements by 1996 had to be made to conform or be phased out by 2005.

Implications of NAFTA and GATT-WTO

Reduction of Quotas and Tariffs Restriction,
Creation of Free Trade Environment

Both NAFTA and GATT-WTO reduce tariffs and nontariff barriers in the textiles sector.

In North America, NAFTA eliminated some tariffs immediately; others were phased out over a ten-year period. Under NAFTA, no new quotas may be introduced and existing quotas were to be removed or phased out. On a worldwide basis, the Uruguay Round GATT-WTO agreement also called for the phasing out of import quotas over a ten-year period.

More important, it provided for the integration of textile agreements into the GATT-WTO scheme and the commitment of all members to provide greater market access in textile and clothing through tariff reductions and the elimination of nontariff barriers. A major impact of such liberalization agreements has been an increase in demand.

The opening of textile and clothing markets has created trade opportunities for exporting countries, many of which are in the developing world, such as Mexico. This liberalization is increasing and has become significant in the early years of the new century.

Development of International Sourcing Capabilities

Within the U.S. textile and apparel industry, the trend toward increased development of international sourcing capabilities in response to high U.S. production costs is continuing. For many American companies, international sourcing has had a positive impact on profit margins due to the reduced labor and manufacturing costs associated with overseas production. Sourcing in Mexico shows particular promise over the next several years and, as has been shown here, the country is already being exploited. As already noted, Mexico's main benefits as a sourcing location are its proximity to domestic U.S. markets and the elimination of tariffs and quotas on imports, resulting in quite a brisk trade in textiles and apparel between the United States and Mexico since 1994.

According to the American Textile Manufacturers Institute, U.S. textile and apparel exports to Mexico amounted to $3.7 billion in 1997, up almost 29 percent from 1996. Mexican producers shipped $5.9 billion of textile and apparel merchandise into the United States in 1997, an impressive gain of 40 percent over 1996 levels. In a few short years, Mexico has become the United States' largest source of imported apparel.

For the fabric portion of the industry, Mexican apparel production means full sourcing of fabrics from the United States for assembly in Mexico. As a result, U.S. fabric exports to Mexico amounted to $1.0 billion in 1997, compared to imports of only $380.5 million.

European Union Impact

Additional opportunities for increased Mexican-European trade have arisen since the establishment of the EU. Adoption of the Euro on January 1, 1999, has had a large impact on tax and accounting practices, as well as on trade agreements, duties, and tariffs. Formerly independent European national currencies are now set at a fixed exchange rate, denominated in euros. On July 1, 2002, all of the national currencies of countries participating in the EU were withdrawn. It was anticipated that this could result in some currency risk for companies with contracts denominated in the soon-to-be-obsolete pre-euro currencies. However, the creation of a single currency zone, a single trading bloc within the EU, and unification of external trade policies have helped to simplify the maze of trade regulations facing companies wishing to export to EU member states. The main risk presented by the creation of a single currency and common market is that the EU, like NAFTA, will enact exclusionary regulations, tariffs, and quotas for non-intra-EU trade.

A November 9, 1998, article from the Xinhua News Agency announced that Mexico and the EU were going to discuss a possible bilateral trade agreement. This agreement established a zone of free trade in goods and services between Mexico and the EU. The Mexico-EU negotiations ended with the hope of opening up markets, stepping up investment, and promoting reciprocal investments.

On March 12, 1999, a second round of talks between Mexico and the EU were conducted. The EU suggested a 66 percent immediate reduction of tariffs, with a total elimination by the year 2003. Mexico responded with an offer of 50 percent immediate reduction in tariffs.

Adoption of such an agreement has had many implications for manufacturers and exporters in the region. The additional influx of countries to the cheap Mexican labor pool has consumed even more worker hours and possibly caused Mexico's labor rates to increase.

Opportunities

Garment Retailer will achieve significant advantage from NAFTA provisions as long as the agreement's sourcing requirements are met. In other words, raw materials will need to be sourced in Mexico or the United States for reduced NAFTA tariff rates to apply. In addition, as the level of Mexican trade increases, Mexico's textile industry will become more sophisticated.

The recent worldwide trend toward freer trade, the elimination of quotas and tariffs, and other trade accords have somewhat reduced the NAFTA-derived tariff and quota-related benefits of Mexican sourcing. However, proximity-derived benefits such as the ability to take advantage of reduced product cycle time have remained and should remain intact.

As Mexico negotiates more trade agreements and the attractiveness of Mexico as a sourcing platform increases, the inherent risk is that sourcing demands in Mexico will increase beyond the ability of the Mexican industry to meet them. This in turn will reduce the Mexican textile industry's capacity to devote its resources to Garment Retailer's production needs. Thus an early advance into the market and a good faith effort to establish good working relationships with vendors in Mexico will go a long way toward securing future capacity for Garment Retailer in Mexico.

The next section contains information gathered from the February 1999 Wharton Economic Forecasting Associates analyst's report on the Mexican economy, as well as from Grupo Bursatil Mexicano, Centro de Analisis e Investigación Económica, Ciemex-Wefa, and Bursametrica Management.

Outlook for Mexican Economic Growth

Expectation of Lower Economic Growth for 1999

Mexican GDP growth for 1999 was expected to slow as psychological and economic aftereffects of the Brazilian devaluation put pressure on interest rates and sent capital out of the country. The following chart shows what analysts projected would be the total Mexican GDP for 1999 and 2000.

The Mexican economy had been growing strongly over the previous four years, following the higher-than-expected growth of the U.S. economy. However, that growth was expected to slow during 1999 and to contribute to a slowdown of the Mexican economy.

Although there were fears that the Russian default in October 1998 and the effects of the Brazilian exchange rate crisis could reduce GDP growth for the year, Mexico in fact had a higher-than-expected GDP growth rate in 1998. This was achieved through an easing of monetary policy during the second half of the year. However, the increase in money supply threatened the government's inflation target for 1998, resulting in an inflation rate that was almost 5 percent higher than the one estimated by the Mexican government for the year.

The Mexican government estimated that GDP growth in 1999 would be 3 percent and the inflation rate would be 13 percent. Mexico was able to reduce the inflation rate the previous two years, but it was not known how monetary policy would be conducted during 1999 and whether the government's inflation target would be achieved.

As stated before, the higher-than-expected inflation rate in 1998 was probably due to the government's easing of monetary policy, resulting in a money supply that was above the level needed for economic growth. High inflation was of some concern as Mexico headed for an economic slowdown during 1999 as a consequence of the Brazilian devaluation, an expected slowdown in the U.S. economy, and political uncertainty surrounding the 2000 presidential elections. Analysts believed, however, that the inflation rate would fall during 1999 and 2000.

Mexico Currency and Inflation Outlook—Continued Pressure over the Mexican Peso During 1999

The Mexican peso was expected to continue suffering from pressure during 1999 and 2000, mainly as a result of weakness in other Latin American and Asian markets. Inflation remained a threat as long as the government continued its loose monetary policy. If the Mexican government were not able to set and follow a clear and transparent monetary policy and keep inflation in check, either inflation or the exchange rate would suffer the consequences.

The Mexican economy is one of the most liquid economies of the region, so the risks of currency flight and continued pressure on the peso in the exchange rate market were best taken seriously by the government as the Zedillo administration approached the end of its presidential mandate. Economic stability was also threatened by market anxiety over who would be chosen as President Zedillo's replacement in the 2000 elections, and over whether or not the Institutional Revolutionary Party (Partido Revolucionario Institucional or PRI) would continue to control Mexican politics.

Forecast Risks

The probability of devaluation in Brazil was no longer one of the biggest threats to the Mexican economy, because Brazil's currency devaluation occurred on January 13, 1999. The risks to Mexico were similar to the risks associated with the Tequila effect (the impact that the 1994

Mexican economic crisis had on the region) and the Cairpirinha effect (or Samba effect, the fallout from the Brazilian currency crisis), because both countries tried to produce a controlled devaluation but later had to allow their currencies to float freely. The next two years would be very difficult for Mexico because it had to show to the world that its political system had learned the lessons from its own currency crisis.

Summary

As part of the fiscal budget approved for 1999, the Mexican government increased import tariffs from 3 to 10 percent for the countries that did not have a trade agreement with Mexico.

The consumer price index during the month of December rose by 2.44 percent after an increase of 1.77 percent during November, taking the year-over-year consumer price index (CPI) to a higher-than-expected 18.6 percent. The government's inflation target for 1998 was 12 percent. The higher-than-expected CPI raised questions about monetary policy. In 1997, the CPI was only 15.7 percent.

Opportunities

Mexico had fully recovered from the 1994 debt and currency crises. As a developing economy, Mexico is subject to economic fluctuations based on world market expectations about the health of its neighboring Latin American countries and to worries about the country's economic policies and political stability. Since joining NAFTA, however, increased trade and tighter linkage to the United States and Canada have resulted in increased economic stability for Mexico and a more fertile environment for FDI. Garment Retailer should thus not be dissuaded from investment in Mexico on account of its economic indicators.

Labor

Because Mexico has undergone so many changes in its government, economy, and trade and tariff agreements, its labor outlook is extremely positive. Some of the factors that have influenced these trends include the increase of textile manufacturing in Mexico, increased vertical integration, increased worker skills, a reduced labor pool because of an in-creasing numbers of plants, and competition from the various manufac-turing industries, including electronics and automotive. At a macro level, it looks as though Mexican labor costs for textiles are dropping.

Costs and Unemployment

As more companies look to Mexico as a source of inexpensive labor, it will be more difficult to hire people and wages will increase. This effect has already been seen in some of the Maquiladora cities, such as Ti-juana, which is home to more than 666 plants employing more than 147,000 people. Company X has already felt the effect of this increase and is finding it more difficult to find and keep employees for its plants.

Another key factor in labor trends is the unemployment rate. Over-all, Mexico has a lot of problems with unemployment; however, when you look at the urban areas, almost everyone is employed.

In 1998, close to 760,000 new jobs were created as measured by the number of both permanent and urban workers registered at Municipal Solidarity Funds. Additionally, the average open unemployment rate of 3.2 percent for 1998 was the lowest figure since 1992. Unemployment had been on a steady decrease, due in part to all of the foreign invest-ment in factories and other businesses in Mexico. Because unemploy-ment had dropped to such a low level in the urban areas, manufacturers were looking for obscure, rural places to set up shop and draw on a se-cure labor pool. Although the owners needed to worry about resources and infrastructure, it was difficult to get inexpensive laborers to offset their costs. Often one company would move in, straighten out the re-source problems, and start to train the local laborers for work, and then another company would move in, set up shop, and take advantage of the path the first company had already beaten. This is how clusters, centrally located groups of similar factories and services, formed.

Absenteeism

A serious problem in Mexico has been absenteeism. Very often, work-ers decide not to show up on given days (taking a long weekend) or some-times never return after vacation. One of the most difficult times of year is right after Christmas. Because the factories can be hundreds of miles away from the workers' families, they tend to work in the factories, save up money, and then return home and stay there for a while. Once they need money again, they go out and find another factory job. Farhad Kashani of Company X stated that there were times when more than one hundred of his thousand laborers did not show up for work after Christmas. This is a plant that is known for retaining its people. Others are having a much more difficult time.

Comparison to Asia

Mexico's labor costs are close to four and a half times higher then China's; however, they are still more then eight times lower then in the United States. By 2005, Mexico's labor rate was expected to increase to one seventh of U.S. labor costs, and China's labor rates were to rise to one tenth of those of the United States. Although Mexico will become more expensive, it is expected that its proximity and convenience will help to sustain production facilities.

Regulations

Labor relationships are established regardless of a labor agreement when there is subordination (employees follow the directions of the employer) and economic dependency on the employer. Under U.S. labor law, commercial agents or sales promoters are considered employees when their activity is permanent.

Employees may be dismissed with fair cause, as statutorily defined. Fair cause basically includes only significant violations by employees of employment terms, to the detriment of the employer. In the event of dismissal without fair cause, the terminated employee will, at his option, have the right to the following:

1. To demand reinstatement because he or she is a trusted employee ("empleado de confianza"), in which case he or she will receive payment of only the following termination indemnities
2. Three (3) months' salary
3. Twenty (20) days' salary for each year of employment

4. Seniority premium equal to twelve (12) days' salary per year of employment

5. Proportional share of vacation, annual bonus, and profit sharing for the year in which the employment was terminated

6. Salaries accrued from the date of termination to the date of payment of indemnities

Opportunities

In the near future, labor will be readily available for Garment Retailer's manufacturing facilities. Adjustments will be needed in worker expectations for a successful relationship to be maintained between the facilities and the workers. However, for the short term it would be better for Garment Retailer to copy best practices of existing successful facilities in Mexico (such as Ford). The labor pool is likely to change over time and should be carefully monitored.

Before a textile vendor can source for Garment Retailer, it must be designated Garment Retailer Certified. This requires Garment Retailer compliance officers to evaluate and rate each potential vendor on the basis of a number of criteria, including facility standards, quality assurance, compliance issues, environmental standards, and resource availability. Facility location is also a consideration.

Resources and Utilities

Water

The primary resource requirement for a textile manufacturer is water. Whether for washing, garment dyeing, or finishing the garment, a source of clean water must be available. The consistency and regularity of color of a garment is critically dependent on this capability.

The water supply in Mexico is very limited, with a constant source available primarily in Guadalajara and in Tamaulipas, as well as minute supplies in Puebla, Cuernavaca, and Aguascalientes. The water in Mexico is high in minerals and is thus much harder than in the United States. As a result, before it can be potable, minimum water processing must be performed. Additional water softening must be completed before it can be used for garments. All purification requirements and pH level adjustments are expensive. Moreover, the government in Mexico owns the natural resources and thus charges a standard cost per cubic meter of water utilized.

The cost of the necessary water treatment facility can be quite high. Few vendors, with the exception of those like UIC (a Hong Kong–based company with operations in Mexico), have the capital to purchase such treatment facilities. However, other vendors must follow suit to remain competitive.

Due to the volume of goods Garment Retailer receives from Mexico, it is imperative that the requisite water and treatment facilities be available. With the ever-increasing demand for Mexican production capacity, one way for Garment Retailer to secure vendor relations could be to fund and build a water treatment facility. This facility could be located in a hub of textile manufacturing or close to a centralized Garment Retailer distribution center. This would allow vendors more vertical integration in Mexico and would help Garment Retailer maintain strong ties in the country. Any excess capacity of this facility could be outsourced by Garment Retailer to other vendors for additional profit.

Electricity

Availability of electricity does not seem to be an issue for the textile industry in Mexico. Even when a facility is built at a greenfield (previously undeveloped) site, electrical requirements are easily satisfied.

Telecommunications and Information Systems

There were 9.5 million telephone lines in service in Mexico in June 1998. Mexico is in the process of fostering competition in telecommunications, and has granted ten concessions to companies who began offering competing long-distance telephone service starting on January 1, 1997. U.S. companies are involved in six of the consortia.

Yet Mexico's information system infrastructure is considerably underdeveloped when compared with that of the United States. Because of the high cost of telecommunications, World Wide Web and other Internet-based services have grown at a very slow rate in Mexico. Few businesses have deemed it worthwhile to invest in the dedicated data lines required to ensure access, and only a few business servers currently exist. Additionally, the current devaluation of the peso has restricted cash available for investment and has made it very difficult for firms to enter the world business market through the Internet.

Mexico is concerned that its lack of telecommunications infrastructure will negatively affect foreign investment. Companies such as Motorola and Qualcomm view this concern as an opportunity to provide services to the general public. Mexican universities are also interested in developing an Internet backbone throughout Mexico.

Motorola will work with Corporación Mobilcom to build a nationwide wireless network, starting in Mexico City and later expanding to other regions. This system will focus on providing basic connectivity, data transmission, and messaging services.

The National Council for Science and Technology in Mexico has been trying to build the national information system backbone with the support of the universities. These efforts have helped raise the bandwidth for the Internet backbone from 64 kilobits per second to 2 megabits per second. In late 1993 the National Technological Network was formed to be the main Internet service provider for Mexico's businesses. Various other regional networks are also being developed around the country. The primary drivers for this are the universities and libraries.

In 1998, Qualcomm, a leading provider of wireless infrastructure, received purchase orders for roughly $200 million in digital cellular technology service equipment. This was the first stage in a three-year, $650 million contract. The project helped to build on Mexico's budding wireless telecommunications infrastructure.

Transportation

Four modes of transportation are available in Mexico for the import and export of textiles. They are air, rail, truck, and water. Depending on the origin or destination of the product and the lead-time flexibility, certain modes may be better suited for a particular part of the journey between different levels in the supply chain. However, while planes, trains, and boats do carry freight between the United States and Mexico, 80 percent of all United States-to-Mexico trade moves by truck.

Trucking and Border Crossings

The most common mode of transportation within Mexico and out-bound from Mexico is trucking. This requires a good network of high-ways and inner-city roads. Additionally, well-equipped and efficient bor-der crossings are requisite for a smooth transition between countries.

Mexico's highway system is a cluttered combination of unpaved roads (157,752 km), highways (94,248 km) and tollways (6,740 km). Parts of the road system have been privatized, resulting in a mismatch in the quality of roads available to commercial interstate transportation. Sev-eral 110-kilometers-per-hour highways are being constructed to reduce travel time from Mexico's east to west coast. To reduce overall transpor-tation costs, some trucks avoid paying tolls by traveling solely on free public roads. This results in higher total transport times and jeopardizes the safety of the goods in transit (due to more frequent incidents of hi-jacking and poor road conditions.)

According to the *Journal of Commerce,* approximately eleven thou-sand trucks cross the border each day from Mexico into the United States. As noted, 80 percent of cross-border cargo moves by truck. Al-though there are twenty-eight border-crossing points, only five are con-sidered major. Texas constitutes 63 percent of the U.S. border and 57 per-cent of the entry points, and handles 66 percent of transborder traffic. California handles 24 percent of the traffic, and Arizona 10 percent. (New Mexico's cross-border traffic is negligible.)

The amount of congestion at these borders causes huge delays. Al-most every day trucks heading south are backed up from the border for five miles or longer. Many border-crossing regions have become giant parking lots, with fume-spewing eighteen-wheelers idling for up to six hours during the peak times of 3 to 9 P.M.

Laredo, the busiest port of entry on the Texas-Mexico border, cleared $21 billion in goods from Mexico in 1997. The border there has never been so congested. Because of budget and staffing cuts, rarely are more than three of the sixteen lanes heading onto the main bridge at Laredo open at the same time during the day. The result is a strained infrastruc-ture characterized by street congestion, lack of alternative freight routes, and deteriorating facilities. In fact, a Texas Department of Transporta-tion feasibility study estimated that between 1995 and 2015, traffic along the Texas-Mexico border between Del Rio and Brownsville would increase by 128 percent. U.S. Customs officials have indicated that more than two million trucks a year will pass through Laredo alone by 2010.

On December 18, 1995, Mexican and U.S. commercial trucks were supposed to have reciprocal access rights to each other's border states under the terms of NAFTA. This was not realized. On that date the Clinton administration announced it would not adhere to that part of the treaty. The expressed reason was concern about the safety of Mexican trucks and drivers. There was also evidence, it claimed, that Mexican commercial trucks were conduits for illegal drugs coming into the United States. It was generally expected that the ban would last until after the 1996 U.S. presidential election. However, it is still in effect.

Inspectors who participated in and observed the Mexican trucks at several border crossings reported that Mexican trucks failed to meet U.S. safety requirements twice as often as the U.S. average (56 percent versus 28 percent). They also reported that 14 percent of Mexican drivers (versus 8.5 percent for the United States) failed to meet U.S. qualifications, and that 50 percent of Mexican trucks were built prior to 1980 (versus the U.S. average of 22 percent). To this day, the principle stated reason for not adhering to NAFTA's trucking provisions is safety concerns.

Under NAFTA's terms, on January 1, 1997, Mexican trucking companies were to be allowed to file applications to operate within U.S. border states and to distribute international cargo (that is, cargo originating in Mexico) within the entire United States. Also on that date, Mexican regular-route bus companies were to be allowed to begin scheduled cross-border service to and from any part of the United States. It wasn't until January 1, 2000, that Mexican truckers were able to file applications to operate within the entire United States, and on January 1, 2001, Mexican bus companies could finally become established in the United States to provide service between Mexico and all U.S. destinations.

There are some major differences in U.S. and Mexican trucking regulations (see Table 3.2). For example, Mexico has a shorter maximum overall vehicle length requirement than does the United States, which effectively bars the fifty-three-foot semitrailers that are becoming the norm in the United States from coming into Mexico unless the trailers are being pulled by so-called snub-nose tractors. More properly called *cab-over engine* tractors, these units are considered by drivers to be especially uncomfortable compared to the more conventional front-engine cabs. The problem with fifty-three-foot semitrailers is highlighted here

Table 3.2
Some major differences in U.S. and Mexican trucking regulations

Regulation	United States	Mexico
Hours of service	10 hours	No limits
Logbooks	Required	Not required
Front brakes	Required	Not required
Maximum vehicle weight	80,000 lbs.	97,000 lbs.

because shortly before the Clinton administration decided against opening the borders, Mexico, which had been largely overlooking the fifty-three-foot restriction, said (or implied) that it would begin enforcing its length-restriction regulations more vigorously. This angered a lot of U.S. truckers, who soon began sending only the less-available (in the Southwest, at least) forty-eight-foot semitrailers into Mexico while at the same time voicing in Washington their displeasure with Mexico's action.

Hijacking

Truck hijacking is causing serious operational and insurance problems for American as well as Mexican truckers and shippers. Other companies, such as Levi Strauss and Sony, for example, are having difficulty getting truckers to transport their freight. Quite a few U.S. shippers of high-value merchandise are shipping by water to the Pacific port of Manzanillo and then beyond via rail. Others are shipping by air. Those that are using truck transportation are taking precautions such as traveling in convoys on the highways and preselecting specific rest points.

Compounding the theft and hijacking problem, Mexico requires that truckers insure cargo for only seventeen cents a ton. The United States, by contrast, requires full coverage, for all practical purposes, and Canada requires $2 per pound. Premiums for additional insurance on cargo going to Mexico are, as might be expected, very high.

Water

There are seventy-six maritime ports in Mexico with thirty-five thousand meters of docking facilities. The major ports are located in Acapulco, Altamira, Coatzacoalcos, Ensenada, Guaymas, Manzanillo, Mazatlán,

Puerto Vallarta, Salina Cruz, Tampico, Tuxpan, and Veracruz. Since June 1993, private sector concessions have been allowed in port operations and development. Six port facilities have been privatized and more privatization is in process.

For textile companies with markets in the United States, the maritime ports in Mexico are used primarily for the import of raw materials. However, as more manufacturers place facilities in the Yucatán peninsula, there is an increasing trend toward sending products by boat for entry into the United States via Miami, Florida, or Corpus Christi, Texas.

Rail

There are three main railways in Mexico:

- Ferrocarril del Pacifico Norte (North Pacific)
- Ferrocarril del Norte (North)
- Ferrocarril del Sureste (Southeast)

On a national level, 100 routes out of a total of 3,741 transport 65 percent of the tonnage of goods. The most important line in terms of cargo is the northeast line, which handles approximately 40 percent of the nation's cargo. It runs from Mexico City to Nuevo Laredo, the border site with the highest trade volume in Mexico.

Air

Mexico has the most extensive airport network in Latin America, with 1,726 runways. Most of the country's eighty-three airports provide passenger and some cargo transportation services. Within this network, fifty-one airports provide both domestic and international flight service, while the remaining thirty-two serve only domestic routes.

Opportunities

The transportation of goods into, out of, and within Mexico is a critical step in the supply chain for Garment Retailer. Transportation has an enormous impact on the cycle time of a product. For a product that is trucked, drivers in Mexico may take either the slower free public roads or the faster, expensive private toll roads. However, the latter choice requires them to carry large amounts of cash (which is dangerous because of hijacking) as well as to stop to pay tolls, which can cause long delays in the time from origin to destination. Crossing over at the border can also add substantial amounts of time to those delays.

New technologies are being developed to help alleviate such problems. For instance, automated toll collection and electronic fare payment initiatives are being investigated and implemented. Vehicles equipped with electronic toll-collection (ETC) tags will be able to use special ETC lanes at tollgates. This will allow for automatic payment without requiring the vehicle to stop. The same electronic fare payment media will also be used to provide financial transactions for other transport-related charges such as transit fares and parking charges and eventually for non-transportation-related purposes as well. One company creating such technology is Bancomer, S.A., which has created a smart card that lets drivers pay tolls electronically. Bancomer is in the process of installing card readers in all thirty-one Mexican states.

Similarly, improvements in border crossing may lie in technology capable of enhancing inspections and routing traffic away from congestion. Garment Retailer could help improve these situations by investing in research to develop these new technologies.

Backhauling

Backhauling is a vehicle's return movement from destination to origin. Following various acts of deregulation from 1970 to 1990, interest in backhaul deliveries has increased. The ability to reduce empty vehicle-miles by picking up and delivering freight on the return trip provides shippers with the opportunity for significant cost savings.

Garment Retailer is interested in determining the potential cost savings of implementing a backhauling program for trucks and containers returning from Mexico to the United States. Raw materials (fabric) are trucked and shipped into Mexico. Investigating opportunities to utilize these vehicles for return trips into the United States will reduce overall transportation costs for both retailer and manufacturer.

Why should Garment Retailer consider a backhauling program? Because each empty mile is a lost opportunity to reduce total trip costs through significant revenue generation. Sending products on the return trip provides an opportunity to reduce cycle time.

The following discussion assumes that the company has its own private fleet of trucks for trucking operations, including moving products to intermediate and final customer destinations. Discussions with Garment Retailer employees suggest that operations in Mexico generally have private fleets. However, Bob Schmaltz at MGD Manufacturing said that a private fleet was too costly for his operations and that the company relied on a common carrier in Mexico. Either way, investigating backhauling opportunities will present cost savings for Garment Retailer, either directly, with a private fleet, or indirectly, when negotiating with a common carrier.

The key reasons for establishing a backhauling operation for a private fleet are to increase fleet revenues from raw materials backhauls and intercompany purchases, to offset fleet operating costs, and to provide fleet stability. The Private Fleet Management Institute estimates that 25 percent of the ground covered on mid-range trips is empty miles. Suppose that half of these miles could be filled through backhaul opportunities. On the basis of this assumption, a private fleet operating one million miles per year might be able to add an additional 130,000 loaded miles annually. Table 3.3 presents a best- and worst-case scenario for additional revenue generation from backhauling. However, other risks and liabilities, such as management commitment, asset utilization, and equipment availability, must also be considered.

In the literature, backhauling is generally not considered for other modes of transportation. However, if a company owns its own vessels or its shipment containers, there would seem to be equivalent opportunity for a backhauling program.

Garment Retailer should consider adding a backhauling program to its operations to reduce total trip costs through revenue generation, to increase efficiency in the supply chain, and to reduce the overall cycle time. A detailed analysis of the actual product flows and current transportation practices of Garment Retailer's Mexico operations would reveal the numeric value of the actual cost savings and revenue generation a backhauling program would provide.

Table 3.3
Private fleet backhauling cost-benefit review

Current empty miles percentage	25%	25%	25%
Annual miles	1,000,000	2,000,000	4,000,000
Empty miles	250,000	500,000	1,000,000
Best common carrier practice empty miles percentage	12%	12%	12%
Best common carrier practice empty miles	120,000	240,000	480,000
Backhaul opportunity miles	130,000	260,000	520,000
Estimated revenues			
Best case ($1.30/mile)	$169,000	$338,000	$676,000
Pessimistic case ($1.00/mile)	$130,000	$260,000	$520,000
Incremental trip costs ($0.02/mile)	$20,000	$40,000	$80,000
Administrative costs			
Administrative	$5,000	$5,000	$10,000
Insurance licensing / pro rate	$10,000	$11,000	$12,000
TOTAL	$11,000	$11,000	$22,000
Estimated net benefits			
Best case	$138,000	$287,000	$574,000
Pessimistic case	$99,000	$209,000	$418,000

Garment Retailer

For the apparel industry, the supply chain begins with the supply of fibers to a mill to be spun into fabric. All of the fabric must then be washed. From there, the fabric is transported to a manufacturer, where it is laid out and cut into the pieces necessary for the garment. The pieces are sown together into the final garment. The garment is then dyed, if required, and screened. It is then packaged and shipped to the retailer. The location of each step in the supply chain will vary by company and by product.

For Garment Retailer products manufactured in Mexico, the supply chains across all business units (including Men's Tops, Women's Tops, and BU1) are almost identical. Raw materials for Garment Retailer originate primarily in the United States; manufacturing (cutting, sewing, and trimming) is completed in Mexico by a Garment Retailer certified vendor; and final goods are shipped to Garment Retailer in the United States, primarily by truck.

Previously, duty had to be paid on cutting operations completed in Mexico. However, as a result of duty releases from NAFTA, these operations can now be completed in Mexico, duty free. Consequently, cutters as well as thread and button manufacturers are moving to Mexico. Border regions, such as Mexicali and Juarez, are avoided because of high turnover (see previous discussion of absenteeism).

Garment Retailer Men's Tops

There are two main mills for men's tops, one in Puebla and one in Navojoa (Ciudad Obregón), both of which are partnered with a U.S.-based company. These mills handle only simple items such as tube tops (which require only four basic operations and no seams). Approximately half of the raw materials are procured in Mexico, while the other half come from the United States. Finished goods are trucked (generally by a private fleet) from Puebla, crossing the border at Laredo, Texas, with one week allocated for customs clearance), and from Navojoa, crossing the border at Nogales, Arizona.

Garment Retailer Women's Tops

Yarn for Garment Retailer's women's tops is spun at a mill in North Carolina. It is then sent to a fabric finishing plant in Mexico for further processing. Next it is sent to a manufacturer to be cut, sown, and possibly garment-washed. At this point the garment may be packed and trucked to the U.S. border; however, if it requires screening, the garment is first sent to Los Angeles for final processing and packaging. From there it is finally shipped to Garment Retailer.

BU1

Garment Retailer's BU1 has the most experience working with Mexico. With more than fifteen plants scattered throughout the country, BU1 not only manufactures in Mexico but sources its raw materials completely from Mexico as well. Unlike the other business units, BU1 produces both basic and fashion items in its Mexican facilities. In fact, BU1 feels that it is better at chasing fashion items in Mexico. Finished garments are shipped to the United States through various border crossings, depending on plant location.

Opportunities

The supply chains for each business unit are evaluated and analyzed separately. Coordinating the supply chains between units will offer synergies for Garment Retailer in terms of price negotiations, transportation of goods, and so on. This will result in cost savings for both Garment Retailer and its vendors.

General

Investing in Mexico

To help reduce operating costs and improve its ability to meet customer needs, Garment Retailer has no choice but to expand into Mexico immediately. Using its own organizational information, Garment Retailer should be able to take advantage of the low-cost labor, short cycle times, and opportunities to improve quality and reliability that are found in Mexico. Although labor costs might be an issue in the future, it appears they will be dropping in the near term. With the Mexican government and economy stable, there is little concern over losing investments because of nonmarket issues.

Billing Concerns

One of the production problems that BU1 is having in Mexico is the billing cycle. Using the standard net thirty days to pay a bill does not work very well in Mexico. Local suppliers do not have the financing to float large orders for thirty days. They need the cash right away. For this reason, they will process orders for only fifteen to twenty thousand units at a time. Even if Garment Retailer wants to order five hundred thousand units of an item, it will have to split the order into twenty to forty orders. This creates a lot of problems with paperwork, lost shipments, and tracking. A cost-benefit analysis should be run to compare the cost of processing so many orders and the inherent inefficiencies of such small batches with the benefit of holding onto the money owed to Mexican vendors for sourcing.

The vendors with which Garment Retailer has contracted to produce their products buy the fabric from a mill, and Garment Retailer purchases the finished goods from the vendor. The disparity in the billing process arises from the fact that Garment Retailer, a $10 billion corporation, sits on one side of the equation and the fabric mills, typically $1 billion companies, sit on the other side; and the mom-and-pop cutting and sewing facilities (which are quickly moving into consolidated factories that are still cash constrained) are unable to carry the costs on their books without returns. Calvin Klein gets around this problem by purchasing the fabric themselves and sending it to their finishers.

Shipping Logistics

As already mentioned, reduction of cycle time is often achieved by making changes in the physical transportation of the product. For goods that are trucked, for example, investigating the operations of the carrier may reveal practices such as using free public routes as a cost-cutting measure that may cause undue increases in transportation time. Negotiating a clause in its carrier contracts that guarantees delivery within a certain time frame may help Garment Retailer reduce its cycle time.

Currently, business units approach their supply chains autonomously. However, synergies between business units in terms of raw materials procurement, production scheduling, and transportation can result in increased efficiencies, reduced costs, and reduction in cycle times.

Production and Sourcing Scenarios

After analyzing all the information gathered, Bridge Consulting considered several scenarios for Garment Retailer. Two main recommendations arose from key tradeoffs between the two main options identified:

1. Garment Retailer should move some of its sourcing to Mexico in the near future by selecting vendors who operate in Mexico.

2. Garment Retailer should strongly consider joint sourcing among its subsidiaries (such as BU1).

Organizational Changes

Because of the interviews we were able to have with Garment Retailer and BU1 personnel during the course of this project, we were able to come to a few conclusions about changes that should be looked into that go beyond the decision as to how many resources should be committed to Mexico. The following suggestions come from our analysis of the Garment Retailer organization in its entirety.

Internal Communication

During our interviews with Garment Retailer, it occurred to us that there are many sources of information that could be leveraged within the company. It seems that every business unit has different areas of expertise and that, properly organized, they could pool their information and move ahead. This would take a lot of effort and could distract key employees from their current roles. In the long run, however, it would help build a more solid foundation within the organization and remove current inefficiencies in Garment Retailer's development process.

For example, each group is looking for information on different aspects of manufacturing in Mexico. Women's Knits may be concerned about water quality, stability of labor, and regional stability, while Basics may be concerned with high-volume production and shipping times. While searching for the information they want, groups may come across information that others would find useful. If there were a formal communication path throughout the organization, these groups could share their findings. This path could be an intranet database that is routinely updated with findings, a weekly meeting, or possibly an ad hoc group set up for the sole purpose of digging up information and disseminating it to the rest of the organization.

A large part of the problem seems to be the way Garment Retailer is organized. It appears that each of the clothing lines is on its own and that the company operates in product stovepipes that leverage only their distribution and sales channels, not their own manufacturing.

In some regards, companies are encouraged to make their business units as small as possible so they can operate nimbly and react to market changes quickly. In essence, this is what Garment Retailer has done by separating its product lines. However, companies are also encouraged to leverage common operations throughout the organization. For example, it does not make much sense for each group to have its own human resources department. Along the same lines, it seems that Garment Retailer could reorganize its groups so that production becomes its own department. The combination of these two theories is known as "patching."

Garment Retailer has three main store chains: Garment Retailer, BU1, and BU2. All have had tremendous success in moving their manufacturing to Mexico from Asia. They are also getting positive feedback from the ramp-up of their fashion lines in Mexico.

BU1's experience could be leveraged by Garment Retailer. Also, the two companies combined could move into Mexican plants and take over entire clusters of factories and services.

It appears that although BU1 has its own product lines, all of its production is lumped together, allowing the unit to bargain with vendors and take advantage of economies of scale. By coordinating production runs, BU1 can also explore new opportunities such as investing in its own plants and moving en masse to other countries. BU1's organizational structure also allows it to see the big-picture issues such as future capacity problems and global trends in textiles. If BU1 could leverage this infrastructure, it might be able to reduce production costs significantly.

In some instances Garment Retailer and BU1 are producing on the same product lines and are operating completely independently. Garment Retailer is paying 50 percent more than BU1 in the same plants for the same items or services. This is clearly suboptimal.

Conclusions

In recent years, the outsourcing of apparel manufacturing to Mexico has become a strategic move for companies such as Garment Retailer that are based in North American markets. This discussion has shown that although labor costs in Mexico are still four and a half times the average labor costs of China, Mexico offers the advantages of short cycle times, improved quality and reliability, reduced operating costs, and increased ability to meet customer needs due to flexibility and fast turnaround time. Additionally, Mexico boasts government and economic stability, so large companies such as Garment Retailer can be less concerned over losing long-term investments due to nonmarket issues.

Case 2: PCH China

RFID Logistics Tracking System

It was the year 1996 and Liam Casey knew that it was now or never. The emerging China market presented an enormous opportunity for entrepreneurs to create tomorrow's company today and he had to act fast. Yet China was a society based on *guanxi* or personal relationships and as a foreigner he had none. He had spent many months brainstorming ideas but each idea led him back to the same question, namely, how could he break into China? Frustrated by his lack of inspiration that morning, Liam decided to take a drive to clear his mind.

As his convertible raced down the Pacific Coast Highway in southern California, it all suddenly came together. He realized he was not alone. From his extensive business relationships in his native land, Ireland, as well as in the United States and Europe, he knew that others like himself had the same problem. They all wanted to enter the China market, but none of them knew how to do so. His opportunity, then, was to be the liaison that bridged the two worlds, and PCH China was born.

Eight years after that fateful morning in 1996, PCH had grown from a $20 thousand bank loan to a $40 million SCM business. Because of the opaque business environment in China, outsourcing was difficult: product quality, reliability, and on-time delivery often varied greatly. Contracts were nearly impossible to enforce and companies routinely defaulted on obligations. Moreover, corporate social responsibility had become an implicit requirement in the new millennium. Image-sensitive global tech firms required disclosure and a high level of openness.[4] Poor working conditions in developing-country plants created public relations nightmares. Through all of this, PCH led its customers through these difficulties by practicing *transparency*. By allowing customers to track products directly from the source all the way to delivery, PCH had become the guiding light in a murky environment for many companies outsourcing work to China.

Yet as PCH's business expanded, Liam faced a critical new question. In 2004, the hot new technology for transparency was radio frequency identification. RFID provided real-time tracking and inventory management capabilities, but deployment in this form existed solely as an emerging technology limited to billion-dollar companies with deep pockets, such as Wal-Mart. While PCH was clearly not the size of Wal-Mart, it was growing exponentially year after year. In 2004 PCH was forecast to make $70 million[5] in revenue and probably hundreds of millions of dollars business within a few years. The question then was not whether PCH could afford RFID but rather when it should deploy an RFID system. RFID could be the technology that cemented PCH as the premier SCM company, but the investment needed in order to implement an RFID system was enormous. Liam wondered, should PCH implement this technology today, or should it wait a few years for the technology to mature?

Industry Background

Commoditization of Technology

The majority of PCH's business is in supplying low-cost technology items such as modem cables and audio-video pods to technology companies. The industry is a highly commoditized market characterized by razor-thin margins and products that differ very little from one another. Market definition plays a key role in a sector marked by frequent acquisitions, rapid spending swings, and bitter price wars. For every market leader there is a hard-charging challenger armed with lower prices or a rival technology.

The intrinsic boom-bust nature of the tech sector challenges technology companies to reexamine constantly the way they do business. Hardware sellers are increasingly turning to contract manufacturers to squeeze the costs in order to keep profits as prices continually fall. Offshore contract manufacturers provide cost-effective means of manufacturing huge quantities of a particular product at a fraction of the cost of manufacturing in the United States. Offshore companies take advantage of the standards of living in the host country and as a result enjoy much lower labor costs. From MP3 players to mainframe computers, from network cards to PDAs, outsource manufacturing plays a role in building the products used by consumers purchasing personal computer (PC) peripherals and by multibillion-dollar global corporations installing entire networks. Some companies have gone so far as to outsource manufacturing completely and focus solely on integration and support services.

Lean Manufacturing

The commoditization of products increases pressure to cut costs. As a result, companies look to their supply chain to increase productivity while eliminating waste. By eliminating waste through increasing inventory turnover, improving inventory forecasting, reducing forecast lead time, and reducing variability in forecasts, it is possible to improve profits and ROI. Many companies adopt a variation of just-in-time management, a philosophy first introduced by Toyota, which strives to eliminate sources of manufacturing waste by producing the right part in the right place at the right time. The general idea is to establish flow processes that optimize efficiency.

Regardless of which management strategy is adopted by a company, one of the necessary effects is that logistics complexity increases exponentially as business grows, requiring expensive investment in information technology (IT) to manage the overall logistics systems. Moreover according to a study by Booz Allen Hamilton, 45 percent of their survey respondents were dissatisfied with the performance of their investments against expectations.[6] Sophisticated IT operations are very costly and require knowledgeable staff on site to customize or troubleshoot potential issues.

The Role of SCM Companies

International Data Corporation (IDC) reports that in 2002, although investment in SCM services had increased by 9.5 percent, buyers were much less receptive to large-scale SCM investments that required complex and lengthy implementations and internal change.[7] As a result, companies were increasingly looking to third-party SCM companies to outsource their supply chain logistics. These companies coordinate and integrate the flow of materials, information, and finances from supplier to manufacturer to wholesaler to retailer to consumer. Specifically, SCM companies provide services that manage all or part of the following:

- *Product flow:* Movement of goods from a supplier to a customer, as well as any customer returns or service needs
- *Information flow:* Transmitting orders and updating the status of delivery
- *Financial flow:* Credit terms, payment schedules, and consignment and title-ownership arrangements

In addition, SCM companies may also provide the following IT-based solutions that facilitate planning or execution:

- *Planning applications* use advanced algorithms to determine the best way to fill an order.
- *Execution applications* track the physical status of goods, the management of materials, and financial information involving all parties.

SCM companies may also support the sharing of data both inside the enterprise and with key suppliers, manufacturers, and end customers. By sharing data with a company's suppliers and downstream with a company's clients, SCM applications have the potential to improve the time-to-market of products, reduce costs, and allow all parties in the supply chain to better manage current resources and plan for future needs.

Market Analysis

China's growth has been driven by manufacturing, and the country's planned economy has tapped into domestic savings and foreign investment to build an impressive infrastructure. Manufacturing has accounted for 60 percent of China's GDP growth over the past decade. The low cost of production, coupled with favorable economic policies and preferential tax rates, is among the drivers behind this manufacturing success. Indeed, China is increasingly becoming an attractive sourcing destination. Shenzhen and Shanghai are leading the way, and since China's accession to the WTO, Mainland authorities have been aggressive in opening distribution centers for foreign companies ahead of the timetables set by the trade body.

As a result, many manufacturers are seeking to reduce supply chain costs through sourcing in China. But if they are to succeed, they must deal with the problems this entails. As a recent report from McKinsey & Company points out, it can be hard to get right the many pieces of a procurement operation in China. Finding high-quality suppliers is a ubiquitous problem, but the great geographic distance between suppliers in China and overseas headquarters makes the job tougher. It is this above all that makes sourcing in China so complicated.

Indeed, this unfamiliarity with the size of the country can be one of the biggest barriers to a Chinese sourcing program. Firms might worry that distant and uncertain supply lines will require them to hold larger inventories, thereby driving up costs and reducing returns. Similarly, logistics managers will warn that using far-flung suppliers will push up costs. Inventory and logistics costs in China will undoubtedly rise, and adjustments will be needed to deal with the new risks of managing suppliers in China. The companies that succeed will be the ones that have demonstrated that the benefits of lower-cost purchasing almost always outweigh an increase in operational costs and risks.

Firms that have built their expertise through association with a wide range of clients and with resources placed in all major Chinese business centers, says the analyst, should have the capability to provide this highly specialized service. According to McKinsey's report, many companies starting up in China will use sourcing agents. It is here that the role of companies like PCH China becomes critical. Certain agents are skilled at handling delicate materials or complex product categories or have exclusive rights to particular factories. Another report, from Pricewaterhouse-Coopers, suggests that Western firms should utilize experienced personnel who are well trained and knowledgeable about local business practices and regulations.

The McKinsey report suggests that if a company sources more than $100 million a year in goods from China, it makes economic sense to have a unit there that can go directly to suppliers, because the cost of running a direct-procurement operation is a third or less of what agents charge. The Logistics Institute-Asia Pacific, a think tank funded by the Singapore government, released the China Logistics Provider Study in January 2002. The study found that revenue growth had averaged 40 percent for the twenty-nine largest logistics providers in China over the previous three years. Growth was projected to level out at about 50 percent for the next three years.[8]

PCH China

PCH is a small, dynamic niche player that offers full SCM service, from design through specification and manufacturing to testing and delivery. Its core competency lies in sourcing and manufacturing such low-cost items as modem cables and audio-video pods. PCH's available manufacturing product categories include:

batteries	microphones
cable assemblies	modem adaptors
connectors	motors
CD cases/sleeves	PCBs
die cast assemblies	power cords and adaptors
flex circuits	power supplies
headphones	speakers
heat sinks	transformers[9]
kitting	

PCH offers customers a complete SCM solution between its Taiwan customers, fifty factories in China that make goods for them, and ultimately its customers in Europe, the United States, and Mexico, who install these components into their finished products. The company offers:

- Competitive pricing, with customers given a competitive quotation for components delivered duty paid
- Quotations preparation within one week
- ISO-approved and -audited suppliers
- Full AutoCAD specifications
- Free qualification samples within two weeks
- Cost reduction analysis of designs
- Source inspection and work-in-progress audits
- Full logistics management, with different freight and delivery options[10]

The current PCH client list includes the following companies:

- Three of the top five makers of PCs
- Two of the top five telecom and networking suppliers
- The world's leading contract electronics manufacturers

A sample exchange of information between PCH and one of its clients can be found in Table 3.4.

Table 3.4
Sample PCH-client information exchange

Client	A drawing and specification for the component required
	Sample component
	The volume and frequency of orders
	The approvals required for the product
	Packaging requirements
PCH	A written quotation in one to two weeks
	Design and support suggestions
	Qualification samples (in three to four weeks)
	CAD specification for approval
	Credit terms and conditions
	Lead time and freight options
	Order acknowledgment
	Source inspection at PCH's specialized factories
	On-time delivery, duty paid to client

Source: www.pchintl.com

Transparency in an Opaque World

Central to PCH's success is its belief in transparency. PCH allows customers to track products directly from the source by providing names, addresses, and photos of supplier plants on an exclusive intranet, and facilitates visits by end users to source factories. Customers can track suppliers' inventories, capacity, and even raw materials. The level of detail at which PCH shares information helps customer planning, and the amount of information available is comparable to what the customer gets from its own internal operations.

Because of the general opacity of business in China, transparency has been a key competitive advantage. Product quality, reliability, and on-time delivery often varied greatly. Contracts were nearly impossible to enforce and companies routinely defaulted on obligations. Moreover, corporate social responsibility became an implicit requirement in the new millennium. Image-sensitive global tech firms require disclosure and a high level of openness.[11] Poor working conditions in developing-country plants created public relation nightmares. PCH shields customers from this messiness by auditing manufacturers and transporters in China to ensure Western standards for both the products and the labor pool.

Underwriting Risk

PCH's business strategy has been to internalize the risk of the supply chain in order to immunize the client from its fundamental risk factors. What is unique about PCH is its strategy of buying the freight in transit. Effectively, PCH underwrites the risk of the shipment and in return earns a fee for managing the risk. This strategy has fueled PCH's growth. However, it introduces a big liability on PCH's side. As a result, the quality of service is of utmost importance, and any issue with shipments translates into direct loss for PCH.

Transflo

PCH provides proprietary software that mimics sophisticated programs but looks alarmingly simple.[12] At the core of the system is Transflo, a Web-based tracking system where customers can obtain up-to-the-hour information about their manufactured shipments. It enables customers to see into the supply chain with a clarity that is unparalleled in manufacturing in China. This service provides a huge competitive advantage for PCH and embodies its mantra of clarity.

Competitive Environment

To succeed in China's market, companies must compete at a lower cost. Clients of SCM are under enormous pressure to cut costs and many may also have cash-flow problems. As a result, clients are consistently looking for low-cost providers of logistics services.

Exel

PCH's major competitor is Exel, a publicly traded British company that provides international logistics services. Exel was created from a merger between Britain's Ocean Steamship Company and National Freight Consortium in 2000. The Ocean Steamship Company was founded in

1865, so Exel was born with a long history in the logistics business. It currently has approximately 111,000 employees in 2,000 operating locations in more than 135 countries. It services more than 75 percent of the world's largest nonfinancial companies and has a yearly turnover of £6.3 billion of goods. Its geographic region of service is similar to PCH's. Roughly 55 percent of its logistics services center around Europe, the Middle East, and Africa; 30 percent of the services are in the Americas; and 16 percent are in the Asia Pacific.

Exel's core strategy centers on what it calls "the four cornerstones of this strategy":

- Global coverage and local strength
- Integrated capability and breadth of solutions
- Consistent processes and occupational excellence
- Skilled people and supply chain expertise

This strategy helps Exel position itself to meet customers' needs with innovative solutions that bring together the best of its people, processes, and core capabilities.

Exel's approach to IT ensures that its services are robust, scaleable, and globally consistent in solution definition, development, deployment, and support, leveraging economies of scale, experience, and knowledge across the company, and maximizing the use of standard technology. In addition to pure supply chain services, Exel also provides the following IT solutions that solve supply chain issues:

- IT product management
- IT service management
- IT infrastructure service delivery
- Enterprise architecture
- IT project delivery
- Systems integration

These IT solutions help customers achieve improved cost-effectiveness and usability in ways that fit the customer's purpose. The company believes in an architecture that reuses existing components and applies them to various customers. This practice results in increased awareness of functionality and availability of information.

Exel has been aggressive in the adoption of RFID. Although the technology is neither proven nor perfected, Exel is gearing itself to meet the challenge. Exel has run eight to ten RFID pilots with other customers worldwide and has expertise that stretches across industries, including automotive and pharmaceutical manufacturing. In February 2004 Exel announced a project with House of Fraser (HOF), a British department store, to test RFID in the retailer's international supply chain. The HOF trial, known as Project China, is an ambitious effort that attempts to track individual garments from the retailer's own brand manufacturers in China all the way back to the United Kingdom.[13] In October 2004, Exel entered a partnership with Energizer Holdings to help it meet an RFID mandate from Wal-Mart. With Exel running three of Energizer's four warehouses, Energizer sees Exel as a strategic partner in its RFID efforts. The scope of the project included plans to test RFID tags under real-world conditions and ultimately to apply Electronic Product Code (EPC) tags to pallets and cases of batteries at Energizer's warehouses.[14]

Exel has also developed an eleven-thousand-square-mile warehouse testing facility designed to give customers a real-world simulation of RFID. In this warehouse, an organization can explore issues raised during RFID implementation, such as chip positioning, pallet configuration, materials handling processes, and distribution center layout. The center also studies RFID issues such as the accuracy, reliability, and security of RFID in delivering supply chain visibility at an affordable price. It provides a major competitive advantage for customers wishing to implement RFID in that it provides a risk-free testing ground for potential implementations.

Project Definition

Determine the Risk and Return of RFID on PCH's Supply Chain

The goal of the Stanford University and Hong Kong University of Science and Technology project was to develop a strategy and implementation plan to help PCH implement RFID technology for tracking goods during transportation between supply chain destinations. The project team was to deliver the following:

- Comprehensive documentation on the current state of the art for RFID technology, including standard, frequency, tag, reader, middleware, and application software
- Best practices in applying RFID technology in both land and sea logistics
- Financial analysis about ROI
- Concrete implementation plan with guidelines to the follow-up project that will realize the proposed RFID system architecture

RFID Technology Overview

RFID technology has been around for more than forty years but did not enter commercial applications until recently. Even now, RFID technology is not commercially mature, because there are still varying standards and deployment is limited. However, in the early 2000s, large industry players such as Wal-Mart and the U.S. Department of Defense mandated that suppliers provide RFID technology on their products, citing the need for more efficient inventory tracking and better transparency and the overall desire for information on the supply chain. Table 3.5 shows a timeline of the major events in the history of RFID.

In the manufacturing and supply chain industry, the specific area of

Table 3.5
RFID Timeline

1940–1950	Radar refined and used, major World War II development effort
	RFID invented in 1948
1950–1960	Early explorations of RFID technology, laboratory experiments
1960–1970	Development of the theory of RFID
	Start of applications field trials
1970–1980	Explosion of RFID technology
	Tests of RFID accelerate
	Very early adopter implementations of RFID
1980–1990	Commercial applications of RFID enter mainstream
1990–2000	Emergence of standards
	RFID widely deployed
	RFID becomes a part of everyday use

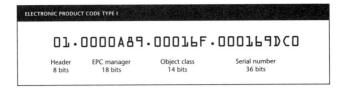

ELECTRONIC PRODUCT CODE TYPE I

01.0000A89.00016F.000169DC0

Header	EPC manager	Object class	Serial number
8 bits	18 bits	14 bits	36 bits

EPC Class 1 (96 bit) tag content

Header: Identifies which version of EPC is being used.

EPC manager: Used to identify manufacturer and even plant.
Capacity for *268 million* companies

Object class: Identifies the unique product family and item.
Capacity for *16 million* objects.

Serial number: Uniquely identifies the specific physical item being read.
Capacity for *68 billion* serial numbers.

Figure 3.1   Sample RFID EPC tag

RFID technology being commercialized is EPCs. EPC is an emerging specification for RFID tags, tag readers (also known as interrogators), and business applications that was first developed at the Auto-ID Center at the Massachusetts Institute of Technology. It represents a specific approach to item identification, including an emerging standard for the tags themselves, including both the data content of the tag and open wireless communication protocols. In a sense, the EPC movement is combining the data standards embodied in certain bar code specifications, such as the UPC or UCC-128 bar code standards, with the wireless data communication standards that have been developed by the American National Standards Institute and other groups. Embedded in the EPC is a series of 96 bits used to provide unique, unambiguous, context-independent, and unduplicated lifetime identification. The EPC standard assigns a uniform way of using the 96 bits to embed in a product information on the manufacturer, product category, and the individual item. Figure 3.1 shows sample data contained in an EPC tag.

The way RFID works in manufacturing or supply chain is that EPC tags containing the product identification are attached to items or group of items. A specialized reader broadcasts radio frequency signals to activate the EPC tags attached to the target items. Once the EPC tag "hears" the broadcast, it sends its identification information back to the reader.

The reader then communicates with middleware software that performs data aggregation and filtering on the raw data. Once a certain predefined event condition is reached, the middleware sends an event notification to a warehouse management system (WMS), enterprise resource planning system (ERP), or manufacturing execution system (MES) for further data processing. The communication is complete once the system receives the notification and users are able to see the item in the system.

Market Trends

Today RFID is poised to enter a period of exponential growth in commercial applications. The RFID manufacturing market is positioned to grow from $99.9 million in 2004 to $3.8 billion in 2008. Table 3.6 shows the projected growth of the overall RFID market from 2003 to 2008. RFID is used in many industries. From military to manufacturing to retail, organizations are waking to the technological, logistical, and cost-saving benefits of RFID. Figure 3.2 shows a histogram of RFID applications in different industries.

Standards

Currently there are competing standards for EPC and RFID, the most popular of which is EPC–ISO18000-6A. The ISO18000-6 standard is the de facto international standard for SCM and parcel tracking. The standard is supported by a consortium of industry and research organizations, including MIT, IBM, Microsoft, Philips, Wal-Mart, and Tesco, and such vendors as Alien, EM, Matrics, and Atmel. Table 3.7 shows a sample EPC specification.

Table 3.6
Projected RFID market size

Year	Revenue
2003	$65.8 million
2004	99.9 million
2005	261.7 million
2006	2,924.0 million
2007	3,344.0 million
2008	3,797.0 million

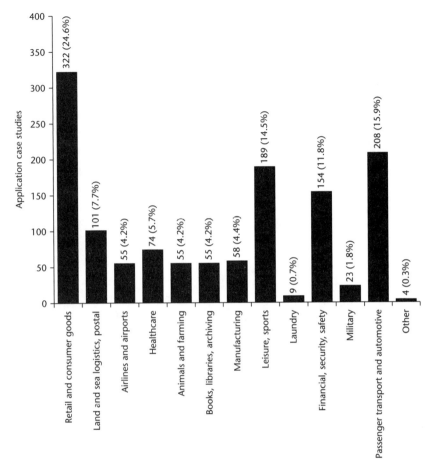

Figure 3.2   Industry applications of RFID

RFID Frequency

As with all wireless communications, there are a variety of frequencies or spectra through which RFID tags can communicate with readers. Depending on the frequency, there are trade-offs in cost, performance, and application requirements. For example, low-frequency tags are cheaper, use less power, and are better able to penetrate nonmetallic substances compared to ultra-high-frequency (UHF) tags. However, UHF frequencies have better range and can have faster data transfer rates. UHF tags are typically best suited for use with or near wood, pa-

Table 3.7
Types of RFID tag corresponding to EPC global standards

EPC class	Specifications
Class 0	Passive Read-only tags (R/O)
Class 1	Passive Can be programmed once by the user
Class 2	Passive Program capabilities Increased memory space for additional user data storage requirements
Class 3	Semipassive tag with embedded battery for long range Program capabilities
Class 4	Active tag Communicates with readers and other tags on the same frequency band

per, cardboard, or clothing products, whereas low-frequency tags are ideal for scanning objects with high water content, such as fruit, at close range. Table 3.8 summarizes the characteristics of different frequency ranges.

RFID Tag

An RFID tag comprises a microchip containing identifying information and an antenna that transmits this data wirelessly to a reader. Figure 3.3 shows an example of an RFID tag and its subcomponents. At its most basic, the chip will contain a serialized identifier, or license plate number, that uniquely identifies that item, similar to the way many bar codes are used today. A key difference, however, is that RFID tags have a higher data capacity than their bar code counterparts. This increases the options for the type of information that can be encoded on the tag, including the manufacturer, batch or lot number, weight, ownership, destination, and history (such as the temperature range to which an item has been exposed). In fact, an unlimited list of other types of information can be stored on RFID tags, depending on application needs. An RFID tag can be placed on individual items, on cartons or pallets for identification purposes, and on fixed assets such as trailers, containers, totes, and so on.

Table 3.8
Summary of frequency characteristics

	LF 125 KHz	HF 13.56 MHz	UHF 860–960 MHz	Microwave 2.45 GHz
Typical maximum read range (passive tags)	Shortest 2.5–300 mm	Short 5–600 mm	Medium 0.6–3 m	Longest 0.6–4.6 m
Tag type	Generally passive tags only	Generally passive tags only	Active tags with integral battery of passive tags	Active tags with integral battery of passive tags
Data rate	Slower	Moderate	Fast	Faster
Ability to read near metal or wet surfaces	Better	Moderate	Poor	Worst
Applications example	Manufacturing processes in harsh environments	Library	Supply chain tracking	Vehicle fleets in/out of yard or facility

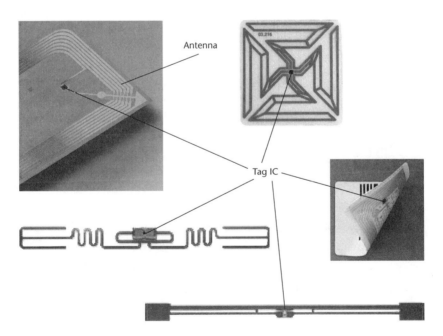

Antenna

Tag IC

Figure 3.3   RFID tag

Types of RFID tag

There are different types of tags with a variety of capabilities, including data capacity, read-only versus read-write, and passive versus active.

Data Capacity. The amount of data storage on a tag can vary from sixteen bits on the low end to as much as several thousand bits on the high end. Obviously the greater the storage capacity is, the higher will be the price per tag.

Read-Only Versus Read-Write. There are three options in terms of how data can be encoded on tags:

1. Read-only tags contain data such as a serialized tracking number that is written onto them by the tag manufacturer or distributor. These are generally the least expensive tags because no additional information can be included as they move through the supply chain. Any updates to the information would have to be maintained in the application software that tracks SKU movement and activity.

2. Write-once tags enable a user to write data to the tag one time during the production or distribution process. Again, the information may include a serial number and perhaps other data such as a lot or batch number.

3. Full read-write tags allow new data to be written to the tag as needed—and even written over the original data. Examples of the latter capability might include the time and date of ownership transfer or updates of the repair history of a fixed asset. While these are the most costly of the three tags and are not practical for tracking inexpensive items, future standards for EPCs appear to be headed in this direction.

Passive Versus Active. There are also three options in terms of how tags manage power:

1. Active tags have their own power supply. They can receive a weak signal from the interrogator, and, because of their own power source, boost the return signal. They have ranges from tens of meters to even hundreds of meters. Due to their size and increased sophistication, they cost more. Moreover, the lifespan of active tags is limited by the lifespan of the battery.

Table 3.9
Active versus passive tags

Characteristic	Active	Passive
Power source	Internal	Transferred from reader
Battery	Yes	No
Range	Up to 100 m	Up to 3–5 m
Multitag reading	Thousand times / sec	Hundred times / sec
Data storage	Up to 128 KB	Less than 128 bytes
Cost	Range US$10–US$50 depends on size of battery, memory, packaging around transponder	Range US$0.20–US$3.00 simplest license plate: US$0.20 thermal transfer label: US$0.40

2. Passive tags differ from active tags in that they get their power from the RFID reader. When the tags are within range of the radio frequency field, the interrogator emits a radio frequency (RF) signal that powers the silicon chip on the tag.
   The chip then sends back information to the interrogator on the same RF wave. The range of the passive tag is lower than that of the active tag because the passive tag does not have its own power source. Its lifespan is much longer than that of the active tag because it does not depend on a local power source.

3. Semipassive tags (or semiactive tags, as some refer to them) are somewhere between active and passive. They have a power source that can be used for in-tag sensing, such as for monitoring temperature, but it cannot be used to boost range. The power source is usually a laminar, flexible, low-cost battery.

Table 3.9 summarizes the differences between active and passive tags.

RFID Reader and Antenna

The RFID reader sends RF signals to tags to request the information contained on the RFID tag. Once this information has been received, it is translated into digital form and sent to the application software. Reader requirements vary depending on the type of tag and application. In addition, readers are divided into three types:

1. Handheld readers are tethered to portable data-collection devices and fixed terminals or PCs running application software. They work almost exactly like handheld bar code scanners.

2. Embedded readers are internal to portable wireless data collection devices such as those used in warehouses, on shop floors, and by transporters.

3. Fixed readers are mounted so as to read tags automatically as the product passes them or passes near them. Examples include readers mounted on conveyor equipment or on entry points to the back room of a retail store, portal readers placed at dock locations to read tags as the product is shipped or received, and readers mounted on material-handling equipment.

Middleware

Middleware is specialty software that sits between the reader network and the true application software to help process the significant amount of data coming from the tags and readers. More specifically, RFID middleware provides the following functions:

– *Reader interfaces:* Middleware provides drivers to retrieve data from the readers of various hardware manufacturers.

– *Data filtering:* Not every tag will be read only once, and sometimes a tag is read incorrectly. Middleware uses embedded logic to aggregate, purge, and filter tag data, thereby cleaning the data feeds to the application software.

– *Reader coordination:* By monitoring multiple readers, middleware can detect the movement of RFID tags as they pass from the read range of one reader to another. This directional movement detection can be captured and passed on to the application software as an inventory movement notification.

– *System monitoring:* Middleware will monitor tag and reader network performance to generate a real-time view of the tags being read. It may also capture history and analysis of tag-read events for application tuning and optimization.

Application Software

The application software is the piece that actually processes RFID data, controls workflows and business transactions, and passes on RFID data to other systems such as electronic data interchange (EDI) translators or ERP software. Thus far, much of the publicly available information on RFID has been on the hardware aspects of the technology (tags and readers) or on the description of business applications at a high level. Yet the requirements and role of application software to utilize the technology and deliver business value are absolutely critical, whether in a compliance scenario or in driving internal supply chain improvements. Some types of application software include the following components:

- *Compliance enablement:* Software to help companies meet the specific RFID requirements of their customers. This software automates processes around tagging for customers that require it, collecting RFID tag data in shipping, printing RFID tags or Smart Labels, creating advanced shipping notice (ASN) data based on RFID reads, and so on.

- *Logistics/WMS:* RFID will enable new levels of tracking and fulfillment in logistics and WMS software. New workflows for taking full advantage of RFID capabilities (such as automated RFID receiving) will need to be created in existing WMS systems to offer advantages beyond those available today with traditional bar coding.

- *Supply chain visibility:* As an extension of warehouse management, RFID will be used to achieve real-time visibility of goods across the supply chain, including international movements and tracking of inventory across company facilities, during the transportation process, and as goods move among trading partners.

- *Shop floor control:* Manufacturing and shop-floor software will enable raw materials, work in progress, and finished goods heading to distribution to be tracked in real time. Production-related data such as lot and batch number might also be written on the tags for downstream use. Asset-tracking software supports tracking of a variety of fixed assets in real time (Where are they now?) and over the entire product lifecycle (How many times has this asset been used?).

Limitations of RFID

One of the biggest limitations in the implementation of an RFID system is the cost of implementation. Today, users can expect to pay about twenty cents for a passive tag and a few dollars for an active tag. Item-level tagging will not become economical until tag prices fall below the one-cent mark. Because of the high costs, current supply chain implementers generally perform tagging only at the pallet level.

In addition to cost considerations, other practical limitations affect the implementation and performance of an RFID system. The lack of globally accepted standards for radio wave frequency causes problems for the implementation of a cross-national RFID system. The lack of accepted standards also means that tags from one provider may prove unreadable by another provider's readers. Finally, RFID is a new technology and not all legacy (existing) systems are compatible with RFID implementations. It may not be possible to implement RFID without expensive system upgrades.

Methodology

Charged with making decisions that should increase shareholders' value, management is always faced with trade-offs when deciding to take on projects. When deciding between multiple projects, only those that promise the most value should be considered in light of limited resources. Management should always ask whether and how much value will be added through the project. In this context, *value* refers to future cash flows resulting from the project, and for management to be able to make correct decisions, analytical tools should be available to compare one project's expected cash flows to those of another project. One of these tools is the ROI analysis. ROI, in short, aids management in quantifying the magnitude of "value created in relation to investment required."[15] In other words, ROI signifies the number of additional dollars generated from one dollar of investment.

When used correctly, ROI becomes a convenient tool for comparing competing projects and benchmarking performance and productivity across multiple projects. A project with a zero ROI adds no value; for projects with positive ROI, the one with highest ROI value relative to others is most appealing. A simple mathematical definition of ROI can be given as:

$$\text{ROI} = \frac{\text{ExpectedGains} - \text{Investment}}{\text{Investment}}$$

For example, consider a project that requires a $100,000 capital invest-ment. If the sum of the gains (cash flows) generated by this project is ex-pected to add up to $125,000, then

$$\text{ROI} = \frac{\$125,000 - \$100,000}{\$100,000} = \frac{\$25,000}{\$100,000} = 0.25$$

A result of 0.25 means that each dollar invested generates an additional $0.25, or equivalently, each dollar invested generates $1.25.

Pitfalls of ROI

This definition of ROI is rather simplistic and lacks accuracy when applied to nonidealized, real-world projects. Considering that most real-world projects are rather complex and involve a stream of cash flows that occur over an extended period, this ROI definition fails to consider the no-tion of the time value of money. This notion, which is one of the founda-tional ideas in finance, states simply that a dollar tomorrow is worth less than a dollar today (or put in more sophisticated language: the present value of a future cash flow is less than the face value of the cash flow itself). In a typical project where the planning horizon could be anywhere from one to thirty years, simply adding all the cash flows for calculating the ROI re-sults in gross overstatement of the project's financial merit, especially if the project becomes fully operational only after a period of implementation.

Modified ROI

To incorporate the notion of the time value of money in an ROI cal-culation, ROI can be redefined as follows:

$$\text{ROI} = \frac{\text{PV(ExpectedGains} - \text{Investment})}{\text{PV(Investment)}}$$

where PV is Present Value

The fundamental difference between this modified equation of ROI and the previous one is that instead of adding all the cash flows, one adds the discounted values of the cash flows. Of course this new definition introduces yet another issue: the rate at which the particular project's cash flows are discounted. Should it be the prevailing interest rate? Is it the firm's hurdle rate? Or a project-specific discount rate based on the financing mix of the project and the risk of the project? There is an ample amount of literature on this subject, and any corporate finance textbook discusses this issue. Specifically, the concepts of Weighted Average Cost of Capital (WACC) and Capital Asset Pricing Model (CAPM) will be used here to address the PCH ROI question. It will be assumed that the best discount rate to use is one that reflects the financing mix and the risk level of the project.

ROI in IT Projects

Characteristics That Affect Financial Decisions. Enterprise-level IT projects are typically long term (once a company commits to a project, it expects the results to be utilized for a long time). These projects usually require a considerable capital investment; and, depending on the nature of the project, it may take months or even years before the project becomes completely operational. For example, it could easily take six months to a year to transfer data from a legacy system to a new enterprise-level application. In theory, IT projects would usually have net positive cash flows (inflows) following the initial capital investment; therefore, an idealized net present value (NPV) profile for an IT project would be decreasing in interest rates. This means that for a given cash flow stream, the higher the discount rate is, the less valuable the project will be.

ROI Calculation for IT Projects. When conducting an ROI analysis for an IT project, special attention must be paid to the fact that calculation of costs is not always straightforward when evaluating an IT project. In fact, IT projects are notorious for being over budget and costing more for implementation than previously estimated. As a result, when conducting ROI analysis, one must carefully examine assumptions made about costs and ensure that costs have not been not under- or overestimated.

It is often challenging to quantify the gains of an IT project in the form of dollar amounts. It is very easy to overestimate the gains of an IT project.

Beta of the Project. It was mentioned earlier that an appropriate discount rate for a given project considers the financing mix (cost of debt and cost of equity) and the risk of the project. The underlying risk of the project affects the cost of equity of the project's discount rate by increasing the value of the project's beta (which in the CAPM is a magnifying factor of the risk premium). One element of risk is the timeliness of implementation: the opportunity cost of overextending the implementation duration constitutes a risk and should be factored in. In this way, when evaluating an IT project, the appropriate beta should be applied to the project. For example, even if the IT project is being implemented in an oil and gas company (the oil industry historically has a low beta), the beta of the project is going to be higher than that of the industry and therefore the appropriate beta should be used.[16]

ROI in Real Time IT System Projects

Application of ROI analysis to IT projects that involve real-time systems introduces issues that go beyond the three already mentioned. This is not to say that the already-mentioned issues do not apply, but rather that other factors must be considered as well. For one thing, the analyst must be very careful when determining the true benefits and gains of the system. The distinguishing feature of a real-time system is its capability to provide data that is up-to-date and reliable. Therefore, the added value of having a real-time system is this very ability to provide data that best represent the current state of the world. In this way, the underlying value driver for a real-time system is the value of the live data. This value can best be captured when analyzing a non-real-time alternative and judging the opportunity cost of not being able to interact with a set of live data. Furthermore, it is often the very nature of a real-time system that it is in constant communication with other systems. With the growing complexity of data, a system designed to deliver real-time data most often has to interact with other systems in a distributed environment to get the most complete set of available data. This feature exposes real-time IT systems to what may be referred to as integration risk. Not only is integrating enterprise systems a costly task, but the reliability of the integration is often an issue. Because a real-time system is only as valuable as the live data it provides, integration failure directly affects the quality of the data and thus could potentially render the entire system useless. An ROI analysis of a real-time IT system must therefore consider this added risk and, in calculating the project's cost of equity (as part of discount-rate calculation), utilize a beta that accurately reflects this risk. One way to quantify the real-time system's risk-adjusted beta is to consider *pure plays* in the real-time IT systems market. Pure plays are firms that specialize in developing and deploying real-time IT systems. The value of their beta would reflect the risk and should be a good reference when deciding the beta for a project.

IT Analysis

After carefully analyzing PCH's IT infrastructure in relation to RFID white papers, the following alternative implementations were proposed as architectural solutions:

– *Batch updates:* Keep the same data movement as the current IT system and replicate the RFID database periodically to the Transflo database through data-flow synchronization services. The benefit of this solution is that it is easier to implement because of its consistency with the current IT architecture. The tradeoff is that updates will not be real-time and will show up in the system only after synchronization. An architecture diagram of this implementation is shown in Figure 3.4.

– *Real time:* Transflo the RFID Information Server (or EPC-IS) directly to get up-to-the-instant information. The benefit of this implementation is that it instantaneously provides users with current status. However, the trade-off is that this system is difficult to set up because it requires reengineering of PCH's current data-movement architecture.

Real-time architecture is most useful to the manufacturer or the end customer in terms of inventory management, reducing shrinkage (theft), and generally where the focus is on the items themselves. Because the goal for PCH is to manage the transportation of the items, the batch architecture would be the most useful. The time scale in tracking data is on the order of days, and the current half-hourly updates have more than sufficient granularity to accomplish this task. In addition, the batch process fits well with the current data flow and will be less disruptive in the implementation phase. On the basis of these considerations, the recommended architecture is the batch architecture.

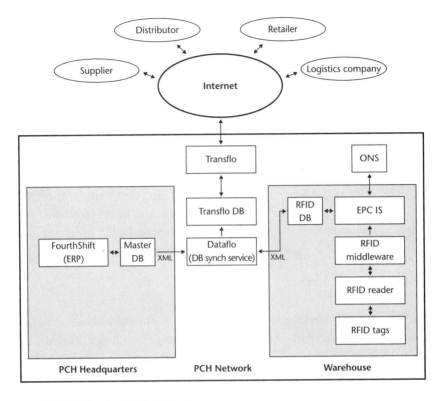

FourthShift (ERP system). Main ERP system.

Master DB. Master database (DB) of the entire system. Currently only the ERP directly modifies the Master DB.

Transflo. Proprietary Web-based tracking system. Has local DB image that is updated from the Master DB on average every thirty minutes.

Dataflo (DB synch service). Proprietary DB synchronization service. Takes XML output from the source DB. Uses XSL to transform the source XML output into a stored procedure call on the target DB. Dataflo is used to synch both the Master DB and the RFID DB with the local Transflo DB.

Tags. Can be passive or active. Passive tags have limited range and data storage capacity.

Readers. Physical device that reads RFID tags.

Middleware. Software layer that filters raw tag data and converts it into useful event data. It is also responsible for registering new tags to the ONS when they appear.

EPC IS. Network infrastructure that enables companies to provide access control policies and to store data associated with EPCs in secure databases on the Web.

Database. Database that stores RFID data.

ONS Service. Similar to the Domain Name Service that points computers to Web sites. ONS points computers to Internet databases where data associated with an EPC are stored.

Figure 3.4 Batch update architecture

Financial Analysis

Using the methodologies described earlier, the team analyzed the potential benefits of RFID to PCH. The revenue model projections were based on RFID benefits in the SCM industry. The model assumes that RFID has essentially two types of benefits for PCH:

- Strictly operational benefits that make PCH's operations run more efficiently
- Strictly business benefits that bring in new cash flows

The operational improvements of RFID are captured as improvements to the current operating margin of PCH, and business benefits are captured as an enhancement to the growth rate of PCH's projected (future) cash flows.

Operational Benefits

Specifically in terms of operational benefits, the model includes improvement to the productivity of customer relationship management (CRM), reduction of claims and credits, and improved diversion management.

Customer Relationship Management Improvement

SCM firms such as PCH must have accurate and responsive CRM. In fact, maintaining good relations with customers, who depend on PCH for their sourcing solutions, is an underlying necessity. CRM is not without costs, however; hiring customer relations representatives and setting up call centers add cost and could become a drag on the business's bottom line. When RFID is deployed as an integrated solution, providing real-time data can streamline CRM by allowing customers to check for the status of the shipments themselves, thus alleviating traffic coming into the call centers. This makes it possible to achieve a higher ratio of customers to CRM representatives and thus improve productivity from a CRM perspective.

Reduction in Credits and Claims and Disputes

RFID can improve tracking across supply chains, allow for better quality by exposing issues early on, ensure that actual shipments match the original purchase order, and allow for a transparent and clear log of activities that could aid PCH in scenarios where problems originate at the client's procurement office. The value of all these services can be estimated by considering the average number of claims that occur every year and the average loss per claim, then quantifying a reduction factor in number of claims. The resulting reduction in the value of claims is a source of improvement for PCH's operating margin.

Improving Diversion Management

Diversion occurs when a shipment goes to the wrong destination. Because SCM is labor intensive, supply chains are at many stages prone to human error that could result in diversions. Diversions are yet another source of liability and risk for PCH. Once again, RFID can help improve the situation by automating a control and checking mechanism, particularly at warehouses, for detecting and preventing diversions. Please see the RFID Technology Overview section earlier in this chapter for a concrete example.

To capture the improved operating margin resulting from this early detection and prevention mechanism, the model employs the following logic: a good estimate of the cost of diversion is the cost of initial freight to the wrong destination added to the cost of retransporting the item express (most likely by air) to the correct destination. Therefore, adding average cost of freight per shipment to the average cost of air shipping per shipment provides a good estimate of cost for a single shipment diversion. Multiplying that figure by the average number of diversions that occur every year will then produce an estimate of the total monetary liability that diversions pose. A reduction factor is then used to capture the improvement possibility offered by RFID.

Business Benefits

RFID contributes to creating new cash by positively affecting PCH's marketing strategy and reducing supply chain pain points.

Marketing Strategy. Successful implementation and integration of RFID can serve as a valuable marketing tool in differentiating PCH from the competition. The transparency that RFID creates can enhance clients' trust in PCH by providing a tangible view of the supply chain as shipments are transported from origin to destination. A successful marketing strategy could assert PCH's responsiveness to clients' needs and concerns and emphasize PCH as the most transparent solution provider. Furthermore, being a niche player, PCH can capitalize on RFID's cutting-edge reputation to differentiate itself from the rest of the competition and establish itself as the most efficient and technology-savvy competitor.

To capture value added by RFID to PCH's marketing strategy, the model attempts to determine the number of new clients who joined PCH as a result of marketing RFID. Clients are divided into three categories: small, medium-sized, and large. It makes sense that RFID would have a more pronounced impact on the success of marketing to medium-sized and large potential clients. The result of new cash flows from these new clients is expressed as an incremental percentage in growth rate.

Supply Chain Pain Points. Every supply chain suffers from bottlenecks that slow shipments and put a limit on its capacity. RFID can aid PCH in identifying these bottlenecks by allowing accumulation of shipping data that were previously unavailable. Additionally, RFID implementation at a bottleneck can improve performance and allow for greater PCH capacity by freeing some of the resources that are allocated to alleviate the problem. For example, if PCH sends a representative to inspect a problem point, not only are there monetary values associated with the employee's cost of travel to the designated location, but there is also the opportunity cost for an employee whose time could have been spent instead working on a project involving incorporating new clients, for example. To quantify RFID's impact on enhancing PCH's capacity (by pushing out the production possibility frontier), the model follows a logic similar to that used in evaluating RFID's marketing strategy:

- Approximate the number and type (small, medium, and large) of new clients whose addition has been possible because of the expanded capacity derived from the introduction of RFID technology.
- Attach a monetary value to these new clients.
- Report the result as an increment in growth rate.

Financial Calculator

Because PCH manages a multitude of supply chains for its customers, it made most sense to deliver a generic tool that can be applied to the different types of chain. An ROI calculator that models the financial implication of implementing an RFID system on a particular supply chain was delivered as part of the overall solution. The financial calculator is specific to PCH and provides a quantitative measure of the financial worth of an RFID implementation. It relies on NPV analysis in which the expected or projected future RFID-generated cash flows are discounted to represent the value or worth of the project today. These expected cash flows include both inflows (the financial benefit of the RFID project) and outflows (the cost of the project implementation). In this way, the NPV analysis provides a neat conceptual framework around which the model is developed: the value added of an RFID implementation is the present value (PV) of the benefits minus the present value of the costs. Furthermore, the model captures the ROI of the project by relying on the NPV analysis in the following way:

$$\text{ROI} = \frac{\text{NPV}_{\text{Project}}}{\text{PV}(\text{Costs}_{\text{Project}})}$$

One key point in the NPV analysis is the determination of the hurdle rate at which the project is to be discounted. The model takes advantage of the WACC model explained later.

Implementation of the model takes shape as an Excel application. The calculator consists of the following elements:

Fundamentals Worksheet. The fundamentals worksheet captures the user's inputs of project-specific and PHC-specific data. These data are used by other worksheets in calculating the NPV. One key measure captured in this sheet is the WACC used for discounting the cash flows once the cash flows are generated. (See *Corporate Finance* by Ross, Westerfield, and Jaffe for an explanation of WACC methodology.)[17] Following are the types of data captured:

– *Project-specific data:* The time it takes for the project to go online when the life of the project is limited to ten years
– *PCH-specific data:* Information about the supply chains that PCH

operates, such as current revenue, current operating margins, and projected growth rate

Revenue Worksheet. The revenue worksheet quantifies the positive benefits of the RFID implementation in terms of the additional inflow of cash. The revenue model is designed to reflect the added benefits that RFID can have for PCH, such as operating margin improvements.

Revenue Increases

Cost Worksheet. The cost worksheet captures the total costs of the RFID system:

- *Fixed one-time costs:* Incurred once in the project's lifetime. Amounts are known and deterministic. For example: the cost of installation and initial training.
- *Fixed recurring costs:* Costs whose amounts are known or predetermined. Incurred regularly during the lifetime of the project. For example: the yearly maintenance costs associated with software upgrades.
- *Variable costs:* Costs whose amounts are not necessarily known in advance because they are directly driven by the volume of the underlying business. For example: the costs of RFID tags that depend on the volume of pallets shipped in a given time frame. Variable costs can be estimated and forecast. For the sake of simplicity, this calculator assumes constant yearly growth of these variable costs.

Cash Flow Stream Worksheet. Three cash flow streams are generated on this worksheet:

- Projected future cash flows without an RFID implementation, based on current margin and growth projections.
- Projected future cash flows with an RFID implementation, based on the growth and margin captured in the revenue model and the projected costs of implementing the system.
- The incremental cash flow generated by the difference between the projection with RFID and the one without RFID. This incremental cash flow isolates the impact of RFID on the bottom line.

The incremental cash flow is discounted at the discount rate determined from WACC (in the fundamentals worksheet). All the discounted incremental cash flows are added to produce the NPV of the RFID project.

ROI calculated on the basis of the equation presented earlier—that is, the NPV of incremental cash flows—is divided by the PV of the cost of RFID. Figure 3.5 shows a portion of the financial calculator.

Recommendations

Depending on the supply chain, business characteristics, and existing technical infrastructure, different strategies may be applied in the implementation of an RFID system. Because of the number of parameters controlling the implementation of the most optimal RFID solution, recommendations for PCH are given in the form of a questionnaire. Using the characteristics of a business or supply chain, the questionnaire provides a best-practice recommendation that will guide PCH in its deployment of the RFID system. Following is a nonexclusive list of the parameters considered in the questionnaire that will guide an optimal implementation of the RFID system:

1. What is the geography of your supply chains?

A supply chain can be defined as a path between two endpoints. Assuming that these two endpoints are located in different countries, there will be a number of points between the two endpoints (transshipping or middle stopping point) where the goods will need to be tracked. These endpoints may not necessarily be in the same countries as the two endpoints. Because different countries have different restrictions on the RFID UHF frequency, the frequency of tags needs to be chosen carefully. A list of frequencies based on geographic location is shown in Table 3.10.

Care must be taken to choose a frequency that is supported by all warehouses in all geographic regions. The following formula can be used to find the appropriate frequency range:

Frequency lower bound = min(frequencies at all supply chain points)

Frequency upper bound = max(frequencies at all supply chain points)

For example, for supply chains between China and the United States via Hong Kong, use 902–920 MHz, and for supply chains between China and Europe via Hong Kong, use 862–915 MHz.

Servers

Cost per server	$2,000
Readers per server	2
ONS per warehouse	1
EPC IS per warehouse	1
Total number of servers needed	14
Total servers cost	$28,000
TOTAL HARDWARE[1]	**$59,600**

RFID software costs

Middleware	$183,000
ERP system	$100,000
TOTAL SOFTWARE	**$283,000**

Installation and integration

Consulting and integration[2]	$128,000
Internal project team	$315,000
Tag and reader testing	$80,000
TOTAL INSTALLATION	**$523,000**

Training

Trainer	$1,000
Training time requirement	1
Lost employee productivity	$4,000
TOTAL TRAINING	**$5,000**

Summary total setup costs

Hardware	$59,600
Software	$283,000
Installation	$523,000
Training	$5,000
TOTAL	**$870,600**

[1] Aggregate of all hardware-related costs, including server costs.

[2] Forrester Research estimate: $128,000 for a $12 billion manufacturer.

Figure 3.5   Portion of financial calculator

2. What transportation methods do the supply chains use? Broadly speaking, supply chains can be divided into two categories on the basis of transportation method:

– *Sea and road*

    i. *Full container load (FCL) versus less than container load (LCL):* Sea and road supply chains may utilize either FCL or LCL shipping methods.

    ii. *Clients using FCL:* FCLs are containers sealed at the manufacturer and opened at the customer's warehouse. The goods might be packed in the container without a pallet, and the contents of the container are not accessible for scanning. The RFID application level will therefore be container or carton. Depending on whether there are additional tracking requirements before packing and after opening the container, the client may choose to tag at both the container and the carton levels. In implementing RFID at the container level, it is suggested that 433MHz active tags, per current industry practice, be used. (There are several reasons for this: first, 433MHz tags are accepted all over the world; second,

Table 3.10
RFID frequencies based on
geographic location

Region	Frequency selection
China	915 MHz
Hong Kong	915 MHz
Macau	915 MHz
Taiwan	915 MHz
United States and Canada	902–920 MHz
Mexico	915 MHz
Singapore	862–870 MHz
Northern Africa	862–870 MHz
Europe	862–870 MHz
Middle East	862–870 MHz
Australia	915 MHz

433MHz tags are less sensitive to metal than UHF tags; third, active tags have a long range.) Clients who decide to augment the container-level tagging with carton-level tagging should refer to questions 1 and 3 for further explanation of optimal tag type and frequency choices.

iii. *Clients using LCL:* LCL containers contain multiple shipment orders and are not sealed. In fact, the containers are likely to be checked in and out of warehouses at different points throughout the supply chain. For this reason, shipments inside the container are usually packed on pallets to facilitate ease of movement. Tracking at the pallet level is particularly attractive to those parties interested in monitoring and tracking items entering and leaving warehouses and distribution centers, because such tracking enables pallets to be identified across the supply chain. For example, the movement of a pallet may be tracked from a manufacturer to a distribution center and then to a store that intends to sell the product being carried on the pallet. The Auto-ID Center's Phase I field trial consists of asset tracking at the pallet level.

– *Air.* This type of supply chain uses air cargo to ship small amounts of cargo quickly to a destination. While the total amount of cargo per shipment is small compared to that of other mechanisms, air cargo requires a more accurate tracking system because the cost of air cargo is considerably greater than the cost of other shipping methods. As a result, the optimal implementation level for RFID tags is at the carton level. Tracking assets at the carton level can be accomplished either in conjunction with pallet tagging or by itself. Carton-level tracking is more specific than pallet-level tracking and may be more attractive for those wishing to track individual cartons of product within a distribution center once a pallet is unloaded. The Auto-ID Center's Phase II field trial consisted of asset tracking at the carton and pallet levels.

3. Do your supply chains move goods that have high levels of metals? Or goods that induce electromagnetic fields, such as power supplies, transformers, and so on? As mentioned earlier,

the detective performance of RFID can be highly affected by metallic material. For classifying goods according to what could affect RFID performance, we recommend the following implementations:

- *Nonmetallic (or low level of metallic components):* The choice of tagging level will not be affected by the material, and RFID implementation at either the carton level or pallet level is possible. Furthermore, for this group we recommend using UHF frequency because of its long read range and low cost.

- *Metallic (or high level of metal present):* Implementation at the carton level is not recommended because of the potential for metal interference due to the proximity of the tags to the metallic goods. This interference could cause the reader not to detect the tags. However, if the client requires carton-level tagging (due to some overriding business requirement), low-frequency tags (13.56MHz) are recommended because they are more resistant to metal interference than the UHF tags. The trade-off with low frequency is diminished range. If range becomes an issue, portable readers are recommended to mitigate any issues with range. Pallet-level tagging should still be acceptable with a UHF implementation.

4. Do your supply chains deal with high-volume, low-unit-cost items or with low-volume, high-unit-cost items? High-volume, low-unit-cost items might be priced individually at such low values that their price might not justify the tag prices. Furthermore, in this situation it is highly unlikely that individual or low-level tracking would be a business requirement. It is therefore recommended that the RFID be implemented at a higher level of tagging, such as pallet or container. Conversely, given low-volume but high-unit-cost items, each unit represents a higher percentage value of the total shipment and low-level tagging (such as at the carton or individual item level) might not only make economic sense but also be highly likely to be part of the business requirements. Of course the client must consider the composition of the items (as discussed earlier) before the actual implementation.

5. *Real-time system versus batch considerations:* The client must consider two aspects when deciding whether to provide a real-time system or put a batch process in place. The client must first consider the business requirements and makes sure that the decision satisfies the underlying business needs. To better clarify these needs, we suggest the client consider the following questions:

- *Do you currently have customer-facing applications that provide order status?* If not, do you plan to develop one? If the client is not planning a customer-facing application or if having such a system is not part of its business strategy, then a batch system should provide adequate support considering the lower average cost of implementing a batch process and the shorter project development period. If, on the other hand, the client already has customer-facing applications or if the client's business strategy requires having customer-facing applications, proceed to the next question.

- *What kind of information do you expect to expose on your customer-facing application?* Having a customer-facing application does not warrant a real-time system. A more important issue is the types of data that will be accessible in the application. If the customer-facing application is a tracking system that shows the flow of the supply chain, then a real-time system is suitable. However, if the online application is simply a portal to input orders and check the accuracy of accounting data, then a batch model will be more appropriate.

- *How much information exchange do you expect?* Real-time systems have limited capacity for data transfer. If data transfer volumes are huge, then a batch system, where data is transferred and persists in bulk, is faster, more efficient, and more reliable than a continuous channel of data communication.

- *What is your budget for RFID?* Generally, batch processors are cheaper and faster to implement. The client must therefore consider the financial aspect of the project and make sure it has the budget to implement the real-time system.

- *Are you planning to replace your current system?* Upgrading from a legacy system is expensive and time-consuming. If the client is dealing with such a scenario, it could get more bang for its buck if it bought a complete solution from a CRM vendor (most CRM vendors provide support for real-time data transfer). Beyond the underlying business needs, to ensure that an implementation is feasible, the client must be aware of the technological realities. The following questions provide some guidelines:

— *What kind of integration technologies are you able to support?* Real-time systems often support some kind of synchronous messaging system under such protocols as Simple Object Access Protocol (SOAP) and therefore usually have Web service capabilities. The client must assess its existing IT architecture and either ensure that it has the necessary technologies for a real-time implementation or acquire or develop those technologies in a way that falls within the project's budget.

— *What kind of rollback and backup methodology do you have?* Batch processes are usually fairly robust, and a correctly designed batch process that creates the necessary backups can be immune from system failures. A real-time system is much more prone to data-write issues due to system failures or network data-loss rate.

6. *What types of warehouses do you have?* The physical implementation of RFID depends on the nature of the warehouse layout. There are four general categories of warehouses and each calls for a different implementation strategy.

— *Separated in and out entrance (SIO):* SIO is the simplest warehouse structure. Goods are checked in through one dock door and checked out through another door. RFID antennas can be installed at both the in and the out dock doors. The recommended practice is to put two readers and four to eight antennas (depending on the power of the antennas) at each gate. In addition, signaling lights should be placed on the door as a visual way for workers to check the validity of the shipment. The RFID system will read the tags as they move in and out of the dock doors. If the shipment is correct, a green light will flash; otherwise, a red light will flash, indicating that the

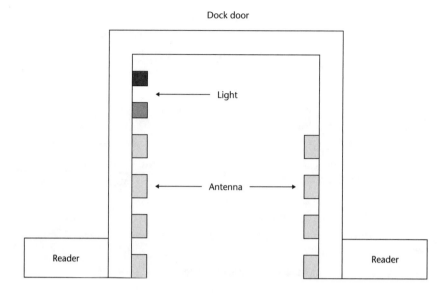

Figure 3.6   Typical dock door implementation

workers need to check the shipment. Figure 3.6 illustrates a dock door implementation.

- Mixed in and out entrance (MIO): At the MIO warehouse, in and out entrances are mixed and the RFID system requires an additional device for detecting whether the goods are being checked in or out. The general solution to this layout is to install infrared detectors at the entrances to detect pallet movement.

Conclusions

RFID technology offers SCM exciting possibilities in process automation, efficiency improvement, speed, and quality control. However, these benefits are not without costs. As a nascent technology, RFID currently requires considerable capital investment and has yet to be fully proved as a winning solution to some of the chronic problems that affect SCM. The question, then, is how an SCM company like PCH China that manages multiple supply chains across the globe could effectively implement RFID in the face of the considerable capital requirements.

Balancing Act

Scale is important when implementing RFID in a supply chain environment. Certain costs, such as for software integration, will not vary given RFID implementation across one or several chains. Additionally, the high cost of the hardware and potential process reengineering may not make economic sense if you are dealing with implementation across only one supply chain. RFID requires scale, and scale is easily achieved if a solution is deployed across multiple chains. In this way, PCH could spread some of the underlying costs across multiple chains. On the other hand, RFID may not be feasible for all of PCH's supply chains. Reasons that can make a particular supply chain less of a candidate for RFID implementation include but are not limited to the following:

1. Too low volume across the supply chain to justify chain-specific RFID costs.

2. Cyclical nature of the supply chain. The customer may be operating in a very cyclical industry; thus the supply chain may experience periodic traffic fluctuations, which means that the RFID infrastructure may be underutilized during the periods when there is not much traffic.

3. An underlying transportation method in the supply chain may pose serious problems for a particular RFID implementation. For example, sealed containers will not fit in an RFID implementation based on warehouses because the contents stay within the containers and never enter many of the warehouses. Another example is that in FCLs there are no pallets associated with any of the cargo; thus a pallet-based tagging system would be irrelevant.

Implementation Policy Suggestions

On the basis of the research presented here it is recommended that PCH use the following approach for their RFID implementation assessment and strategy:

– *Categorize supply chains on the basis of their geography.* Because PCH is largely a China sourcing solution provider, it makes sense to base the geography of the supply chain on the location of the customer. For example, consider North American supply chains as those with customers in North America and European supply chains as those with customers in continental Europe, the Republic of Ireland, and the United Kingdom.

– Considering PCH's strategy in underwriting risk by actually purchasing shipments, it is our recommendation that PCH consider the amount of liability induced by a given supply chain. This means considering a supply chain's cost of freight. Obviously those supply chains that see large numbers of shipments are going to be more costly in the sense of the underlying risk.

– We then suggest normalizing these costs across all the supply chains to come up with a portfolio weight for supply chains. Considering PCH's supply chains as a portfolio and then considering how much weight each supply chain adds to this portfolio could be helpful in distinguishing those chains that are candidates for an RFID implementation. If the portfolio weight is too low, that is, if the relative cost and liability of the chain is miniscule, then an RFID implementation may not be the optimal solution for the chain.

– For those chains that are relatively low volume but could still utilize RFID we recommend centralizing part of the chain into another chain if operationally feasible. For example, consider a chain in which the port of entry is Rotterdam and a marginal supply chain that has Hamburg as its port of entry. The question is, Can the marginal supply chain be redesigned to share facilities and go through Rotterdam as well? The process of centralizing operations across multiple chains must be carried out with care because of the potential for creating new bottlenecks in the chain. One advantage that PCH enjoys is its strong relationships with regional forwarders such as ATE Group in North America and Bax Global in Europe. PCH could capitalize on these relationships to centralize operations at designated warehouses. This could increase the volume at designated warehouses to a point where RFID implementation makes sense. The designated warehouses would provide benefits to the partners and thus make cost sharing a viable mechanism for lowering the cost of implementation.

Once PCH decides on the chains it finds optimal for RFID implementation and solidifies the scope of the project, it can then assess the project's ROI using the model provided earlier. The questionnaire can be used as a guide in devising a technical implementation strategy.

4　Information Technology

Information technology (IT) has had a profound impact on many aspects of day-to-day life. But it's not just individuals who are benefiting from IT. Companies also have benefited greatly from the proliferation of IT, particularly in the past fifteen years. Information technology has not only enabled large corporations to automate their back offices and such essential functions as accounting, human resources, and other enterprise resource planning (ERP) tasks, but it has also, because of "killer applications" (programs that people want so much that they will buy hardware or software just to be able to run them), allowed many firms to acquire competitive advantage in their specific area or core focus. These new tools have tremendously increased efficiency, allowed for better management of resources, and therefore made firms more efficient in allocating scarce resources. Huge quantities of data can now be stored, mined, analyzed, and presented to decision makers within the firm. In fact, a particular IT value added has been the unlocking of data the firm either had stored but could neither retrieve nor analyze efficiently, or could not store in the first place. Illustrations of how valuable data can be are easy to find. Financial service companies are excellent examples of how the implementation of IT systems has leveraged considerable value for firms considering the importance of information in such areas as asset pricing, transaction monitoring, and tracking.

An important subset of IT, known as real-time systems (for their ability to deliver live data), are increasingly playing pivotal roles in delivering information within firms and changing the very nature of organizations. The most valuable aspect of a real-time IT system is its ability to provide data that are up-to-date and reliable. The added value of a real-time system, then, is this ability to provide data that best represent the current state of the world. This value can be better captured when analyzing a non-real-time alternative and judging the opportunity cost of not being able to interact with a set of live data. Furthermore, the very nature of a real-time system often implies that the system is in constant communication with other systems. With the growing complexity of data, it is most often the case that a system designed to deliver real-time data has to interact with other systems in a distributed environment to get the most complete set of available data. This has given rise to and become an underlying factor in integrating IT processes and systems across firms and in creating comprehensive end-to-end solutions. These live-data systems are enabling decision makers to make decisions not only on the basis of an existing set of data, but additionally on the basis of having a realistic picture of the existing condition of the world.

This chapter presents two case studies in which consulting teams worked with the clients to solve two entirely different issues pertaining to information systems. The first case examines GTP USA (a fictional name), a small and fast-growing subsidiary of a global supply chain management company. The study focuses on the IT organization and how best to integrate it into the overall strategy of the firm while leveraging the parent company's IT resources and putting in place a structure for a scalable IT organization. Furthermore, the case focuses on the governance issues within an IT organization that arise from competing projects in need of funding. The consulting team that studied this company soon realized that there was no formal process in place for mapping the IT function to business strategy and no systematic ways for management to filter through opportunities. The consulting team therefore suggested formation of three committees: am executive committee, an IT steering committee, and an IT council to give management more insight into IT organization and to create a systematic response methodology to facilitate resource-sharing efforts. The team also suggested that formal project management be applied to strengthening the ties between IT and business strategy, and that a portfolio management approach be created for selecting projects so that those projects with the highest return on investment (ROI) would be selected.

The second case is much more concentrated in that the consultants helped a region in southwest China create a platform to provide services for companies that are intending to source and invest in this region. Most of the economic growth and prosperity in China have been focused in the eastern region, especially in the coastal areas. The government of this southwestern region has been seeking foreign direct investment to spur further economic growth for the province. As part of this effort, the region is seeking to develop a hosted IT platform to provide comprehensive solutions for the global sourcing industry. This platform is to facilitate different steps in sourcing to the region and provide for better communication between general buyers (companies that are sourcing) and suppliers (local manufacturers) of the sourcing solutions. The Stanford–Hong Kong University of Science and Technology team began by analyzing the business process flow that takes place in a typical sourcing situation between the supplier and an internationally based buyer. The team conducted extensive interviews and market research to better understand user requirements for such an IT platform in terms of functionality and user interface. On the basis of the gathered data and the existing platform developed by a local university, the team made a series of feature suggestions targeted to address specific supplier and buyer functional needs of an outsourcing platform. In addition, the consulting team developed a detailed marketing plan and discussed the product adoption life cycle, consumer analysis, product development schedule and planning, partner analysis, distribution channel analysis, and pricing suggestions.

Case 1: GTP USA

IT Organization and Governance

On a weekday in February 2005, John Taylor returned to his office in downtown Los Angeles after a long morning of meetings with the senior management of GTP USA.[1] As the newly appointed chief information officer (CIO), Taylor was responsible for managing all the IT systems and resources for the Americas. GTP USA was in the process of implementing a new global strategy and was poised for a period of rapid growth. Taylor's technology resources would need to scale to accommodate this phase of growth, and he faced a number of organizational challenges as he sought to plan effectively for the next few years.

GTP USA is the Los Angeles–based subsidiary of a Shanghai-based supply chain management (SCM) company that U.S. and European companies in many industries, such as furniture, consumer goods, automotive, and apparel, use as a service provider. The smallest and fastest-growing subsidiary of its parent company, GTP focuses on providing sourcing solutions to China and SCM solutions for the American apparel market.

Initially, GTP USA developed capabilities in product design, import management, domestic distribution, and other related services to broaden the parent company's offerings to its U.S. customers. These capabilities well positioned the parent company to diversify beyond its core business. The time was ripe for the parent company to enter wholesale businesses to capture higher margins than it had previously experienced. GTP USA's management team hoped to grow the business into a substantial part of the overall parent company's business within a few years.

Taylor was energized to tackle this significant market opportunity, but he knew that major challenges lay ahead. As a company quickly expanding its presence in the United States, GTP USA had many competing priorities for utilizing its IT resources. Its global IT governance process, which had worked well for an established global consumer goods sourcing company, was being challenged by GTP USA's new dynamic business environment.

Taylor faced critical decisions at this juncture. How could he create a responsive IT organizational framework for sustainable growth while ensuring that business needs were met in a scalable manner? Furthermore, what is an optimal process for prioritizing projects within a dynamic organization in a way that best addresses the business needs?

Industry Overview

Industry Trends

The apparel industry is traditionally one of the largest industries worldwide. In the United States alone, the garment industry reached $295.7 billion in 2005, a 4.7 percent increase over the preceding two years. Increased domestic competition and cost-effectiveness had forced apparel manufacturers to expand beyond their national borders. The biggest benefits of this global trend were the emerging economies that offered cost advantages to the developed nations. In 2003, more than 50 percent of the apparel sold in the United States was imported and the vast majority of this clothing was from China.[2] Over the last few decades, this growing reliance on China as a low-cost producer had resulted in a competitive combination of pricing and quality products.

To safeguard against domestic production, several countries, including the United States, established the Multifibre Arrangement (MFA) in 1973. This agreement brought into effect a quota system that limited the maximum number of products a country could produce and export to the MFA's member countries.

However, the WTO's Agreement on Textile and Clothing defined a ten-year phase-out of the MFA quotas, finalized on January 1, 2005, giving the WTO member-countries unlimited access to the MFA countries. This unrestricted access to resources to and from any country affected the global apparel and textile industry.

China, a member of the WTO since 2001, is expected to be the largest beneficiary of these government deregulations due to its large installed base of textile manufacturing plants, low-cost skilled labor, and high-quality production. Since the end of the quota system, China's export of baby clothes has already surged by 826 percent. China is now taking vast strides toward being the world leader in the garment and apparel industry. In fact, a Plunkett Research report estimates that China will control as much as 50 percent of the world's clothing market by 2010. This is a significant increase when compared to its modest share of 17 percent in 2003.[3]

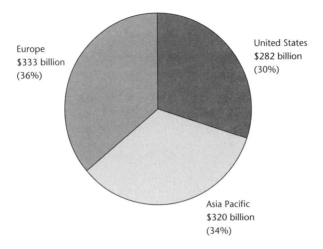

Figure 4.1   Apparel and textile market by share, 2003

Market Analysis

A market study by Datamonitor revealed that the world's apparel and textile market for 2003 was worth $934.7 billion, of which the United States represented 30.2 percent ($282.3 billion). The Asia Pacific represented 34.2 percent and the remaining was accounted for by Europe (see Figure 4.1). In the United States, the apparel sector formed 75 percent of the market. Further, an in-depth study by *DSN Retailing Today* reported that the discount apparel market constituted around 40 percent of the total apparel market. The market share was distributed mostly among the supermarkets. Wal-Mart stood at the top with 24.6 percent, followed by T.J. Maxx and Marshall's with 10.1 percent. Target, which offers designer-name products, stood third with an 8.6 percent market share, followed by Old Navy with 7.8 percent and Kmart with 6.1 percent.

It is estimated that the total apparel and textile industry in the United States will see higher growth in the next few years and reach $320 billion by 2008 (see Figure 4.2). On the other hand, in the Asia Pacific region, the industry is expected to reach $416.7 billion, a rapid growth of 30.4 percent from 2003 (see Figure 4.3).

The apparel industry has always been driven by manufacturers who constantly compete on lower price points. These price wars have helped consumers enjoy a wide selection of economy clothing at moderate prices.

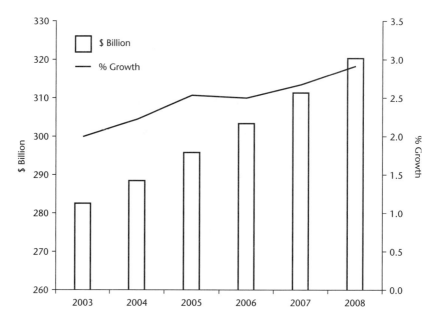

Figure 4.2   U.S. apparel and textile market value forecast, 2003–2008
SOURCE: Datamonitor

The largest beneficiaries, however, have been the retail stores, who have been able to capture increased profit margins due to hypercompetition at the manufacturing level.

Some of the biggest players who keep the profit margins low are Wal-Mart, Costco, and Kohl's. These retail stores operate on economies of scale because they rely on large volumes of sales to compensate for relatively small profit margins. On the other side, successful chains like Sears and JCPenney target middle-market consumers with pricier and higher-margin products. Companies like Spyder, Victoria's Secret, and Chico's FAS focus on premium niche markets with attractive high-end products catering to wealthy individuals. The growing demand and the competition in apparel have forced many department stores to shift their focus primarily to clothing and textile accessories.

Globalization

The increase in globalization has been a blessing to both consumers and retailers. Retailers now have access to a rapidly growing global pool

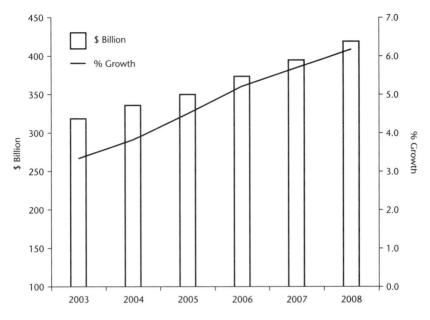

Figure 4.3   Asia-Pacific apparel and textile market value forecast, 2003–2008
SOURCE: Datamonitor

of manufacturers who offer reliable services at fractional costs. Retailers are also at liberty to outsource operations that are not directly related to their core business. For example, a U.S.-based apparel retailer could outsource its manufacturing to Japanese factories, its sewing to Taiwan, and its division of labor to South Korea. This would help it focus strongly on designing better products at cheaper prices. Consumers, as a result, enjoy the price cuts resulting from heavy competition among retailers.

Leading Companies

Vanity Fair Corporation. The international giant of the apparel industry, Vanity Fair, designs, manufactures, sources, and markets its products in many countries, including the United States. For 2004, its U.S. market capitalization was $6.7 billion. Products include consumer, occupational, outdoor, and sports apparel and equipment.

Liz Claiborne Inc. Liz Claiborne designs and markets women's and men's fashions, accessories, and fragrances. Its U.S. market capitalization for 2004 was $4.5 billion and it has a presence in thirty-six other countries.

Polo Ralph Lauren Corporation. Polo Ralph Lauren designs, markets, and distributes specialty lifestyle products including women's, men's, and children's apparel; home products; and fashion accessories. Its operations include wholesale, retail, and licensing. It does business in twenty-three countries and had a market capitalization of $4.1 billion for 2004 in the United States.

In the retail industry, the biggest player is Wal-Mart, which is also the largest importer of Chinese goods. Ten percent of all Chinese imports are imported by Wal-Mart, which has established its own global procurement division.[4] In 2003, Wal-Mart imported 471,000 containers and reached $256 billion in annual sales. Target ranked second, with 48 billion in revenues; Sears Roebuck ranked third, with $41 billion; and JCPenney ranked fourth, with $32.9 billion.

These large retailers are expected to increase their global sourcing in low-cost manufacturing countries. It is important to underline the bargaining power of these giant retailers in driving down prices and shifting the risks back to the vendors.

Barriers to Entry

China wanted and gained a position in the WTO after serious efforts at liberalization of its economy. The country is now passing laws endorsing private ownership and intellectual property as well as embracing public-private and domestic-foreign partnerships.[5]

China's economy has boomed since it became the world's biggest factory and most important destination for foreign investments. This exponential growth has led to a sharp rise in the prices of raw materials such as petroleum, and to burgeoning inflation rates in both China and Western countries. This effect has led Chinese officials to undertake serious measures to contain price inflations that will eventually erode China's competitive advantage in cost leadership in manufacturing. However, even with an expected 8 percent annual increase in gross domestic product and price inflation, China is still expected to be the worldwide leader in 2010.

Offshoring to China

Outsourcing to China is not necessarily the lowest-cost alternative. There are four important criteria for trade management success in China: lowest total delivered cost, delivery reliability, supply chain flexibility and regulatory compliance, and risk minimization.[6] The points to consider before offshoring are the following: legal issues, theft and piracy, shipping losses, additional administration and paperwork, employee morale, layoff and severance, cultural and communication difficulties, loss of manufacturing control, training, and startup and transition costs, as well as increased labor costs as supplier relationships mature and increased inventory costs due to longer lead times. To do business in China, it is also important to have leading people in the sourcing process who know the customs and culture.[7]

Third-party logistics companies are quickly gaining prominence because of the specialized services they offer that help the apparel companies concentrate on their primary business. Since its inception in the early 1990s, the logistics services industry has grown rapidly, at the rate of 20 percent each year. A study conducted by a logistics consulting firm found that about 37 percent of the companies with large shipping activities outsourced their SCM to logistics companies. This outsourcing was estimated to reach 73 percent by 2005.[8]

Value Chain

To determine how global the value chain is, we need to compute the ratio of trade (including trade in product components as well as final goods) to sales. A ratio above 100 percent means that the industry is very global.[9]

Consumer electronics, for instance, boasts a trade-to-sales ratio of 118 percent, which means the industry generates 18 percent more value from trading components and finished goods among global business partners than from sales of final goods to consumers. The reason for this is a globally disaggregated low-cost consumer electronics value chain. U.S. desktop components are very likely to have been manufactured in Taiwan, China, Thailand, or South Korea, reckoning on the cheapest price for each component. The reasons behind this globalization of consumer electronics parts are that they are lightweight and easy to ship and that they have standardized specifications.

Not every industry is prone to such high levels of globalization, however. The apparel industry, which employs forty million people worldwide, falls in the middle, with a high trade-to-sales ratio of 77 percent, for two main reasons: on the one hand, labor, which accounts for the bulk of production costs, is very cheap; on the other hand, clothing is lightweight and thus easy and cheap to transport.

The January 1, 2005, expiration of the MFA quotas, which protected textile and apparel producers in thirty developed countries, was predicted to lead to a consolidated industry with fewer producing countries. Needless to say, China, with its access to cheap labor and mass production capabilities, is the favorite and will get the lion's share of this global market.

The dynamics of fast-fashion retailers like H&M, Old Navy, and Zara, which focus on trendy, economic clothes, are likely to take advantage of the MFA expiration and drop their prices due to their cost-plus pricing models.

GTP

GTP USA is the smallest and fastest-growing wholly owned subsidiary of GTP, a Shanghai SCM company active in many industries, including hard goods such as furniture, consumer goods, automotive supplies, and apparel. GTP was founded in the first half of the twentieth century as an exporter of raw material from China. With the gradual opening of China and the rise of Shanghai as a regional center for manufacturing, GTP, under the control of the Chinese government, began to focus on low-margin consumer goods such as toys and plastic flowers assembled in China. The company continued to modernize and was privatized in the early 1990s.

Since privatization, GTP has acted as an end-to-end service provider for overseas companies (mostly in the United States and Europe) that wish to outsource and need help with logistics. The company has offered services that cover every part of SCM and serves a number of well-known clients. The company's main focus is in the area of hard goods, but it also has the capabilities to source apparel through GTP. In 2004 the company had a thousand employees and revenues of $250 million and was supported by a global network of thirty-eight offices in thirty countries around the world.

GTP USA

GTP USA consists of an office of fifty employees in Los Angeles that provides a variety of value-added services to the apparel industry.

It is common practice in the apparel industry for customers to take ownership of goods on a free-on-board (FOB) basis, which means that customers are responsible for shipping goods from the port of export in the country of origin. Some customers, however, wanted to take advantage of the economies of scale offered by GTP and outsource their import logistics. To meet this demand, GTP provides SCM services that deliver goods directly to customers' distribution centers or stores in the United States on a Landed, Duty Paid (LDP) basis.

As an agent, GTP USA followed traditional business models that involved no inventory risk; regardless of the product's performance at retail, GTP USA would still be paid the same fee for its services. This business model exemplified the classic risk-reward tradeoff. The branded retailer who ordered from GTP had the potential to earn gross profit margins of more than 50 percent, while GTP USA's core business generally had single-digit profit margins. The retailer, however, carried the overstock and markdown risks, while GTP USA and its parent company would always be paid their service fee.

Changes in the Global Apparel Industry

For many years, exports of textiles and apparel from many countries (including China) into the United States and Europe were limited by global quotas. GTP USA's business was a beneficiary of the quota system, because it helped its customers manage the complexity surrounding sourcing products from a number of countries. Several developments in the early 2000s, however, set the stage for the transformation of the global apparel industry.

Many forecasters expected apparel production in China to rise sharply at the expense of other developing nations, as had happened in other industries in which trade quotas had been lifted. Some analysts expected GTP USA's business to be threatened by this structural change in the industry, because branded retailers could now source apparel directly from China, bypassing sourcing and SCM companies like GTP. However, GTP expected to thrive in the new environment without quotas because this environment created more new customers in search of outsourcing solutions.

Global Brands Group

To take advantage of capabilities developed over the last few years, GTP USA launched its Global Brands division in 2004. The company acquired exclusive licenses to design and market certain categories of clothing for global apparel companies, along with some textile brands. GTP's management team hoped to build a portfolio of global brands, leveraging the company's existing expertise in global sourcing and logistics management.

GTP chose brands with global reach, high consumer recognition, and perceived quality. In addition, only the product categories in which it already had sourcing expertise were licensed.

The Global Brands strategy marked a significant departure from both GTP's and GTP USA's traditional business models. Historically, the company refused to take inventory risks. However, with this new strategy, GTP USA would be responsible for sales, design, logistics, marketing, and inventory planning and would effectively become a customer of the parent company, placing orders with it, importing goods, and in some cases holding inventory for domestic replenishment.

The new business model carried several new risks, including dilution, credit, and inventory risks. Dilution risk, the lessening of merchandise value, included markdowns, shortages, and damages—new risks the company had never faced before. Furthermore, it was customary when selling to retailers to extend trade credit, so GTP USA faced the additional risk that its customers would default on their payments for goods. Finally, with inventory risk, GTP USA faced the possibility that it would produce too much inventory or the wrong inventory, or have inventory returned, which it would have to write off.

The company would be able to mitigate some of the business risk by partnering with a few key retailers in the United States and staying with familiar product categories. Furthermore, despite the business risk generated by the Global Brands strategy, moving up the value chain was a significant business opportunity for the company. The gross margins generated by the new strategy were in the double digits, compared to the traditional margins in the single digits from the core business. Thus the management team was highly committed to pursuing this new growth driver for GTP USA.

Global Organization Structure

GTP USA's operations were largely independent of those of its parent company, GTP, due to differences in the industries each served. The subsidiary offered a set of services complementary to the core business in hard goods, and thus its business processes were decentralized and managed locally.

GTP USA's president and executive director, Roger Page, served on a global executive board with eight other executive directors and the company's chief operating officer (COO), Adam Castille. The global executive board reported to Byron Horowitz, the parent company's president, and Brandon Ricardo, the company's managing director.

The parent company also had a Shanghai-based Global CIO, Albert Chen, who oversaw the company's global IT strategy. Taylor reported directly to Chen under loose formal structures within the parent organization. In turn, Chen reported to the COO in Shanghai. Taylor determined the IT strategic direction with the GTP USA management team, then worked with Chen's Hong Kong IT team to determine a technology solution.

Due to business model differences between GTP USA and its parent, the two companies' business systems were entirely separate, with minimal functional overlap. GTP USA reported financials to the parent company by extracting files from its databases and sending them to Shanghai. Orders and shipments under the Global Brands strategy were handled in a similar manner. Within GTP USA, to manage its core business, Taylor had the opportunity to set new IT standards for the new business model without regard for the existing technology platforms in Shanghai. To a large extent, GTP USA was treated as a retail customer of the parent company due to the disparate nature of the parent company's business and logistical constraints.

GTP USA's Organizational Structure

Within GTP USA's newly created Global Brands division, Taylor's IT organization served five brand managers and a senior vice president of operations. Each brand manager had profit and loss responsibility for a specific brand. In addition, the brand managers controlled the design, sales, and marketing resources for their respective brands. They reported directly to Roger Page. Operations was responsible for processing orders and budgeting in support of the brand managers, and relied on Taylor's IT systems to facilitate these transactions. The senior vice president of operations also reported to Page.

Taylor had four direct reports, all IT directors. One director was responsible for IT infrastructure, a second for IT program management. The other two directors were organized according to IT systems that supported the business process—one supporting all activities up to placing the order with Shanghai, the other supporting all activities from tracking inbound shipments through customer invoicing. The organizational structure was highly effective for eliminating redundancies across the business process, and helped IT align closely with the brands and operations.

As a rapidly growing operation, GTP USA's IT organization faced challenges in choosing between a myriad of competing priorities. Taylor prioritized IT projects by bring together the senior management team on an as-needed basis whenever there was a significant IT event. This method of project prioritization would not be sustainable as the business grew, and many, including Taylor, were concerned that IT resources were not being properly allocated across divisions because the company lacked a formal method of evaluating IT projects.

The company also lacked a forum for the system's users to suddenly increase IT opportunities and potential problems. Although Taylor's IT directors participated in regularly scheduled cross-functional meetings with the directors and managers across the brand organizations, IT issues and opportunities were not discussed in depth. This lack of formal communication processes would likely hinder ability to proactively address IT and business process issues.

Diagnosis

Project Definition

The objective of the consulting team's project was to recommend an organizational structure and a set of processes that would allow GTP USA's IT organization to identify and manage issues and opportunities in order to improve its IT and business processes.

Identifying and managing issues and opportunities are critical to the success of Taylor's IT organization, as well as of GTP USA as a whole. To sustain the rapid growth necessary to implement the Global Brands strategy, it is important that Taylor's IT strategy be highly aligned with the needs of the business while at the same time being highly responsive to changes in the business environment that also cause changes in the IT strategy.

Because GTP USA has no formal forum dedicated to identifying opportunities and communicating IT issues, and because of the organization's rapid growth and change, key issues are brought to senior management mostly only when they become urgent. This as-needed system of escalation is not sustainable in the face of rapid growth.

A second motivation for implementing organizational structures and processes is to allow Taylor to manage numerous competing priorities with advocates from across the organization. With the organization's growth, Taylor needed a way to measure objectively the benefits of projects across brands and divisions so that project prioritization would be defensible to other organization stakeholders, such as brand and operations managers.

The team's deliverables consisted of a set of specific, actionable recommendations. Furthermore, Taylor wanted to be able to implement the recommendations within a year, and see organizational benefits within three months of implementation.

Methodology

To gain a picture of the global IT organization, the team relied on interviews with Taylor and Chen. They also interviewed Ricky Wei and Yang-Chi Hua, two vice presidents of the parent company. To develop its understanding of the company's global business, one team relied on the company's Web site as well as on a number of published articles in trade publications.

In developing a competitive analysis, the team interviewed IT executives at VF Corporation, General Electric, DuPont, ING Direct, Carlson Companies, JPMorgan, UNICEF, UPS, Campbell's, State Street, Manheim Auctions, Hershey's, Humana, DHL, Meta Group, Mutual of New York, Freeborders, Spyder, Gerber Technology, and Sears—spanning the apparel, retail, manufacturing, financial services, IT consulting, and supply chain industries. They also drew on best-practice articles from CIO.com.

In applying academic frameworks to this project, the team found several papers to be particularly useful, including "A Matrixed Approach to Designing IT Governance," published in the Winter 2005 issue of the *MIT Sloan Management Review.*[10] An extensive study by MIT scientists Peter Weill and Jeanne Ross, it found that large organizations need a matrixed approach to designing IT governance, and while there is no single best formula for governing IT, companies can rely on a multidimensional strategy that best suits their business.

Analysis

Organizational Structure and Processes

In their analysis of the company's organizational structure, the team found that GTP USA's operations unit was largely independent from the parent company due to differences in business models. The analysis focused on specific, actionable recommendations that Taylor could implement with or without input from GTP USA's parent.

As part of the senior management team, Taylor had an excellent grasp of the company's overall business strategy, but the company did not have dedicated meetings with senior management in which they mapped IT strategy to the business strategy on a regular basis. Because effective IT strategy must map closely to the business strategy to be effective, especially in a rapidly changing environment, this was a substantial deficiency in the organizational structure.

Within the Global Brands division, Taylor's main customers were the brands and operations managers. A major part of his job was to enable these managers to do their business as they saw fit, and to provide them with the IT tools they needed. However, these operations managers did not have a formal forum in which to provide regular feedback to the IT organization.

One formal method of tracking issues within GTP USA's IT organization that did exist was a software system called Remedy for resolving bugs and problems within existing production systems. Taylor's IT team used reports from this system to identify common and high-priority problems that business users were experiencing.

As GTP USA's IT organization primed itself for growth, the single most prominent missing ingredient was the lack of formal communication structures. Because the firm had been smaller, informal communication was the norm at the time and was likely more efficient and effective than formal channels would have been. However, as the firm prepared to grow rapidly and add head count, formal communication would need to play a much larger role in preparing the organization for scalable, sustained growth.

Project Prioritization

Taylor also faced challenges in deciding how to allocate his scarce IT resources across the many competing demands in the company. He had developed a framework for project prioritization that had worked well, but projects were evaluated and justified using different metrics, which made evaluation of their relative priorities challenging.

GTP USA needed an approach to project prioritization that was more scientific and defensible to business stakeholders. The rapid, intuitive approach to resource allocation and project prioritization also would not scale with the company's growth trajectory. Taylor needed an approach that would satisfy stakeholders and convince them that he was using his limited resources in the best way possible.

Finally, the team felt that the question of who should ultimately own the project prioritization decisions had not been satisfactorily determined. At the time, Taylor somewhat unilaterally made IT prioritization decisions, with input from the brand and operations managers. Given that Taylor was charged with supporting the strategic direction of the business, it seemed appropriate for the brand and operations head to have additional involvement in the resource allocation and project prioritization process.

Sharing IT Resources Globally

Because GTP USA was operating in an environment of rapid growth, Taylor discovered that his IT resources where insufficient for meeting the demands of his current business. Taylor knew it would be of paramount importance to get the required resources so that future expansion and development would not be hindered. He believed that he could leverage the existing base of IT support staff and the infrastructure of his parent company to help mitigate these concerns. However, the identification and appropriate allocation of resources across the two businesses was a challenging task. Taylor turned to the research team to devise a framework and recommendation on how his business could introduce cross-pollination of resources to best address problems in IT-resource sharing across both enterprises.

An analysis of the wholesale and trading business of the parent company and the business requirements of GTP USA revealed, however, that there were few direct resources that could be shared. The companies' business-specific ITs were fundamentally different from each other. However, the GTP had recently revealed plans to expand its wholesale business into Europe. There was therefore a strong likelihood that GTP USA and its sister company in Europe could begin positioning their IT-resource sharing policies immediately to leverage each other's resources in the future.

Recommendations

Organizational Structure and Processes

To support the aggressive growth that its management team wished to pursue, GTP USA needed to implement a number of organizational structures and project processes to facilitate the alignment of IT with the business. As mentioned earlier, the consultant team recommended that Taylor institute three committees—an executive committee, an IT steering committee, and an IT council (see Figure 4.4). This three-tier committee structure was an integrated framework for formalizing disciplined communications within the company and across functions. The formation of the committees would allow for rapid responses to problems and opportunities, and greater management visibility and insight.

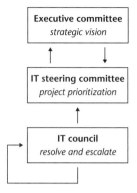

Executive committee to steering committee. Sets business strategy, aligns IT strategy with business strategy, identifies strategic IT initiatives.

IT steering committee to executive committee. Escalates strategic IT initiatives and IT/business strategy issues to executive committee.

IT council to IT steering committee. Escalates IT problems and opportunities requiring additional resources or support to resolve to IT steering committee.

IT council. Works within organization to rapidly resolve IT issues and opportunities within scope of IT director's power.

Figure 4.4   Three-tier committee structure

In addition, the team recommended that Taylor use a more scientific approach to project and portfolio management processes for prioritizing, facilitating, and measuring the success of IT projects. The project management process would level the playing field for different types of IT projects. Furthermore, it would ensure that stakeholders were informed and involved in the decision-making process; business strategy informs IT strategy, but strategy also supports the operational demands of the business.

Executive Committee

The team proposed that Taylor institute monthly meetings with an executive committee consisting of GTP USA's president, Roger Page; its CFO, Alan Brighton; the senior vice president of operations; and other yet-to-be-hired strategic business heads such as vice presidents of sales and marketing. The committee was to involve individuals who set the company-wide strategic direction, and only high-level context makers for the IT strategy were to be included in the meetings. The goal of the meetings was to align IT strategy with business strategy.

In each meeting, the president would set a clear and unambiguous strategic vision for the organization from a business perspective. The president and other externally facing executives would inform Taylor of changing business conditions and their effect on the company's business strategy. Furthermore, the CFO would inform the executive committee of changes in the company's financial goals. The group would discuss strategic IT initiatives and investments, aligning IT with the business. Finally, the executive committee would discuss issues escalated by the IT steering committee.

The impetus for implementing an executive committee was clear: in a rapidly changing, high-growth business environment it would be critical for the IT strategy to be continually realigned with the business strategy. Furthermore, as Taylor worked with the managers on the IT steering committee to prioritize IT work, he would be armed with knowledge about the relative strategic importance of various lines of business.

The research team felt that instituting an executive committee for IT would be a marked improvement over the ad hoc manner in which communication of the business strategy and agenda was being handled at the time. With regular meetings, Taylor could stay abreast of recent developments as the strategic direction of the organization changed. Furthermore, Taylor would be able to raise awareness with GTP USA's senior executives about the strategic importance of IT as a source of competitive advantage, and about its ability to align with and effectively cater to the strategic direction of the business.

IT Steering Committee

The research team also recommended that GTP USA implement an IT steering committee as a complement to the executive council. The IT steering committee would consist of Taylor, as CIO, and the brand managers, as the heads of GTP's business units. The main goal of the IT steering committee was to manage the portfolio of IT projects, initiating, prioritizing, allocating resources for, and killing projects within the IT portfolio as necessary. The committee's decisions would be informed by the strategic direction set by the executive committee. Furthermore, the committee would also be responsible for confronting issues escalated by the IT council. The team recommended that the committee meet on a biweekly basis.

The primary benefit of the IT steering committee was to tie the allocation of IT resources and projects to the operational needs of the business units. Taylor would be aware of the company's latest business strategy from his meetings with the executive committee. He could then combine that knowledge with input from the heads of the business units to create an IT portfolio that matched the ongoing operations of the business units.

As a service provider to the brand managers, Taylor could use the IT steering committee meetings to decide on priorities with the business unit heads so that IT reflected both the company's overall strategy and its daily operational needs. Thus the key business stakeholders rather than IT would have to be the primary drivers of IT portfolio management.

The IT steering committee was an improvement over the traditional process of IT-driven decision making because it ensured that the company's IT portfolio reflected the values of key decision makers. The end product of the committee's decision-making process should be an IT project portfolio that flows from the company's overall business strategy and effectively supports the business units' operational needs.

IT Council

The third and final committee recommended by the research team was an IT council consisting of a cross-functional team of director-level managers from IT, the business units, and the operations and supply chain. The team would meet on a biweekly basis, prior to the IT steering committee's meeting. The goal of the IT council was to identify and rapidly resolve or escalate critical issues and opportunities in the daily operational units of the business and operations.

The business and operations managers would come to the meeting prepared with their top pain points and potential opportunities in their businesses. The job of the IT directors in these meetings would be to listen and look for synergies and commonalities in problems and opportunities across the business units, focusing on issues that applied to two, three, or more business units. Discussions about pain points for single business units would be conducted immediately after the meeting with the individual business managers and the relevant IT director. Issues within the scope of the IT director's power could be resolved within his team, but issues requiring additional resources within the organization would be escalated by the IT directors to the IT steering committee through Taylor.

The research team believed that the IT council would have an immediate, tangible impact on GTP USA's ability to support and sustain growth from a technology perspective. By instituting a regular forum in which middle managers could share their concerns and identify opportunities, Taylor would create formal channels through which he and his managers could hear about problems surfacing across the organization before they became crises. Issues from end users could be resolved more quickly and information would be filtered to senior management when necessary.

The IT council was a significant improvement over the approach of using on-demand communication to surface issues to middle and senior management. By instituting formalized, regular communication structures, Taylor would encourage the sharing of information across the organization and speed up solving problems within the IT organization. The input of operational users would be of substantial help in improving the alignment and responsiveness of his IT organization with the business's operational needs.

Portfolio Management

GTP USA needed a methodology for prioritizing projects and managing a portfolio of IT projects that served the needs of the business and aligned with business strategy and operational needs. The portfolio management initiative would be led by the IT steering committee and rely on mutually agreed-upon metrics to evaluate different types of projects across functional units, essentially leveling the playing field.

Further, to measure the value of an IT project—whether it was a new project, an upgrade to an existing system, a break fix, or an infrastructure project—the research team recommended that Taylor use a business value approach.

The heart of the business value approach is to estimate the value of the world without an IT project and then with an IT project, expressed as the net present value of the value delivered, discounted for time and uncertainty. The difference between the two sums would be the business value. Without a project, the business value could be negative—there is a cost to doing business as usual (that is, adding manual resources to cover automation). Or the business value could be slightly positive, but the fully implemented project might have a much higher payoff.

To illustrate, let us consider the value of a break-fix of a computer network. If the network is not operational, no business can be transacted; thus the business value of the break-fix would be the total value of the transactions lost if the network were not fixed. Clearly the business value of fixing the network would be quite high (nearly the full value of the business).

The research team recommended that Taylor use the ratio of business value to implementation costs, including capital expenditures, IT implementation man-hours, and business implementation man-hours, as a metric for measuring the ROI. This ratio would be useful for comparing various kinds of IT projects, and it would be especially important to consider hidden costs.

In addition to business value, the team recommended that for new projects Taylor consider a number of issues having to do with strategic alignment with the business as well as existing IT infrastructure. The team created a weighted average, with business value being the largest component, but also considering the strategic importance of the business, the strategic alignment with IT, the ratio of system lifetime to implementation lifetime, the implementation risk, the urgency, and the impact on business resources. By instituting this metric across all IT projects, Taylor could effectively capture the tangible value and strategic alignment that a project would bring to GTP USA. Furthermore, it would aid in managing competing priorities for resources across the IT project portfolio. For these reasons the team believed that this metric would be effective for portfolio management at GTP.

Project Process Methodology

In addition to the organizational structures just described, the research team recommended that Taylor institute a formal project process methodology that fit into a larger strategy for portfolio management. The project management team would consist of a project manager, an IT implementation team, and business stakeholders who would report to the IT steering committee at critical business decision points. The goal of instituting this team was to create a highly effective project engagement team that would involve key stakeholders and enable delivery of needed IT projects with the right features on time and on budget. The team would shepherd a project through all phases of the project management funnel, with team members added or subtracted as the project needs changed.

The project process consisted of six phases (see Figure 4.5). Successful projects would go through each of the six phases, with business decision points occurring at the conclusion of each phase. At these decision points, the project team would report to the IT steering committee and discuss progress to date, budget and schedule changes, and organizational and resource challenges. At these critical points, the IT steering committee would reevaluate the project value under the portfolio management methodology and reprioritize IT resources as necessary.

The research team recommended that the IT steering committee have final say on overall project budgets, but that the budget allocation should be done as a joint exercise, with the IT project manager responsible for the project budget line items and the IT steering committee responsible for the overall budget allocation. Furthermore, the team recommended that Taylor emphasize that the decision to terminate a project midstream did not imply the failure of the project management team; rather, changing business conditions or strategies often can derail a project with a highly effective project team.

The value of the project process was the ability to iteratively evaluate projects as business conditions changed and as project teams learned more about the scope and difficulty of their projects. Ideally, the vast majority of the projects that were approved through the first two stages of the project process and commenced implementation would be fully implemented through all six stages. The process, however, left the IT steering committee with the option and the power to eliminate projects that no longer fit with the strategic direction and operational needs of the business.

The project process methodology provided a framework for Taylor and the brand managers to evaluate individual projects in their project portfolio and to examine whether the solutions being delivered were meeting the managers' hoped-for goals. The formality in the process should en-

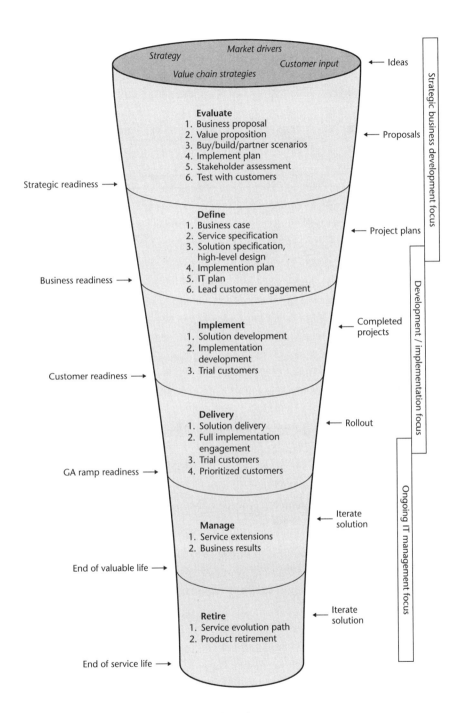

Figure 4.5 New project management funnel

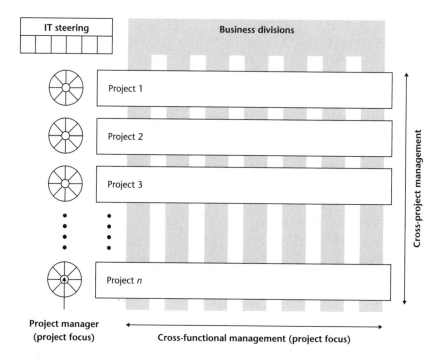

Figure 4.6   Project portfolio management

able clearer thinking and substantially better decision making in the project prioritization process (see Figure 4.6).

The IT committees work in concert with the project management frameworks discussed here to map IT processes to the company's strategic vision, to prioritize projects, and to drive new product development from concept to implementation.

Sharing IT Resources

The research team recommended an IT-resource-sharing decision-making process that would be customized across the IT infrastructure for GTP USA (see Figure 4.7).

The research team recommended that Taylor identify the business functionalities, business requirements, data flows, and network architecture design in order to identify potential applications that could be shared among entities, because it is impossible to share without any commonali-

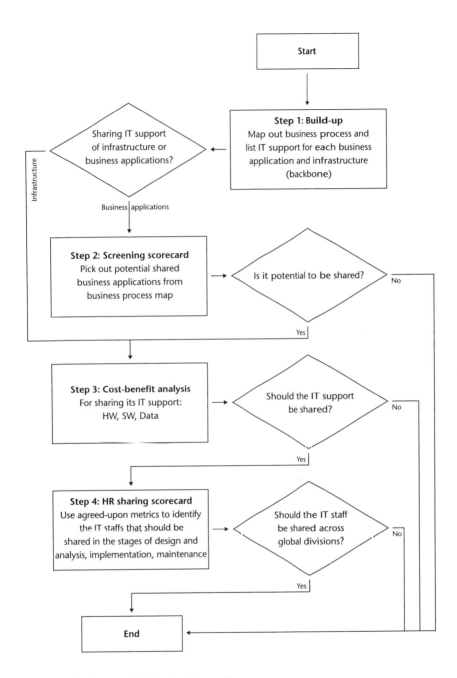

Figure 4.7 Resource-sharing decision-making process

Table 4.1
Screening scorecard

	weight (%) (total 100%)	Sharing score (5 = best, 1 = worst)
Alignment with business strategy		
Commonality		
1. Data information input *Is the content of the input the same?* *What about the format?*		
2. Process functionalities *What are the business requirements of the system?* *What are the processes?*		
3. Entities involved *Are the target customers (wholesaler, retailer, etc.) the same?* *What are other stakeholders of the system?*		
4. Data information output *What is the required output format?*		
Competition impact *Will the sharing trigger internal competition?* *Is it a sensitive issue among the entities involved?*		
Alignment with existing network architecture *Whether the existing architecture is suitable for sharing; what is the impact on performance after sharing?*		
1. Security		
2. Scalability		
3. Flexibility		
4. Bandwidth		
5. Reliability		
TOTAL score		

ties between two areas. Notwithstanding, factors other than commonalities also have to be considered when we make decisions about sharing. Alignment between business strategies and the approach of sharing are key issues. It does not make sense if the sharing approach is not strategically aligned with the business strategies. Synergies and competitions induced by the implementation of resource sharing are another aspect considered by the team. Network architecture appropriateness, commonalities in data input, processes, entities involved, and output format were also identified as factors in the weighted score (see Table 4.1).

The team recommended that, after areas have sharing potential have been identified, Taylor should follow the business value approach to evaluate the benefits and costs of the sharing decision. The differences in costs between a world with shared resources and one without, taken as the net present value, are the benefits of sharing the resources. A thorough consideration involves different perspectives, including on hardware, software, data, and people. The economic impacts of sharing—such as maintenance, retraining, and compatibility costs—on hardware, software, and data were measured through the business values (see Table 4.2). Moreover, it is also important to pay attention to other implicit factors when talking about human-resource sharing. The risks of cooperating and

Table 4.2
Cost-benefit analysis

	Cost-benefit		
	Share (US$)	Not share (US$)	Difference
Hardware			
Maintenance cost			
Upgrade/new hardware cost			
Server reliability (downtime) cost			
Availability cost			
Impact on HR sharing			
TOTAL hardware			
Software			
Licensing cost			
Maintenance cost			
Compatibility cost			
Impact on HR sharing			
TOTAL software			
Data			
Setup cost			
Maintenance cost			
Impact on HR sharing			
TOTAL data			

Table 4.3
HR-sharing scorecard

HR-sharing criteria			
	Weight (%)	Score (1–5)	Weighted score
Return on sharing			
Familiarity of business			
Risk of cooperating failure			
Availability			
Urgent/strategic importance to business			
Return on sharing HR			
Cost of capital:			
Risk discount factor:			
			Dollar value
Sharing			
Reduce hiring cost = # of shared people x man hours x delta labor rate			
No sharing			
Outsourcing cost			
Business value of sharing			
Training cost			
Transportation/communication cost			
IT task man-hours x labor rate x # of shared people			
TOTAL cost			
Return on sharing HR			

familiarity with business, cultural, and language differences were taken into account in the research team's weighted score model (see Table 4.3).

The process just described constitutes a framework for identifying and deciding the appropriateness of resource-sharing opportunities. Through instituting the metrics, Taylor and Chen could determine whether a process should be shared on the basis of tangible values and strategic alignments. What's more, this generic methodology applies not only to GTP USA, but also to the global GTP. As the company further develops globally, this framework could be an effective tool for leveraging scarce IT resources around the world.

Conclusions

GTP USA's parent company is leveraging product development and other U.S.-based value-added services it has developed over the last few years to enter wholesale businesses in the United States under its subsidiary GTP USA. John Taylor, GTP USA's CIO, is particularly concerned with issues surrounding IT governance, organization, and project prioritization in a rapidly growing enterprise in a new business arena. Taylor wants to ensure that GTP USA's IT function is well-positioned to support the company's explosive growth.

This chapter has presented the research team's threefold recommendation for addressing these concerns. To reiterate, first, GTP USA should design three committees to facilitate formal communication channels within the organization, make project prioritization recommendations, and establish formal IT implementation strategies: an IT steering committee, an IT council, and an IT executive committee. Second, new project development should adhere to six phases of development spanning from idea generation to implementation—a process that is considered state of the art. Finally, GTP USA should operate largely as a decentralized entity and command most of the decision making necessary from its parent company in Hong Kong. This position will allow GTP USA to retain the operational flexibility it needs to succeed in a rapidly changing business environment.

Case 2: ABC

Global Outsourcing in China

A massive shift of economic power is currently under way in China. At its current rate of expansion, China will soon be the world's largest economy, followed by the United States and India. China's phenomenal growth is largely driven by corporations outsourcing their supply chains to this low-cost country at a time when trade barriers continue to come down, which was part of China's agreement to enter the WTO in 2001.

Most U.S.-based companies are aware that they can sharply increase their return on capital by off-shoring to lower-wage countries, although many companies still have not taken any formal initiatives to outsource their manufacturing and production services to China. Most companies cite a variety of factors that hinder their efforts. Now the Chinese government and private sectors in ABC,[11] a development zone and hub of commercial activity in China, are seeking an IT solution for reaching out to foreign companies and attracting international business to the region.

Global Outsourcing in China

Industry Trends

Global outsourcing has allowed companies to draw resources, both physical and human, from anywhere in the world, thus facilitating the growth of global value chains. Outsourcing activities that can be better performed by others makes businesses more effective and thereby better able to focus on their core competencies. Thus, companies that outsource are competing with their whole value network.

The pace of China's development is enormous. Today China is the world's largest manufacturing base for consumer goods and its exported goods account for nearly one-third of the world's manufacturing economy. China is trying to stimulate and attract international businesses to its shores by introducing free-trade zones. This will result in the modernization of China, bringing Chinese companies up to international standards.

The greatest advantage that has been identified to outsourcing components and finished goods to China is cost savings, the result of three primary factors:

– Savings on labor costs and raw materials

– Capital avoidance, that is, lower setup, land, and factory expenses

– Low-cost product design[12]

The cost savings, however, are not the main motives behind companies choosing to source to China rather than to other developing countries. China is not a cost leader. Instead, China is advantageous because other benefits are provided in addition to low cost. In particular, China shows enormous capability in manufacturing products that are highly competitive in quality as well as variety.

Current Trends

Today, China is the world's leading manufacturer of products such as air conditioners, motorcycles, and televisions.[13] Recent studies have shown that companies are starting to outsource even more high-tech products, such as automobile parts, to China. This is evidence that China has huge potential to meet international standards and quality concerns.

In recent years, the Chinese government has organized a number of multinational retailers' sourcing fairs and international sourcing promotions in Nanjing, Xiamen, Shenzhen, and other cities to assist Chinese enterprises in establishing contacts with global sourcing groups.[14] It is hoped that these events will help bring Chinese suppliers into the international sourcing network of multinational retailers. Currently, areas around Shanghai and Beijing, where huge new industrial parks are being formed, are developing most rapidly.

ABC is one of the most industrialized and developed areas in southwest China. It is one of the country's high-technology industrial development zones, resulting from a policy designed to attract and take advantage of foreign capital in order to modernize China's international configuration. According to the Boston Consulting Group, most firms realize the importance of China, but many have not taken any formal initiatives in China. However, the global sourcing trend is very clear, and international companies need to aim high and act fast in order to grasp the business opportunity.[15]

ABC is currently the number one producer of motorcycles in China and one of the biggest machine tool producers, exporting to the United

States, Japan, and Southeast Asia, among others. However, the region has not been able to profit fully from the increasing global sourcing trend, owing mainly to its geographical location. To address this problem, the government and private sectors are working together to utilize an IT platform to increase visibility and reach out to global companies.

Diagnosis

Problem Definition

There are some disadvantages that hinder foreign companies from sourcing from ABC as well as from other remote areas in China. Namely:

- *Poor linkage to the international market.* Currently, it is difficult for sourcing companies to get into direct contact with Chinese manufacturers. Thus the sourcing companies are not familiar with the manufacturers' products, which makes it difficult for these companies to take full advantage of the potential of sourcing in China.

- *Lack of professionals in international trade.* Domestic production enterprises lack marketing channels and networks in the opening of overseas markets. They also lack understanding of relevant foreign technological standards and have limited knowledge of the sourcing procedures and methods of multinational retailers.

- *Global sourcing requirements.* Some domestic production enterprises cannot meet the requirements of global sourcing groups in terms of innovation, trends, and dependable quality of their products, and in their batch production capability. This makes it difficult for foreign enterprises to know which domestic companies to trust, and they are therefore reluctant to source from China.

- *Other prohibiting factors.* Language and communication barriers, distant geographic locations, and separate time zones hinder foreign companies in initiating business.

- *Distribution concerns.* Some companies are reluctant to source from China because even though China is providing high-quality products, it is historically poor at delivering them in a timely, reliable, and consistent manner.

   – *Cultural differences*. China is a relationship-oriented country that emphasizes the importance of *quanxi* (see discussion of this term in Chapter 3 of this volume). Not knowing the business culture and not having the appropriate contacts and relationships makes it difficult to do business in China.

ABC's objective is to design an integrated global sourcing platform to improve the effectiveness and efficiency of businesses and to develop a marketing plan for the platform.

Methodology

The approach in developing this platform is first to study the business flow of global sourcing to identify the essential processes, functions, and services that need to be supported. On the basis of this study, first the system requirements will be defined, and then the system architecture will be designed. The platform developed will support all key business processes in global sourcing and enhance the understanding, communication, and trust between business partners—buyers, suppliers, and service providers. Finally, a marketing plan will be developed for the platform.

The methodology used to collect data is primarily literature study as well as empirical study (that is, interviews and surveys). Also, currently available platforms used for global sourcing have been considered. Surveys have been conducted of buyers in the United States to understand and address their needs. Finally, experts in global sourcing businesses have been interviewed.

Business Process. To understand the mechanisms behind a platform and identify the functions that need to be provided, business process outsourcing was studied (see Figure 4.8).

Purchasing Process. An adequate purchase is accomplished only when the source is qualified and the need is legitimate.[16] If a business relationship between the buyer and supplier has already been established, the purchasing process goes more smoothly. However, challenges still exist between the buyer and supplier because communication between the business partners needs to be upheld. Major challenges that need to be dealt with are the distances, time differences, cultural issues, and means

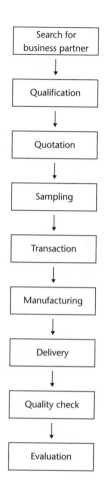

Figure 4.8   Overall business process flow

of conflict resolution. Systems that facilitate communication are advantageous under these circumstances. However, if we are talking about a new supplier or a new product, a lot of questions and uncertainties need to be clarified before an order is placed. For example, one critical aspect to consider when sourcing is the strategic decision of whether to use single or multiple sourcing partners.

Search for Business Partners. The first step in the purchasing process when undertaking a new purchase is to find a list of potential business partners. Traditionally, finding the most qualified source is very difficult and time consuming, especially when sourcing from an international market. However, the fast evolution of information systems and the IT-era has made it possible to get access easily to online sourcing directories that provide comprehensive company information, such as Alibaba,[17] an Asian source.

If business is conducted in the traditional way, the buyer first needs to narrow down the list of countries before looking for a specific supplier. Language barriers might result in the involvement of a third party in the purchasing process to conduct the search or offer translation services.

Qualification. In the qualification phase the potential business partners will get a basic impression of each other on the basis of the information provided in the directory used for the business partner search, as well as the partners' own due diligence when a buyer searches for a potential supplier. Both parties should request financial information and third-party references from previous clients or sourcing partners. The financial information is a good indicator of whether the buyer or supplier is financially sound, and the references can validate the buyer or supplier's past performance. The information can be used to determine if the supplier has a history of not delivering on time or has a record of consistently not meeting quality assurance standards. Financial information can be difficult to interpret because government reporting standards in China are different from those of other countries.[18]

The sorts of problems encountered in this phase are evidenced by the fact that most sourcing company Web sites in China are in Chinese. The visual layouts of these Web sites are also different from the international standard, which may give the impression that the supplier is unprofessional. A global platform could mitigate these problems by standardizing the information and helping suppliers design professional Web sites.

The second step in the purchasing process is to establish contact with potential suppliers to request project bids. This step is often achieved by making an inquiry before sending out a request for quotation (RFQ).[19] Typically, buyers prefer the first contact to be initiated via telephone in order to get preliminary information about the supplier. Using a Web-enabled IT solution can allow the buyer to access basic company information expeditiously.

Request for Quotation. When sending out an RFQ, buyers are unlikely to rely only on traditional mail. Instead, they will often send a request by fax to expedite the delivery and response time. Faxing documents can be impractical when many drawings or specifications need to be sent. Another alternative is to follow up the mailing with a phone call to ensure that the request was received. Several platforms, such as Webex, are available that facilitate the sharing of drawings and specifications. It is important to note that many companies are hesitant to share information with the supplier because of a lack of trust over intellectual property (IP) in China, where IP regulation and support are not enforced well by the government. Companies that outsource a component of a product are less concerned that the business partner will engage in illegal business practices if the business partner is using the company's IP.[20] The Chinese government has started to show concern for this issue with its entry into the WTO.

The bids obtained should be analyzed for qualifications so that the number of potential suppliers can be reduced. After asking for quotes, the supplier should get a price quotation. This is an iterative process in which the price and the contract terms are negotiated. Here the direct sourcing costs will often be a combination of a fixed setup fee and a variable cost for each unit produced, which is invariably lower when producing higher volumes due to economies of scale. When purchasing from an international source, the total costs of outsourcing will also include import duty, transportation, insurance, and paper-handling costs. Also, the risks of fluctuating monetary exchange rates as well as uncertainties associated with long-distance business relationships, such as lead time, should be considered. After getting the price quotation, the list of potential partners should be further reduced.

Requesting a Sample and Ordering. The next step in the purchasing process is to ask for a sample of the item the buyer wants to purchase (see Figure 4.9). The sample is an important indicator of whether or not the supplier will be able to meet the buyer's product quality expectations. This is an iterative process that can be significantly time consuming. If there is no problem in this phase, a contract will be signed between the involved parties. However, the parties need to make sure that the contract is recognized internationally. Also, they should address the problem

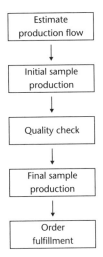

Figure 4.9   Order process flow

of who is held accountable if the component or product is subcontracted to more than one supplier and a production problem arises.

The decision-making process for the supplier begins with reviewing order information from the buyer that contains drawings and product component specifications, material requirements used for manufacturing, measuring and testing methods, and production timelines and dates of delivery (see Figure 4.10). After reviewing this information, the supplier will evaluate the feasibility of meeting the buyer's requirements and specifications. When doing this evaluation, the supplier will consider its capability. For example, does it have enough production capacity (machines, labor, and raw materials) to meet forecast product demand on a timely basis? How many of its projects are a work-in-progress?

Transaction. After the parties agree on the sample, they will decide on the mode of transaction. If they have not done business together before, they might feel a bit uncomfortable confiding in each other because of the lack of trust. Thus, the normal way transactions are done is through bill of credit, by which a credit agency makes the transaction before the goods are actually transferred. In return, a fee will be charged corresponding to a usaul small percentage of the total amount transferred.

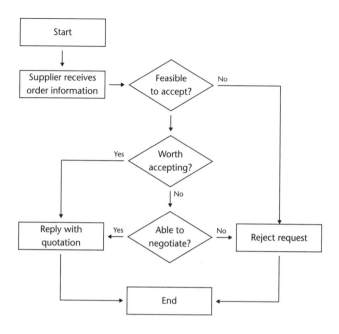

Figure 4.10   Decision making in business process flow

The other usual alternative is for the buyer to transfer money when the order is placed or when the goods are delivered.

Manufacturing. After the buyer has approved the sample, the sourcing is assigned to the supplier and the supplier starts to manufacture the product. Once the supplier has signed the contract, the product has to be delivered on time and meet the agreed-upon specifications. Otherwise, the supplier will be fined (as stipulated in the agreement) and its relationship with the buyer will be harmed. Nevertheless, there can be a lot of disturbance in the manufacturing process. The supplier may need to acquire planning software or other means by which to handle its manufacturing processes more efficiently. If the supplier is not able to perform according to the agreed-upon terms or if the supplier cannot manufacture the entire product itself, it has the option of deciding to subcontract to other business partners.

Delivery. The buyer and supplier should already have agreed on who should be responsible for the shipment—the buyer, the supplier, or a third party. The delivery is often regulated in the contract and includes transportation mode, shipment costs, delivery time, and so on. If the supplier is taking care of the delivery process, it has to assure that the goods are delivered to the buyer safely and on time (see Figure 4.11). The transportation infrastructure in China, especially in more remote areas, is not satisfactory when it comes to delivering on time. Therefore, it is critical to have an order-tracking system. Furthermore, the insurance issue needs to be dealt with. For example, who is buying the insurance? How valuable are the goods?

Quality. The buyer does a quality check when it receives the goods. However, some buyers require that the supplier conduct this inspection before delivery and submit a quality report along with the goods. This practice increases customer satisfaction because the value of the service increases. Accountability for defective units should also be negotiated in the contract because in most cases a buyer is not willing to pay for damaged goods. If the entire assembled or finished product is purchased from a single source, then it is fairly straightforward to identify who should be held accountable. However, if production is subcontracted to several sources, it can be complicated to determine who is held responsible for a defective unit. This is often the case because many small suppliers in China are not capable of manufacturing the entire product.

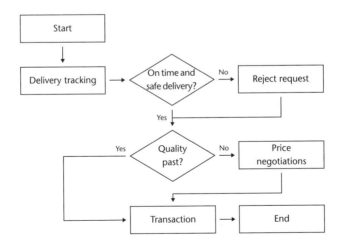

Figure 4.11   Decision making in business process flow: Delivery

Evaluation. After the transaction is completed, the involved parties will evaluate the purchasing process and their compatibility. This will determine whether the buyer and supplier or suppliers are satisfied with the current business relationship and whether they will continue to do business with each other.

IT Platform Design

Overview

The IT platform should be designed to support the entire business process of global sourcing. The intention is not to replace the activities in the process but rather to enhance them. Different companies or industries have very different practices and operate at varying degrees of detail. Moreover, business practices change rapidly, which could make the platform less flexible in meeting all users' needs. Therefore, ABC's proposed platform should facilitate its current activities and improve business efficiency and effectiveness. It should also provide a solution for integrating with existing systems.

The users of the platform will include parties at all stages of the global sourcing business: buyers, suppliers, third parties, and service providers. The supplier will use the IT platform for advertising and promotion as well as to look for potential buyers, reply to quotations and samples, check its own capacity and capability, and report on order status and quality results. The buyer will use the platform to search for suitable suppliers, check order status, clarify engineering drawings, and so on. The platform should also be able to incorporate global sourcing service providers such as the providers of logistics services, banking services, rating and grading services, and customs services.

Because business practices vary across industries and companies, the platform may change rapidly in the future. It is therefore essential that the platform be flexible and adaptable to different business practices. To ensure that it is, the application layer for end users should be as light as possible and provide an easy-to-use graphical user interface.

Because such a platform is comprehensive, it is not practical to develop all of the subcomponents of the IT architecture at the same time. It is therefore recommended that development and deployment of the system be divided into multiple phases with clear and specific deliverables.

Functional Requirement Analysis. The functions supported by the platform should be divided into two parts: basic and advanced. The basic
functions should allow the supplier and buyer to search for business
partners and communicate with each other, which will support the basic
requirement of global sourcing and be provided at no cost. Additional
and more sophisticated functionality should be available only to sub-
scribed users at a premium price. Advanced functionality may include
enabling the supplier to integrate the platform with its existing ERP system, optimize transportation and logistics, and so on.

Functions for General Users. Most of the buyers and suppliers in the business need to manage their own information as well as that of their business partners. In addition, simple communication using popular tools
such as instant messenger and e-mail will be necessary to link buyers and
suppliers. To facilitate the business search process, the platform should
also support requesting quotations and product samples. Additionally,
order status tracking will be very important for monitoring product departure and arrival times.

The platform should allow the buyer to post its company profile on
the Web site in order to connect with potential suppliers. The buyer
should be able to post a list of products wanted so that interested suppliers can contact the buyer directly. Of course, all of these kinds of information are dynamic and the platform should allow the buyer to edit
them. When the buyer "owns" a lot of suppliers, it should be able to
manage the suppliers' information. The buyer should also be able to
search for suppliers capable of producing the products it is seeking. The
search tools should be comprehensive and powerful enough that buyers
can find suppliers with the desired capabilities and capacities and in the
right location. The ideal IT solution would allow the buyer to search for
sourcing partners on the basis of product specifications, geographical location, and quality of products, and would prompt the user with a list of
all qualified suppliers. To keep a historical record of the suppliers, the
platform should also help buyers to qualify suppliers. If this information
is released to others, it will greatly improve the efficiency of other buyers' search for partners. (See Figure 4.12.)

Suppliers too should be able to publish company information, such
as the products they offer, their capabilities, any certificates, and contact
information, on the platform. This kind of information will help the sup-

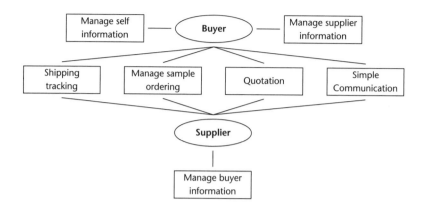

Figure 4.12   Use case diagram for general buyer and supplier

pliers attract the right buyers because this is what buyers want to know when they search for a potential supplier. Providing the right information will not only improve the efficiency of the partner-searching process but will also bring great business opportunities for the supplier. Essentially, the platform should act as an advertising medium for the supplier. It should also help the supplier seek business opportunities. The supplier should be able to search for buyers and, in the process, receive real-time marketing information. Like the buyers, the suppliers might want to qualify the buyers and keep a record. This should also be supported by the platform.

For common users, the platform should offer instant messaging and e-mail to enhance communication. Users should also be able to send RFQs and samples, and give feedback on RFQs and samples through the platform. Once an order is confirmed, the platform should enable the buyer to track the status of the order. Diagrams detailing these processes are shown in Figures 4.13 and 4.14.

Functions for Registered Buyers and Suppliers. Users that choose to register for the platform should be provided with more sophisticated and comprehensive functions that support the whole business process and all its major activities. Besides posting their own information, suppliers should be able to manage their own product data, monitor their orders, check the inventory point, and view statistics. Another advantage would be the provision of advanced communication functions. Even translation services, such as translation of terminology and material names, are possible. To improve efficiency, e-transactions should be provided by the platform for payments. These functions are described in greater detail later in the chapter.

Quotation Support. For a supplier to a quotation, it is necessary to know the due date and the amount of the quotation. To determine the due date, the supplier needs to check its own inventory level and capacity. The platform should ensure that any other orders will not be affected if the order is accepted. Because some materials may play a major role in costing, their prices will change dynamically in the market, making it difficult for the supplier to quote a proper market price for its product or component. To aid in this task, the platform should have a function that helps the supplier to do a rough cost calculation. This could be made possible by linking the platform with markets such as

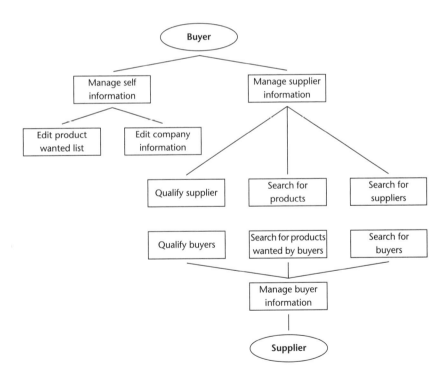

Figure 4.13   Use case diagram: Ordering

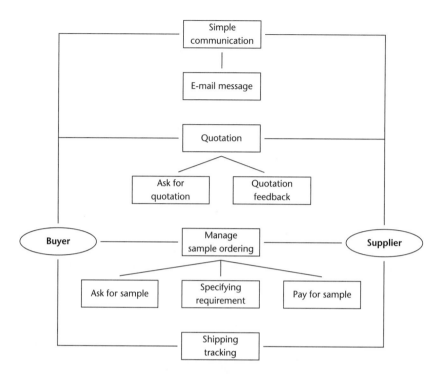

Figure 4.14   Use case diagram: Communication

the London Commodities Exchange. Then both sides would be aware of the price and transparency would be increased. The record of pricing would be a valuable reference. The platform would also provide history data, accompanied by analysis tools, to facilitate the costing (see Figure 4.15).

Manufacturing Support. Once an order is confirmed, the supplier begins the manufacturing process. The platform should provide functions to support this process. By integrating with the supplier's ERP and material resource planning (MRP) system, the platform can check the inventory and notify the supplier if raw materials replenishment is required. It can also link with the production schedule—the labor loading status of the factory—to ensure that the product can be delivered on time. Of course, if the supplier does not have an ERP/MRP system, the platform will not be able to provide these functions (see Figure 4.16).

Transportation Support. According to the research team's interviews with experienced global sourcing people, many suppliers in China are facing logistical problems, such as difficulty fulfilling the buyer's delivery requirements. This is especially true for small and middle-sized companies because they do not know which transportation approach is the most cost-effective. It is also difficult for suppliers to determine real-time transportation schedules, such as departure time, arrival time, and frequency. To help users overcome these difficulties, the platform should provide tools and optimization models to help them choose the most economic

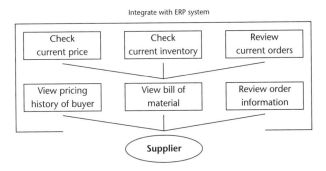

Figure 4.15   Use case diagram: Quotation

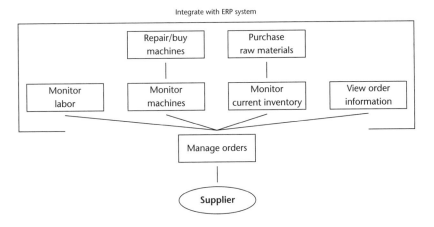

Figure 4.16   Use case diagram: Manufacturing

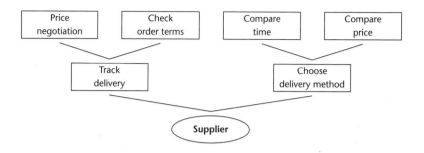

Figure 4.17   Use case diagram: Transportation

delivery method and deliver the goods on time. The tools should compare the price and time differences of different scenarios. The platform should also interface with logistics service providers so that instant information about shipment schedules is available to users. Thus, both buyers and suppliers will be able to track deliveries (see Figure 4.17).

Transaction Support. To meet the transaction requirements of global sourcing, the platform should support electronic transactions (e-trans-actions) by incorporating both e-payments and e-contracts. Since the de-velopment of these technologies, e-transactions have become more and more popular. The advantages of using this technology are that it is more cost- and time-effective than doing payment the traditional way, and the "paperwork" for such transactions is less likely to be damaged or de-stroyed compared with conventional contracts. More important, the se-curity of e-payment has been greatly improved by advanced technology. Data transmission through electronic data interchange (EDI) is by way of a specific channel and a specific format. Initially, e-payment used a digital signature to encrypt the contracts through public or private keys. Electronic signature technology is now available, however. The contract can be verified by the user's own unique information, such as voice, fin-gerprint, and so on. This will ensure that the content of the contract will not leak out or be modified or replicated. Moreover, more countries, such as China, the United States, and the European Union, are recogniz-ing and protecting e-payment legally, and companies, such as Contract Management, License Technologies Group, and Electronics Contract, are providing commercial software solutions. The Canadian Wheat Board (CWB), an agricultural products seller that buys grain from farmers and sells it to other countries, has been using an e-Contract system since fall 2002. All the farmers manage their contracts with CWB online. Ponton X/E is one example of commercial software, developed by Ponton Consulting.[21] The user can create a contract by template, and both parties can review the contract and sign it. AOL Time Warner is one of its users.

E-payment is also becoming increasingly popular. It is much more efficient and could reduce the transaction cost. According to Boston Consulting Group,[22] U.S. B2B online purchasing increased greatly from 1998 to 2003. And it was likely to increase further in 2004. (See Table 4.4.)

Nonfunctional Requirement Analysis. To be successful in doing business in China it is very important to have a well-established business network, that is, to form relationships with the government, with its officers, and with potential business partners. This is because, as was noted earlier, China is a relationship-oriented society and values *guanxi*. According to the CIO of ABC Ford, "The government is pervasive in the business life." The government plays a central role in ensuring that businesses will run more effectively and smoothly. Trust plays an essential role in building this business network. Thus, *trust* is always a key word in global sourcing. For example, the partners in a global sourcing business may wonder whether the information provided on their client's Web site is correct or not. They might even go to the extreme of questioning whether the companies posted on the Web site really exist or not. During the quotation stage, the supplier may question whether the buyer is a real buyer or just a competitor who is interested in finding out their price. Furthermore, the buyer may wonder whether the price is fair or not. And even after the contract is signed, the buyer might be concerned about whether or not the law is protecting the contract.

Table 4.4
Online business-to-business purchasing in the United States

	Online sales	Offline sales	Percentage
1998	$0.67 trillion	$9.0 trillion	7%
2000	$1.20 trillion	$9.7 trillion	12%
2004	$4.80 trillion	$12.1 trillion	40%

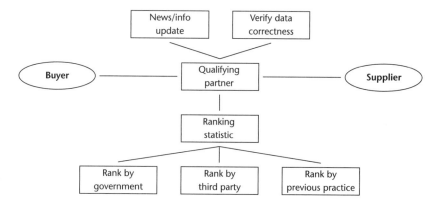

Figure 4.18   Use case diagram: Supporting unit functions

In the global sourcing business, there normally is poor linkage between buyers and suppliers due to geographical and culture barriers. Hence, it is very difficult for U.S. and European buyers to establish relationships with Chinese suppliers and the Chinese government. Moreover, there are large cultural differences between the partners. Building trust between them may be quite difficult.

Event Monitoring. To enhance understanding and build trust between the buyer and the supplier, the platform will need to provide as much information as possible to both parties (see Figure 4.18). It should have a search engine for locating all the relevant information about the partner and dynamically updating it. It should also help the partner find specific information, such as the financial condition of the business partner, and it should incorporate the rating of the partners. Government or third parties can perform the rating. After the business process has concluded, the partners may evaluate each other. The evaluation should be recorded for later users. The IT platform should verify the partners so that the ratings presented are correct and valid. These kinds of information will greatly increase understanding between buyers and suppliers, and eventually help in the establishment of trust.

Sometimes it is very difficult for the IT platform user to know exactly the status of each order and what kind of action should be taken. The platform will monitor the status of each order and automatically notify users when certain actions must be taken. This action will greatly synchronize the order processing. Another difficulty is that when exceptional events happen, all relevant users should be aware of them and take appropriate action. Without system support, any responses will take longer to coordinate. To overcome these difficulties, the platform should provide event monitoring, by which the platform will notify the relevant users when something exceptional happens and request the appropriate actions. This will simplify the decision-making process and the efficiency of the business. Events that should be monitored include inventory status check, stock out, delivery delay, ranking updates, and material price change, among others.

Summary

The IT platform should be based on the current ABC platform, which was developed by ABC University (see Figure 4.19). The research team

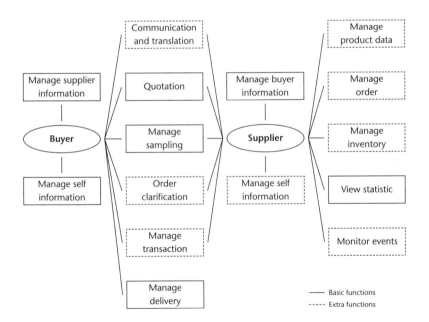

Figure 4.19   ABC platform

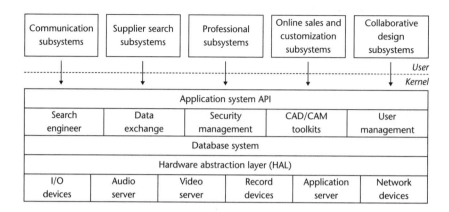

Figure 4.20   System architecture: current ABC platform

studied the functions included in that platform and the way they are deployed. The current platform has five subsystems: communication, supplier search, online sales and customization, collaborative design, and professional. To the users, these are the application layers. Behind these layers is the database system and kernel functions such as the search engineer, data exchange, security management, and so on.

The current system is comprehensive and incorporates a lot of advanced technology (see Figure 4.20). Some parts, like the communication subsystem, are quite mature. Their architecture is very flexible because it decouples the application layer and kernel layer. But the major problem with the current platform is that it is not integrated. The lack of integration can be revealed by two aspects: one, the functions provided are not tightly or seamlessly linked, and two, the functions provided are not integrated with the business process. The users of the platform therefore have to find the right functions and then apply them to their problems. These aspects greatly constrain the usability of the platform. But there is no doubt that the current platform is a good starting point for developing a comprehensive and integrated global sourcing platform.

Overview of System Architecture. As mentioned in the system requirements analysis, the new platform should be divided into two parts: the basic functions that will enable the buyer and supplier to search for partners and communicate with each other. This function should be provided in the ASP application server. Then both the supplier and buyer will be able to access it through the Internet. The functions for the buyer, such as checking order status and sending quotations, should also be put on the ASP applications server. To increase system flexibility, the applications and middleware layers should be decoupled in the ASP server. Of course, the ASP server should have a database system that maintains the supplier and buyer information, rating information, and so on. The ASP server should also link with third parties such as logistics companies to enable online order tracking, and with London Commodities Exchange, so that critical material prices can be acquired by users.

Other advanced functions should be installed on the supplier's side. This has several advantages:

- Greater security for suppliers because they can update secure data themselves.
- Greater adaptability to different business practices. The functions provided can be customized according to different suppliers' requirements.
- Better integration with the suppliers' ERP/MRP systems.

Again, the supplier platform should also be shown as a Web site so that the ASP server can be easily linked with it, and the application layer and middleware layer should be decoupled to achieve better flexibility and reduce development time. Private data, such as engineering drawings, may be kept in the local database on the supplier site.

Detailed System Architecture. As mentioned before, the most important aspect of the platform is that it is integrated with the business. Therefore, the whole architecture should be consistent with the business model. The application layer should support all key activities in global sourcing, according to the process. Because business process activities are very dynamic, the layer will be as light as possible so that it can easily be customized for different users. On the other hand, most of the technical support will be put on the middleware layer. The middleware can be reused by different applications. Some of them may include complicated technology and consume long development and implementation time. Users can then seek professional software companies and simply buy middleware from them. In the following paragraphs, the functions will be deployed along the major business process.

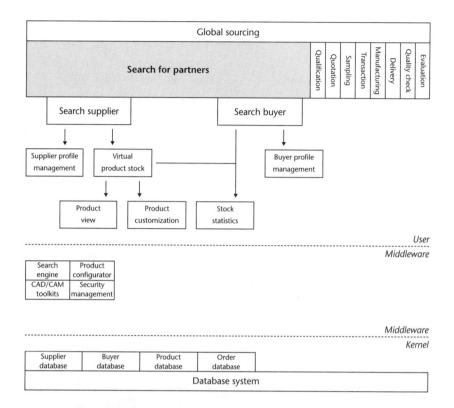

Figure 4.21   System architecture: Search for partners

Search for Partners. The buyer may search for suppliers and manage the supplier's profile. The buyer may also view the supplier's products on the Web site through virtual stock, by which the buyer can customize a product if the desired one is not available. The platform should also enable the supplier to manage its buyer. The platform should help the supplier seek potential business opportunities by providing the statistics of virtual stock. To support all these applications, search engineer, CAD tools, product configuration, and security management will be deployed in the middleware layer. And the supplier, buyer, product, and order data will be put in the database as the data source (see Figure 4.21).

Qualification. To qualify the partners, as much information as possible is needed, that is, the more they know of each other, the easier it will be to build mutual trust. News and information updates will help the user find

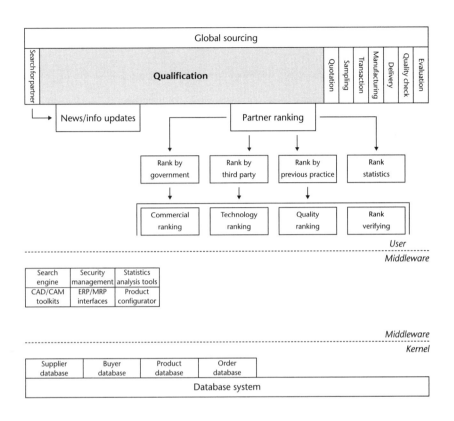

Figure 4.22   System architecture: Qualification

useful partner information. Ranking too will help the establishment of trust. According to industrial practice, ranking includes the following types:

- *Commercial ranking,* which assesses the partner's financial and commercial performance
- *Technology ranking,* which evaluates the partner's technological capabilities
- *Quality ranking,* which indicates whether the partner can provide products with high quality

Ranking may be conducted by the buyer or supplier who has done business through the platform and can rank on the basis of experience. Some third parties can also provide more comprehensive and professional rankings. In addition, the government can provide rankings for

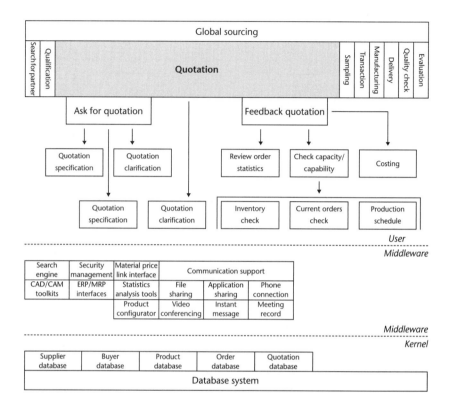

Figure 4.23   System architecture: Quotation

local companies. The platform should provide a checking mechanism to ensure users that different rankings are valid. All the rankings should be stored as a record. Analysis tools can help reveal the trend of one company's ranking and provide management with more insight.

In the middleware there should be an ERP/MRP interface and statistics tools to support qualification. All rankings will be put in the supplier and buyer databases accordingly (see Figure 4.22).

Quotations. The buyer needs to ask for a quotation once he has found potential suppliers. In the quotation the supplier needs to specify product information, materials, engineering drawings, reply date, and so on. Some engineering drawings may be quite complicated. The content of the quotation may not even be clear to the supplier. In that case, the buyer needs to clarify the meaning with the supplier. Once quotations

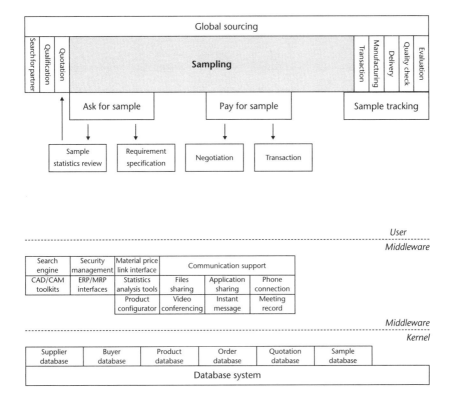

Figure 4.24   System architecture: Sampling

from different suppliers have arrived, the platform should help the buyer assess and compare them and make the best choice.

When a supplier receives a request for quotation from a buyer, the platform should first help the supplier verify his capability and capacity, such as inventory position, current order status, and production schedules, in order to decide whether or not to accept the order. If the decision is yes, the platform should help the supplier calculate the cost, including labor, materials, and overhead. Once the cost is determined, the statistics of orders and quotations can help the supplier offer the correct price.

In the middleware, to support quotation clarification, communication functions should be provided so that the buyer and supplier can clarify the quotation by instant messaging or videoconferencing and application sharing. An interface for linking with the materials pricing market, such

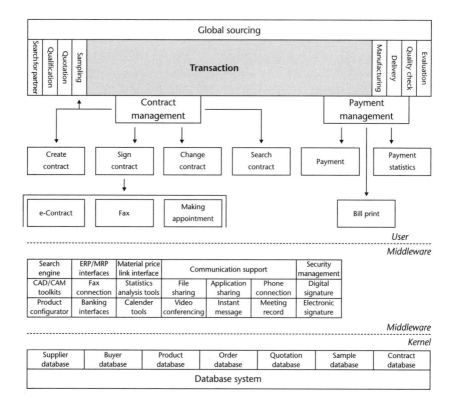

Figure 4.25   System architecture: Transaction

as London Commodities Pricing Stock, can help the costing process (see Figure 4.23). The quotation should also be put in the database.

Sampling. After the buyer decides to accept the quotation, he will ask the supplier for a sample. The platform should help him specify the requirements of the sample, such as delivery time, quality, and so on. The platform should also let the buyer track the sample's status, and support payment for the sample through an e-transaction. The sample information should also be put in the database system (see Figure 4.24).

Transaction. Once the sample meets the quality requirement, the platform should enable the buyer and supplier to create, sign, change, and view the contract electronically, as well as to make and view the payment and contract statistics. To keep security high, the middleware must sup-

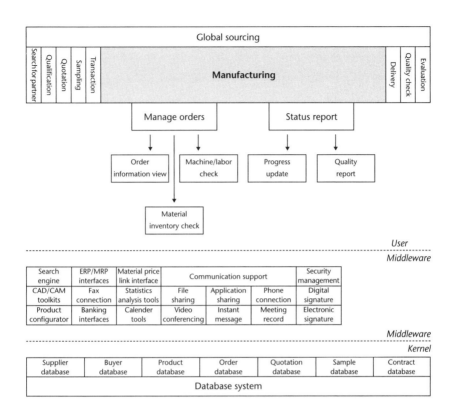

Figure 4.26   System architecture: Manufacturing

port both digital and electronic signature. The contract and payment re-cord should be put into the database system (see Figure 4.25).

Manufacturing. When the order is in the manufacturing stage, the plat-form should help the supplier manage the order. The manufacturing sta-tus should also be reported so that the buyer can track the order (see Fig-ure 4.26).

Delivery. After the product has been manufactured, the order will be at the delivery stage. The platform should provide tools for supplier analysis, as well as offer routing and shipment methods according to cost and lead-time analysis. The supplier will then be able to create the shipment schedule with the help of the platform. By linking with the lo-gistics service provider, both the supplier and the buyer can track the

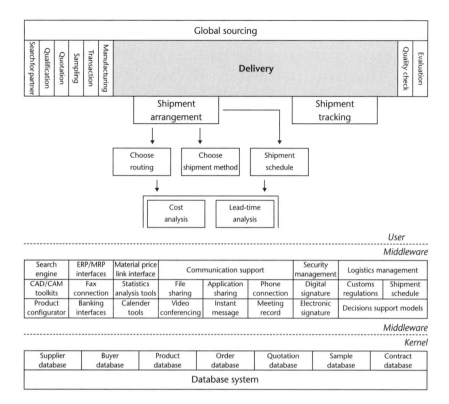

Figure 4.27   System architecture: Delivery

shipment status. In the middleware, logistics management should be included to support these functions (see Figure 4.27).

Quality Check. Before the shipment, a quality check should be conducted. Some suppliers perform the quality check right after manufacturing—a so-called on-site check. When the product arrives at the buyer, another quality check is performed. These quality checks should be reported so that both the buyer and supplier can view them simultaneously. All the quality reports should be recorded in the database system (see Figure 4.28).

Evaluation. After the process has been completed, the buyer and supplier will use the platform to evaluate each other and decide on a long-term relationship. The evaluation can focus on commercial, technological, and quality aspects.

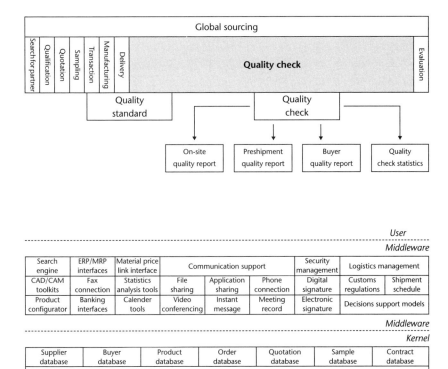

Figure 4.28   System architecture: Quality check

Event Notification. To handle the exceptions in the process, the event should be monitored by the platform. Then, according to the dispatch rules, the platform should automatically notify the relevant actors about the exception event and request the appropriate actions.

Market Analysis

Methodology

The methodology the research team used to conduct its market research included Internet research, Forrester and Gartner databases, publications, interviews with experts and customers, and online questionnaires.

Interviews. The team conducted interviews with people who are experienced in global outsourcing to explore experts' opinions and potential buyers' perspectives. Interviewees included the executive director of the US-Asia Technology Management Center at Stanford University, CEOs from U.S. global outsourcing companies, and managers in SCM at U.S. manufacturing companies.

Questionnaire. The research team designed online questionnaires for both Western buyers and Hong Kong vendors to collect information about the nature of customer demands for a global outsourcing platform.

Publications. The team utilized business databases like Gartner and Forrester, researched existing similar platforms, and used outsourcing associations' resources to explore outsourcing trends and the latest news.

Product Adoption Life Cycle

U.S. Market

According to *E-Commerce Times,* the total global outsourcing market is $5 trillion. This market is growing by more than 15 percent per year. Although offshore outsourcing is just one small part of the market, the offshore component is growing the fastest.

As this chapter has discussed, the research team's product was a global outsourcing platform that aimed to attract U.S. and European buyers to outsource in China and to improve business efficiency by providing transparent information about vendors and manufacturers as well as communication tools to build the initial relationship.

ABC was certainly not the first in this market. A lot of firms have reported that they outsource their functions. There are significant variations in outsourcing practice depending on the size of the outsourcing contract, where a company is headquartered, and the size of the company. Take the IT industry as an example. Companies with large outsourcing contracts ($10 million or more annually) are outsourcing user support, data networking, and disaster recovery more than firms with small outsourcing contracts. U.S. firms outsource data center operations less than non-U.S. firms. Large companies use outsourcing more than small firms as an opportunity to focus on core businesses.

In the United States, outsourcing is rapidly approaching commodity status and this will transform the outsourcing value equation from high margins and vendor control into a classic buyers' market with competition driving down margins, companies adding more features and services, and ever-proliferating options increasing buyer choice.[23]

The transformation from regional economies to a single, integrated global economy is still at a fundamental and early stage. Using the framework that Geoffrey Moore presented in *Crossing the Chasm,*[24] the research team determined that in terms of level of technology adoption, the outsourcing platform industry is in the early market and has yet to cross the chasm into the mainstream market.

In order to better understand its position in the outsourcing platform industry, ABC needs to identify which stage it is at in the technology adoption life cycle.

The technology adoption life cycle may be viewed as a bell curve that illustrates when users adopt a new technology. Moving from left to right, one-sixth of the curve is the early market, one-third is the early majority, one-third is the late majority, and one-sixth is the laggards.

- *Innovators* are technology enthusiasts, the first to try every cool new gadget. They make up a very small percentage of the early market.
- *Visionaries* are the first real customers. They are on a mission. They can and will pay large amounts of money for new technology that fits with their products. They can be very difficult customers to manage.
- The customers in the early majority are pragmatists. They represent the largest source of revenue. Competent consumers of technology, they will only buy proven technology from market leaders. They are very loyal.
- The customers in the late majority are conservatives. They come late into the game, so they expect very mature technologies at commodity prices. There is still money to be made here, but it comes in much smaller baskets.
- The customers in the laggard segment are skeptics. They will never intentionally be your customers. They will buy technology only when it is buried so deep in a product that they do not

know it is there. Their role is to discourage every possible application of your product.

Geoffrey Moore's technology adoption life cycle is built on the idea that the rate of adoption of products is not continuous in high-technology markets. Moore argues that there is a chasm between the early adopters of the product (the technology enthusiasts and visionaries) and the early majority (the pragmatists). This is because visionaries and pragmatists have very different expectations. Moore exposes those differences and builds from there to suggest techniques for crossing the chasm, including choosing a target market, understanding the whole product concept, positioning the product, building a marketing strategy, choosing the most appropriate distribution channel, and pricing.

Through its market research, the team found that the outsourcing platform industry is still in the early market stage. The market has been penetrated and there are innovators and early adopters using a similar type of platform. But the majority of the people who are engaged in global outsourcing are still hesitating. They still have doubts about the functionalities and risks associated with such a platform. They are waiting for references from the early adopters. The platform is about to cross the chasm, so our task is to find the best way to capture the pragmatists and try to capture the majority of the market share in the outsourcing platform market.

Consumer Analysis

Although outsourcing functions vary according to the type of industry and the size of the contracts, there are several key findings about consumer behavior in outsourcing practices. The most important factors for buyers in outsourcing are product quality, reliability in meeting schedules, flexibility in adjusting schedules, lowered product costs, and time-to-market for new products. The relative importance of these factors is shown in Table 4.5.[25]

Customer Satisfaction. In current practice, customer satisfaction with the different functionalities of a platform varies. According to recent research conducted by Forrester Research Inc.,[26] overall customer satisfaction with the outsourcing process is only 3.7 out of 5. (See Table 4.5.)

Table 4.5
Key concerns of customers

Functions	Satisfaction
Product quality	4.0
Reliability in meeting schedulers	3.8
Flexibility in scheduling	4.0
Lowered product costs	3.0
Time-to-market	3.1
Overall satisfaction	3.7

Contract Continuity. Companies are cautious about remaining in outsourcing contracts. None of the participants in a previous outsourcing survey said they would bring an outsourced function back in-house. In a more recent survey, a quarter of companies who have made a decision about future outsourcing plan to reduce outsourcing or bring operations back in-house. Respondents who are reluctant to outsource again cite lack of cost savings, difficulties in vendor management, and poor strategic alignment.[27]

Competitor Analysis

Existing Platforms

The team conducted research on the existing platforms to compare the competitors' strengths and weaknesses. There is no other competitor offering an integrated platform with both a database and communication functions, as ABC's proposed platform does. The strengths of these competitors are their early entry into the global outsourcing market and a broad client base. Their weakness is that they have only limited functionalities and customer support.

Global Outsourcing Companies

There are also a lot of global outsourcing companies, such as Pacific High Way, Group China, Global Outsourcing Group, and so on, that provide outsourcing services to U.S. and European buyers and to Asian manufacturers. The current practices of global outsourcing companies basically follow this cycle:

– *Engagement.* The company makes a visit to potential clients to discuss requirements, which may include drawings, samples, and volumes. Any particular quality approvals and special packaging requirements are communicated at this stage of the process.

– *Evaluation.* The company performs a comprehensive evaluation of potential suppliers along with a formal audit of those suppliers.

– *Pricing and sampling.* The company supplies the customer with a written, competitive quotation to any global site along with credit terms and conditions, freight options, and subsequent lead times. They also deliver qualification samples. Advice is given on supply design in order to further reduce the unit cost.

– *Qualification.* The customer evaluates the samples and adds the company to their qualified vendor list on approval.

– *SCM.* Customer orders are received and acknowledged promptly with an agreed-upon shipment schedule. The outsourcing company also manages everything from the supplier relationship schedule to the delivery process.

– *Strengths.* These sourcing companies have established personal relationship with clients. Because of their frequent client visits and face-to-face talks, it is easier for them to create a reliable image. During their client visits, a lot of detailed information can be exchanged faster than on the Internet.

– *Weaknesses.* Because of the constraints of time and labor, outsourcing companies can possess only a very limited manufacturer base. Sometimes they offer only about ten manufacturers to choose from. But a software platform can include thousands of manufacturers. The buyer's options are more restricted with outsourcing companies, and product quality is consequently influenced.

Target Customers

When ABC is in the chasm of the technology adoption life cycle, its product has some early adopters but has not yet crossed the threshold into the mainstream market. The goal in this stage is market penetration.

Paul Wiefels uses the analogy of the bowling alley to describe the strategy for establishing a beachhead in the mainstream market. In the bowling alley, when a product is still untested, potential customers look toward one another to gauge whether or not they should adopt the product. Each segment of the market has a referential relationship with its neighboring segment. These referential relationships are based on either shared applications or word-of-mouth.

Shared applications are applications that two different but similar segments can both use. In this case, a platform to promote auto parts manufacturing is one application that can potentially be used by different segments: existing parts manufacturers serving joint ventures between foreign and Chinese companies in China, U.S. and European buyers, and buyers from the rest of the world. Due to ABC's capabilities and the existing joint ventures that need manufacturers to supply parts, the research team determined that the first application of the platform should be the auto parts manufacturing industry. From there it would pursue the longer-term goals of using the platform to promote ABC and afterward expanding the platform to China.

Word-of-mouth is the phenomenon whereby the two similar segments each use each other as points of reference when seeking new applications to use. In this case, joint ventures and U.S. and European buyers might expand their use of the platform from just simple auto parts to other products that ABC is capable of delivering, such as auto engines, by talking to each other. The team identified the customer segment most likely to adopt ABC's platform: the auto parts manufacturers in China, who can supply parts for companies that already have joint ventures in China (such as Ford and Peugeot). Conversely, the foreign companies with joint ventures in China can use the platform to outsource the manufacturing of auto parts to local manufacturers. The next potential segment, simply due to economic potential and buying power, is U.S. and European buyers, followed by buyers in the rest of the world.

To bridge the chasm, ABC needs to establish a beachhead on which to cross—in other words, to identify the customer niche we should target first. This first customer niche is represented by the headpin—once the headpin is knocked down, ABC gains momentum through the referential relationships that exist and thus can more easily knock down the pins next to it. As just described, the headpin that would make the most sense strategically to target is the niche of automobile companies with joint ventures already in China who want to outsource the manufacturing of noncritical auto parts to local suppliers. This strategy also makes sense in terms of what the experts the team interviewed suggested. The interviewees suggested that this would be a good first niche for ABC's platform.

Compelling Reason to Buy

From analysis of ABC's competitors, the research team saw that the field of outsourcing platforms was fairly crowded. However, from the customer interviews the team found that there was demand for a product that addressed some unmet customer needs. These needs fall into three main categories: functionality, trust, and usability.

The proposed ABC platform will offer a unique combination of functionalities currently unavailable on the market. The competitive field that overlaps with the functionalities that ABC wished to provide with its platform is roughly divided into business-to-business portals and Web meeting software. Currently there is no product that combines both of these into one platform, as ABC's product would. In addition, the platform would have a wide, comprehensive range of functionalities to provide support throughout the entire outsourcing process.

Doing business in China can be extremely complicated and daunting. Because the proposed platform is the only one supported by the Chinese government, ABC aims to ease some of these anxieties and use its resources to encourage and help the buyer conduct business successfully. In addition, the platform would offer authentication services to guarantee the trustworthiness of Chinese manufacturers listed on the platform's database.

Usability, in terms of a Web site that reflects understanding of how Westerners like to conduct business and of Western culture, was also a major concern among the interviewees. The issues ranged from confusion due to Chinese companies that have Web sites that are incomprehensible or unprofessional-looking to other language and cultural barriers. The team wished to apply its research on users to address those concerns in ABC's platform.

Whole Product

The ABC platform can be conceptualized as a "whole product"[28] (see Table 4.6)—a core product (the global sourcing online platform) along with a set of services that would fulfill the customer's compelling reason to buy. According to Wiefels, during the bowling alley stage, when products have not yet crossed the chasm, the whole product is especially important, because pragmatists demand a complete solution before they will adopt the product. Although the core product is certainly the focus of ABC's product development, these complementary services and products are what will change a customer's decision from "don't buy" to "buy."

One product that ABC can offer is professional-looking Web sites for Chinese manufacturers listed on its platform database. As previously noted, the interviewees stated that the websites of Chinese companies often do not look professional and are thus difficult for the Western buyer to understand and navigate. A professional-looking website would also help to build trust and raise overall sense of quality.

Integrated Supplier Platform and Additional Software Features. The integrated supplier platform being developed for ABC would have additional features and functionalities that would be added on for the second release of the platform. For example, it would have a webcam showing the factories of the listed Chinese manufacturers.

Communication Facilitation Features. Cultural sensitivity is not gained through education alone. Tools to facilitate cultural sensitivity can be built into ABC's platform. Examples from interviewees' suggestions include a pop-up window that will remind Western buyers to speak more slowly while conducting an audio conference with Chinese manufacturers, or an e-mail template with fields such as "date due," "feedback needed," and so on. The interviewees brought up the fact that different styles of communication can often block the successful exchange of ideas. For instance, a Chinese worker may send a Western boss information without specifying what feedback is needed. Westerners, on the other hand, like to have everything spelled out very clearly—What feedback do they need from me? When is it due?—so an e-mail template can help to clarify what information is needed and in what detail.

Complementary Services (Consultants or Professional Agents). Situating a group of consultants and professional agents in an office near where customers are located helps to build trust. These agents should be reachable when customers have concerns and should also understand the customers'

Table 4.6
Components of the whole product

Item	Description	
Core product	Global outsourcing online platform	Web meeting software + database of Chinese manufacturers
Complementary products	Professional Web sites	One product we can offer is professional-looking Web sites for Chinese manufacturers listed on the database of our platform. Our interviewees stated that the Web sites of Chinese companies often do not look professional and are thus difficult for the Western buyer to understand and navigate. A professional Web site will also help to build trust and raise overall sense of quality.
	Integrated supplier platform and additional software feaures	This refers to the Integrated Supplier Platform we have been developing as well as additional features and functionalities that will be added on for the second release of our platform. An example is a webcam showing the factories of the listed Chinese manufacturers.
	Communication facilitation features	Cultural sensitivity is gained not just through education. We can also build tools to facilitate cultural sensitivity in our platform, such as a pop-up window to remind Western buyers to speak more slowly while conducting conducting an audio conference with Chinese manufacturers or an e-mail template with fields such as "date due" and "feedback needed." Different styles of communication can block successful exchange of ideas. For instance, a Chinese worker will often send a Western boss information without specifying what feedback is needed, whereas Westerners like to have everything spelled out very clearly: What feedback do they need from me? When is it due? Thus, an e-mail template can help clarify what information is needed and in what detail.
Complementary services	Consultants or professional agents	A group of consultants or professional agents who have an office where customers are located helps to build trust. These agents should be reachable when customers have concerns and should also understand the customers' culture. Additionally, these agents can facilitate trade shows and follow up to make sure the right people meet each other at the trade shows.

Table 4.6 *(continued)*
Components of the whole product

Item	Description	
Core product	Global outsourcing online platform	Web meeting software + database of Chinese manufacturers
Complementary services *(cont.)*	Authentification/ verification	Having a third party verify the trustworthiness of Chinese companies is crucial to building trust with buyers. Other ways to achieve authentication/ verification that our interviewees brought up include establishing a bond rating for Chinese manufacturing companies, an approval system by the Chinese government, or insurance for both parties involved in the transaction.
	Translation services	Buyers stressed the importance of overcoming language barriers. One thing that would help is if the Chinese government could provide translation services free of charge, especially during the buyer's initial factory visit.

culture. Additionally, these agents can facilitate trade shows and follow up to make sure that the right people meet each other at the trade shows.

Authentication and Verification. Having a third party verify the trustworthiness of Chinese companies is crucial to building trust with buyers. Other ways to achieve authentication and verification that the interviewees brought up include establishing a bond rating for Chinese manufacturing companies, an approval system for use by the Chinese government, or insurance for both parties involved in the transaction.

Translation Services. Buyers stressed the importance of overcoming language barriers. One thing that would help is for the Chinese government to provide translation services free of charge, especially during the buyer's initial factory visit.

Product Development

For the first phase of product development, ABC will roll out the core product. Subsequent complementary products and services will be introduced. A Gantt chart and table that describe the functionalities and services

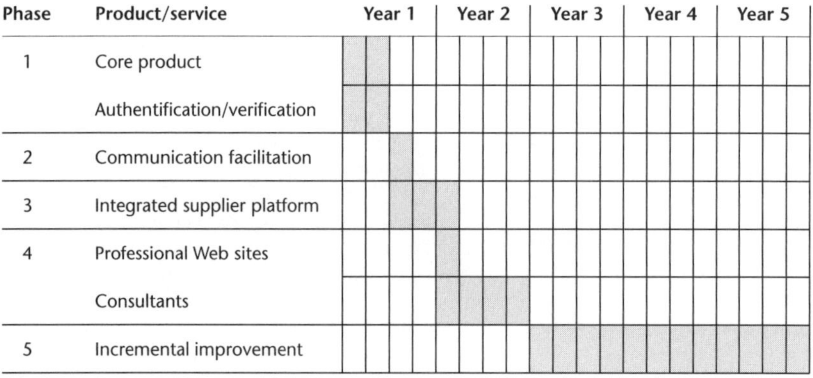

Phase	Product/service	Year 1	Year 2	Year 3	Year 4	Year 5
1	Core product					
	Authentification/verification					
2	Communication facilitation					
3	Integrated supplier platform					
4	Professional Web sites					
	Consultants					
5	Incremental improvement					

Figure 4.29   Gantt chart

offered in each phase of product development, along with the goal we wish to achieve with each phase, are shown in Figure 4.29 and Table 4.7.

Products and services that support product promotion need to be available early, because staff training may take some time to complete. However, promotional staff do not need to be ready for the first target customer segment because business will be conducted in China, which is why this service is in Phase 4 rather than earlier. Promotional staff, however, are crucial for the next target segment, U.S. and European buyers, who will not be in China and will thus need this level of support in their home countries.

Partners

To bridge the chasm, ABC will need to recruit partners to help it penetrate the mainstream market. The immediate goal is to fulfill the needs of the targeted niche markets and provide them with a whole product. The long-term goal is to create a market ecosystem that will expand into a durable value chain. Some goals in choosing partners is to choose those that will (1) help complete the product, (2) help deliver the solution to the target segments, (3) find complements to the whole-product solution, and (4) benefit economically from their participation.[29]

Another way to evaluate potential partners is with a partner matrix, in which partners are evaluated on the dimensions of learning and earning. High-earning partners are those with the potential to add value to

Table 4.7
Definition and duration of each phase of product development

Phase	Time needed	Product/service	Goal
1	6 months	Core product (Web meeting and database	Get product working as quickly as possible and conduct user testing.
		Authentification/ verification	Trust needs to be established for any product to be adopted.
2	3 months (no overlap with phase 1)	Communication facilitation services	Need to conduct more user research and testing in order to provide these additional functionalities.
3	9 months (overlap with phase 2)	Integrated supplier platform and additional software features (such as webcam)	Provide complementary products and services to complete the whole product.
4	3 months (some overlap with phase 3)	Professional Web sites	Provide promotional Web site services for exclusive members first, then extend the service to all other manufacturers once the system is set up.
	1 year (some overlap with phase 3)	Consultants or professional staff translation	Products and services that support product promotion need to start early, because training of staff may take some time. However, the promotional staff does not need to be ready for the first target customer segment, because business will be conducted in China, which is why this service is in Phase 4 rather than earlier. Promotional staff, however, is crucial for our next target segment, U.S. and European buyers, who will not be in China and will thus need this level of support in their home countries.
5	After year 2	Incremental improvements	Extend platform to China, extend to other industries, broaden customer base to United States and Europe. Establish platform as the Yahoo of China.

ABC's product or services and thus increase its earnings; high-learning partners are those that can add to ABC's knowledge base.

Potential partners include the following groups:

- *Chinese government.* Government support is a major factor compelling ABC to buy. Because no other platform has support from the Chinese government, and because uncertainty about the logistics of doing business in China is a major concern for buyers, this partnership will add greatly to ABC's earnings (because it will attract a lot of customers) and knowledge (because ABC will learn about the intricacies of Chinese policies directly from the source).

- *Website design companies.* ABC can partner with companies that specialize in Web site design to help Chinese manufacturers listed on the platform create professional-looking Web sites that are user-friendly to appeal to Western buyers. Because Web site design is not one of ABC's core competencies, these companies will be strictly earning partners. ABC is hoping not to learn Web site design but rather to outsource it to these partners.

- *Consultancies.* In order to build a staff of promotional agents, ABC needs good consultants who have experience with and knowledge of Western culture. ABC can either partner with existing consultancies that have this expertise or train its own staff. In the long term, ABC wants to have staff of its own devoted solely to promoting its platform; but in the short term, because it will take time to train and hire such a staff, a partnership may be the best option. Such a partnership has high earning and learning potential because it will help ABC gain customers and gain knowledge it can use when building its own staff.

- *Hong Kong vendors.* Because many Westerners currently do business in China by going through vendors in Hong Kong, these vendors are an important gateway to potential Western buyers. Thus they are high on earning potential.

- *Engineering and outsourcing professional organizations.* There are many organizations that Western buyers turn to for advice about outsourcing or about doing business in China. Partnering with these organizations will help ABC to promote its platform and increase its earnings.

- *Authentication and verification credit agencies.* These agencies are an essential part of the whole product because trust is one of the major concerns of Western buyers. ABC needs to partner with a reputable outside authentication and verification agency; for conflict-of-interest reasons, this part of the whole product must come from a third party. Therefore, there is no learning involved in the partnership, only earning potential.
- *Academic institutions.* As the team learned when conducting its market research, academic institutions, professors, and others can be a valuable source of knowledge that can keep the platform and marketing plan at the cutting edge. ABC should continue to tap this source of knowledge by forming partnerships with academic institutions or hiring as platform development consultants (not as promotional agents) professors who are experts in the field. These are strictly learning partnerships, because ABC will also have to pay for this knowledge. Although the advice of these partners will help the product earn more money in the long run, for now these institutions and consultants will be classified as learning partners.

Strategic partners are the most important type of partners to have because they are high in both earning and learning potential. In ABC's case, these partners are the Chinese government and consultancies. Earning partners and learning partners are also important to have, but limited partners should not be pursued, because they are not high on earning.

Positioning

ABC's position is determined by how it differentiates its products from those of its competitors or its competitive advantages over those of other products. The competitive advantages are derived from the customer needs that are addressed (their compelling reason to buy) as well as from the product provided by ABC to address this need (the whole product). The company's competitive advantages include:

- Comprehensive platform providing both database and Web meeting tools
- Order tracking systems and ratings that build trust

- Government support in promotion on the Chinese side and favorable regulation policies
- Representation by a promotional agent in both the United States and China to facilitate communication between customers and manufacturers; results guaranteed through the signing of a contract

Next Target. As discussed earlier, ABC's first target niche will comprise companies with joint ventures in China who want to outsource their manufacturing to local Chinese companies.

Long-Term Strategy. The next target niche will be U.S. and European buyers. In this segment, first to be targeted will be small to medium-sized businesses (SMBs), who have the most need for ABC's platform. Large companies often have the money and resources to travel to China and find a suitable outsourcer, so they may not see an immediate need for the platform. After targeting SMB companies in the United States, the services could be extended first to Europe (which represents 60 percent of potential customers) and then to Japan. In Europe, the first countries that should be targeted are Germany, Italy, and France. They are currently outsourcing in China and have strong mechanical or appliance industries that would benefit from outsourcing standard parts. Volkswagen (at 40 percent) is the market-share leader in the Chinese automobile market,[30] and the French company Peugeot is currently investing more than $80 million in Wuhan.[31]

Long-Term Applications Strategy. The platform itself should be extended beyond ABC to China and to new vertical markets such as the electronics, apparel, or chemical industries. Nevertheless, the expected growth should not undermine quality standards or the reliability of the platform. As discussed before, one of the key factors in this market is to build trust with customers who may have a negative opinion of outsourcing in China. Such trust can be built only through transparency and high commitment to quality standards.

Distribution Channel

ABC's first and main distribution channel is the Internet. Its core product includes business-to-business and Web meeting tools that can best be distributed through the Internet. Nevertheless, according to Richard

Dasher,[32] director of the U.S.-Asia Technology Management Center at Stanford University, the information present on a database is not sufficient for U.S. buyers to make a decision; neither is it a guarantee that trust issues will be resolved. As suggested by one customer and used by some competitors, the Web site, which is ABC's first distribution channel, should be used as a way to attract customers to the platform and create awareness.[33]

For the Buyer. Besides the Web site, a staff of experienced bilingual consultants headquartered in the United States would help customers to find the right companies to which to outsource their products and be a reliable contact in case of difficulties with suppliers. They would be a direct sales force that would guide the customer from choice of manufacturer to shipping. The platform would serve as a convenient tracking system for the order, and the customer service provided would intervene in case of problems. Customers have shown strong interest in having a contact who can facilitate the choice of outsourcer and develop trust.

For the Manufacturer. The Chinese government would promote the platform among ABC manufacturers by encouraging subscription to the database. In Chinese offices, both government officials and bilingual employees would help local companies to improve their Web sites and to contact Western buyers directly.

Sales Force. Many of the buyers interviewed stated that the sales force is a very important consideration for them when choosing a manufacturer to outsource to, especially an overseas manufacturer with very different cultural norms. The sales force has the responsibility of delivering the product message to the buyers as well as calming their anxieties about adopting the product. In this case, the main concern that came up across interviews was the issue of trust in Chinese companies.

Interviewees proposed that one way to deal with the trust issue would be to have a group of promotional agents headquartered in the United States. Not only would this group's proximity to buyers help them understand the way Westerners prefer to do business, but the geographic proximity would help the buyers by providing a point person close by to go to.[34]

The sales force should be bilingual in order to deal more efficiently with potential problems arising between buyers and customers. Their role would be to deal directly with the manufacturer so that buyers would not have to travel to China themselves to communicate a change in design, for example, as is sometimes the case today. Nevertheless, there is a strong demand for the buyer to be able to communicate directly with the manufacturer using the other communication tools. The sales force is a guarantee for the buyer in case of problems. If the buyer wants, the sales force, through its experience, can also provide help concerning the choice of manufacturer and its financial practices, work methods, and other conditions. Ideally the sales force should be knowledgeable in the way business is conducted in both the West and China and should provide more detailed information, if required, about the manufacturer and its work methods.

On the manufacturer's side, government officials will promote the platform among Chinese manufacturers and offices, first in ABC and then in the rest of China. The Chinese offices will be in direct contact with their Western counterparts, providing first-hand information about manufacturers and conveying feedback from Western companies to the Chinese manufacturers. They would also be responsible for the control and local certification of manufacturers. Finally, in association with the government, they would coordinate the IT services (such as professional Web site and Web meeting tools) needed to support the platform and to facilitate communication between buyers and manufacturers.

Pricing. The pricing models for the United States and China will be different. Competitors like Alibaba charge a US$5,000 fee per year for Chinese SMBs to set up their Web sites and have access to Alibaba's platform. Moreover, they propose consulting services to U.S. buyers who want more support by providing translation services or organizing factory visits. Other platforms propose advertising banners and charge Chinese manufacturers for getting better visibility through their platform.[35]

Assuming that ABC's platform will be supported by the government, the following business model can be proposed:

Manufacturers

- An annual fee would be paid by Chinese manufacturers to set up and maintain their Web site and communication tools. The exact amount would depend on the government's commitment, as well as on the operating costs of maintenance and installation.
- The service provided could also include seminars about the way to do business with Western buyers, with a stress on quality, IP, and trust issues.

U.S. and European Buyers

- Subscription fees would be charged for Western buyers to have access to online, translation, and legal services. Moreover, an agent could be named to follow up on the buyer's request and to serve as a point of contact in case of problems between buyer and manufacturer.[36]
- A variable fee could be applied at the signing of an outsourcing contract between the buyer and the manufacturer; the amount would depend on the level of service provided.

Advertising and Promotion

Using the different means at its disposal, ABC can try to estimate the total cost of advertising for the second year. Alibaba[37] alone claims more than 1.2 million registered customers. ABC's goal is to reach 300,000 one year after the release of the core product. To increase efficiency and reach the largest number of clients possible, the research team recommended diversifying its methods of advertising, as shown in Table 4.8.

Web Advertising. Considering that the platform is not enough to drive customers to contract, the Website could be used first to create awareness. In order to attract a broad audience, advertising banners or key words could be bought on search engines such as Google or Yahoo. Web advertising is certainly the best and most convenient way to be in contact with the largest number of buyers, but its efficiency is hard to estimate and can fluctuate.

Table 4.8
Advertising and promotion

	Price per click	Conversion rate	Cost per download	Customers	Total cost
Outsourcing Web sites	20	20%	1	50,000	$50,000
Search engines	20	10%	2	25,000	$50,000
Print advertising				50,000	$50,000
Other (trade shows)				200,000	$150,000
TOTAL				300,000	$300,000

Source: http://www.epaynews.com/statistics/transactions.html and www.google.com

Print Advertising. Printing ads or banners on specialized magazines can enable ABC to target the audience and industry better than Web advertising. Nevertheless, its efficiency is hard to measure and it is a relatively costly means of advertising. Articles in news magazines, newspapers, and television are particularly attractive because they provide both free advertising and recognition from a broad segment of customers.

Trade Shows. The research team recommended, in addition to the means already described, participating in trade shows such as the Chinese Export Commodities Fair (CECF) at Guangzhou (84,530 visitors in six days with an $18.47 billion trade volume) or Taitronics at Taipei (20,000 visitors in five days).[38]

Given the high trade volume and the number of potentially interested customers, trade shows are a good way to create business and raise awareness. The buyers who participate in these forums are mainly professionals with specific needs and requirements, and the number of contacts that can be made is much higher than in Web advertising. Alibaba alone claims to have distributed 30,000 CD-ROMs and gotten 2,500 subscriptions during the first session of the CECF.

In addition, conferences in the United States such as the Chemical Processes Industries Exhibition (Chem Show) for chemical products in New York can create contact and recognition.

Government Promotion. In China, the government could support the platform by facilitating contacts between manufacturers and buyers. Moreover, incentives for tax reductions or less rigid legal regulations would help increase trust. Nevertheless, there is a need to clarify the relative powers of local government to determine its efficiency. Actually, such incentives were tried in Japan but failed because the local government had no real power, so there is a need to examine carefully the leverage of authorities.[39]

Conclusion and Discussion

The outsourcing of manufacturing and production services to China has caused a surge in the Asian economy. U.S.-based companies are capitalizing on this trend by decoupling many of their domestic services through contracting them to companies in China, a provider of high-quality goods at low costs. Although the benefits derived from outsourcing services are highly visible in today's economy, many U.S. companies have been reluctant to initiate business in this region.

To address this problem, the Chinese government and private institutions in ABC are turning to a Web-enabled IT global sourcing platform to assist foreign companies in establishing business in China. This chapter has presented the basic requirements of an IT platform that is capable of facilitating the search for business partners and the establishment of processes. Specifically, the IT platform will provide digital services for the entire global value chain of business process outsourcing. The ramifications of this IT strategy will enable value creation and cost benefits, two key drivers for long-term economic growth.

5 Manufacturing

Manufacturing represents a vital stage in the value chain of firms engaged in production and manufacturing operations. Considerable value is added as raw materials are converted, through the manufacturing process, into finished goods that can be used directly by the customer, or into intermediary goods designed to be used in the production of a final good. The production decisions and efficiency of the manufacturing process, on the other hand, have considerable financial implications for the firm. An important determinant in a manufacturing firm's operating profit is the firm's ability to control the cost of manufacturing and to produce a higher gross margin. The nature of manufacturing processes and of the technologies used in those processes varies greatly depending on the industry in question. Addressing a comprehensive array of production operations across different industries is not the focus of this chapter. Rather, the three cases presented here focus on the garment production process. This concentrated approach will help to provide a more in-depth understanding of how general principles of optimizing production can be applied to a particular industry. Furthermore, it is important to notice that the manufacturing process is not simply a monolithic stage in the value chain. On the contrary, manufacturing processes often involve many complicated subprocesses that constantly interact with each other and could include multiple stages in which successive intermediate goods converge toward a final finished product. In many manufacturing firms these stages are captured by work-in-process inventories. A manufacturing firm maximizes profits by first deciding on an appropriate production level and then optimizing the production process for that level. A firm could optimize the manufacturing process for a given level of production through such tools as cost minimization and quality control measures. Two of the chapter's cases focus mainly on the optimization of production processes. Both involve the Esquel Group, a leading private garment producer with vertically integrated operations from cotton farming to retailing.

In the first case, Esquel is trying to optimize its spinning mill processes and process planning through efficient utilization of information parameters about cotton at different stages of spinning mill operations. The case presents an investigation of utilizing radio frequency identification (RFID) to capture information about the quality and color of cotton at a granular level (bale level instead of lot level) and then an investigation of how best to integrate this detailed information across such spinning mill operations as cotton usage classification, heather yarn process planning, and white yarn process planning. Integrating the information captured by the RFID system proves to be a crucial part of the case study and requires further analysis due to the fact that the RFID system would not be complete without the spinning mill operations reflecting the new state of information. The consulting team, as a result, explores algorithms and expert-system implementations for automating the information integration process. Several algorithms are introduced and analyzed for different spinning mill operations, including support vector machine learning, nearest neighbor algorithm, and clustering through neural networks.

In the second case, a different consulting team focuses on how to manage and reduce waste across the garment manufacturing phase. (Note that both of these cases reflect the vertically integrated nature of Esquel operations; while one group focuses on the spinning mill operations that deal with the raw cotton coming into the mill, the second team focuses on processes involved in making the garments from produced fabric). The team focuses on specific processes of cutting, sewing, and washing to provide a new model for waste identification. It conducts cause and effect analysis, process stability and capability analysis, correlation analysis, and hypothesis testing as a part of its data analysis efforts. Finally, a rigorous regression model based on analysis of variance (ANOVA) is conducted to examine the underlying waste factors and produce a new waste model.

The last case in the chapter focuses on Sterling Products Ltd., an apparel manufacturer that is trying to improve its processes in order to shorten production prototype lead time. The improvement will have a direct impact for the company considering the highly competitive nature of the industry.

Case 1: The Esquel Group—Applications of RFID in Spinning Mill Production Planning

The spinning mill is an age-old industry that has survived generations of economic downturns and uprises. In recent years, however, the competitive forces shaping the industry have placed an enormous amount of pressure on companies to be cost leaders in order to survive. The Esquel Group, a renowned garment manufacturing company, has considered innovative ways to increase the efficiency of its operations to reduce costs and to market its new business.

At this time, operations departments around the world are turning toward a new technology that has the potential to revolutionize the industry: RFID tags. The basis of this technology is the ability to query items using passive electromagnetic waves that ping RFID tags to obtain real-time data. The technology enables instant feedback for monitoring activities and opportunities for improving efficiency in the spinning mill by using RFID applications where they appear promising.

The Esquel Group[1] is a world-famous garment manufacturer with annual production of sixty million garments. It is a privately held and vertically integrated company with more than 47,000 employees located in eight countries. With such a unique integration, from cotton farming to retailing, this apparel manufacturer aims to capture all value-added processes within its business model to maintain and control the quality delivered to its high-end customers. However, as a traditional, labor-intensive, original equipment manufacturer (OEM), Esquel faces high demand uncertainties as well as production uncertainties. To achieve high efficiency and responsiveness, and to leverage its competitiveness, it is important for this company to enhance its production management system.

With an ambitious mind-set, the company works with the understanding that the proprietary technology, the recipes, the formulation, and a certain skill level in the labor base, all combined, can make it more competitive. Under this closed-loop model, it needs to operate as the lowest-cost producer in order to have a competitive and profitable production management system. A critical success factor for organizations pursuing this strategy is to integrate and standardize acquired operations as quickly as possible.

This is where RFID comes in. RFID implementation, in its completed form, will enable Esquel to deal with standardized data across the organization. By improving communications from one process to the next and by enabling new opportunities for efficiency at every stage of production, RFID technology will help Esquel meet its objective of lowering costs and seamlessly integrating manufacturing operations.

Esquel is by no means alone in its efforts to take advantage of RFID technology. In the United States, major retailers such as Wal-Mart are requiring that suppliers implement RFID tracking into products. The United States and Europe both have established standards for RFID implementation, and China is quickly following suit. The size of the RFID IT service market alone is expected to reach $4.2 billion by 2008.

Problem Definition

As with most breakthrough technologies, the implementation of RFID requires fundamental redesign of business processes in order to accommodate the potential inherences and attain optimal RFID benefits. Let's take a closer look at how Esquel is currently implementing this technology on its cotton farm.

To date, Esquel uses RFID passive tags to track cotton from Xinjiang coming into its Guangzhou Esquel Spinning Mill, or GES. The Xinjiang cotton farm is the starting point of Esquel's vertically integrated supply chain, followed by its spinning mill in Guangzhou. In brief, the cotton farming process includes operators harvesting, cleaning, drying, extracting, and packaging cotton. It seems relatively simple, but cotton quality information passed forward needs to be unique and strategically defined by a high-volume instrument, or HVI—a spectrometer used widely to reliably identify cotton quality information to world standards. Traditionally, the cotton information is described in terms of lot level, or at-harvest level, with cotton weighing twenty tons per lot on average. With RFID, Esquel is able to describe the cotton in terms of bale level, with a bale weighing eighty kilograms on average. In fact, Esquel is currently working closely with EPCglobal, Inc., managers of the electronic product code (EPC) system, to help standardize the coding system. Esquel envisions that in the near future every cotton bale arriving at its spinning mill will be RFID-tagged with cotton quality information, which will be electronically sent in real time. This technology will be an asset to Esquel in

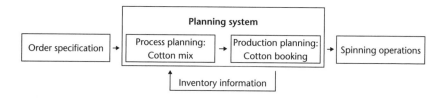

Figure 5.1   Overview of Esquel's planning system

terms of better quality description from lot to bale level, elimination of redundant quality testing in the spinning mill, and better utilization of human resources. GES, however, still does not use bale level information. Decisions are still based on lot level because no further plans have yet been made to implement RFID.

The team's conjecture is that the information associated with the cotton, such as color and quality, can be utilized via the RFID tags in order to synchronize and improve the efficiency of the current process planning system. In other words, RFID will enable a "smarter" process of choosing the cotton to fill any particular yarn order. Intuitively, such a process would reduce time spent and cotton wasted in determining the correct cotton mix.

The project assigned to the research group was to create a bridge from the use of RFID at Esquel's cotton farm to its use in Esquel's spinning process (the creation of yarn from cotton). In essence, the aim was to design a systematic and automated process planning model integrating RFID information to improve yarn quality and reduce cost. An important assumption in this project is that all incoming bales are RFID-tagged. Although this is not yet implemented, Esquel envisions this to be the goal of their strategic supply chain.

Figure 5.1 shows a typical process from cotton mixing to yarn spinning, given customers' specifications. More precisely, the core of this project lies in proposing data management models that will capture and integrate the enriched and real-time data to facilitate the decision-making processes enabled by RFID implementation.

In the following discussion, first the current planning practices in the spinning mill are summarized. Then opportunities for planning process improvements with RFID integrations are identified and addressed. Next, the approaches of planning process redesign are described in detail. The benefits of RFID implementation in the spinning mill are then analyzed through cost simulations. Finally, major findings and results are summarized.

Current Spinning Mill Practices

The project began with on-site observations and interviews of experts from many Esquel departments, particularly production planning, re-dip, IT, and supply chain. Like many other highly varied product manufacturing processes, the yarn manufacturing processes in the spinning mill can be categorized into two stages: make-to-stock and make-to-order. In the make-to-stock stage, raw materials are made into intermediate parts and stored in inventory. Safety stock levels are kept for commonly used materials such as different colors of dyed cottons. In the make-to-order stage, intermediate parts are further processed to make into yarns according to yarn order specifications.

There are two big categories of end products: heather yarn and white yarn. The heather yarn is a mixture of dyed color cottons (as well as white cottons). The white yarn is a mixture of white cottons. Within each category there are thousands of varieties of SKUs with differentiating factors such as color, quality, and usage. The two categories of yarn are compared in Table 5.1.

A conceptual framework for the two production stages in the planning processes in the spinning mill is shown in Figure 5.2. To begin with, approximately eighty to one hundred tons of cotton arrive at the spinning mill every week. Before they are used, the technical engineers judge

Table 5.1
Comparison of heather and white yarns

Item		Description
GES production period	75% year-round	25% July–October
Order size	Small: Generally this is done through partial mixture of cotton lots.	Large: Generally this requires several mixtures of cotton lots.
Quality requirement	High: Color mixture is the most critical with every order.	Low: With large order size, cotton mix is critical in order to maintain consistent quality.

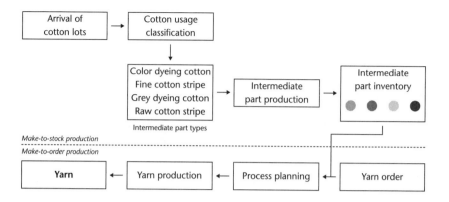

Figure 5.2   Current cotton-to-yarn planning model

their potential direction of usage based on guidelines and experience. This process is called cotton usage classification (see Figure 5.2) and is considered the major planning process in the make-to-stock production stage. These cottons are processed and stored as intermediate parts in the inventory pending orders. When yarn orders arrive, the requirements are fed into the IT system to initiate the make-to-order stage. This process requires experienced technical engineers to decide the cotton mixture recipes for both types of yarn production.

The three key process planning modules—cotton usage classification, heather yarn process planning, and white yarn process planning—determine the quality and cost of the spinning mill's final products. We will focus more closely on three aspects of process planning: current cotton usage classification, consolidated process planning flow, and process variations between heather yarn and white yarn.

Current Cotton Usage Classification

As mentioned, the cotton usage classification process classifies incoming cottons into several categories according to their potential usage. The process flow shown in Figure 5.3 maps the procedures.

The cotton usage classification process is a weekly and manual process carried out by the technical engineers. As noted, an average of eighty to one hundred tons of cotton arrives at GES every week. Each lot is sampled with a specific HVI procedure. That is, 10 percent, or about twenty

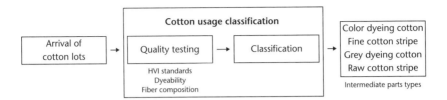

Figure 5.3   Overview of cotton usage classification

bales, of each lot undergoes a quality identification of HVI quality, dyeability, and three-fiber composition. The numerical and text-represented results are manually scanned by technical engineers to classify the yarns into four grand-usages—color dyeing cotton, fine cotton stripe, grey dyeing cotton, and raw cotton stripe—in terms of lot level. Further classifications of each usage exist—all lots are characterized by sixteen parameters—but not all parameters are relevant for this project. For example, a lot from Africa is always chosen as dyeing cotton because of its particular characteristics, that is, it is high in sugar level. If mixed with water, it will dissolve.

The well-trained technical engineers follow certain guidelines; however, most of the time they simply glance at the values and justify their decisions on the basis of a few of the more important parameters. Though highly dependent on experience, this classification system is well organized and flexible, with well-defined cluster formations and a virtual prioritized list of classification parameters.

These justifications of cotton usage are stored in a tabular format. Table 5.2 shows a simplified version of the output of this process.

It should be noted that this process is independent of the yarn process planning. It does not initialize the decisions made in meeting order

Table 5.2
Simplified version of cotton usage

Lot number	Cotton usage	Weight	Area of origin
854762	Color dyeing	86	Xinjiang
847728	Grey dyeing	228.9	Xinjiang
143101	Fine cotton stripe	20,000	Xinjiang

specifications. Rather, the output, which affects the raw material inventory, influences the decisions.

Consolidated Process Planning Flow

The consolidated process planning flow is initialized by the placement of yarn orders, whether for heather or white yarn. (For simplicity's sake, the two types of yarns—heather and white—are consolidated in this description because the general procedures are similar for both. Their differences are distinguished following this discussion.) The order specification (that is, the color code from the heather yarn order, for example) triggers the contract judgment and sample-making processes. At the same time, the availability of materials is also checked. The process flow is shown in Figure 5.4.

Contract Judgment Process. The purpose of the contract judgment is to suggest a preliminary plan that specifies the types and compositions of cottons needed to meet order requirements. For instance, when order ABC arrives with a color code requirement of 123, that number is fed into the spinning management information system (SMIS) to retrieve two important composition plans: reference and historical. The reference plan is a guideline for technical engineers that serves no particular value. Often, the historical plan is more useful and is automatically retrieved from the most recent order with the same order requirements.

The Re-Dip Process (Sample-Making). As a rule of thumb, before any samples are made, technical engineers always check the availability of the cottons. If the amounts of the desired cottons available are insufficient, samples are not made. Unless the technical engineers are certain about the supply of cotton (the exact cotton bale is selected), the process cannot proceed. If the correct cotton is available, the re-dip process is preceded by five to six iterative tests until technicians are satisfied. They select at most six rectangular-shaped fabrics and yarns that are sent to the customer for final approval before a material requirement notification sheet is generated and the bulk production process begins. The notification sheet is used to confirm the cotton mix recipes and specify the cottons needed to proceed to production.

In general, the yarn production process depends solely on the techni-

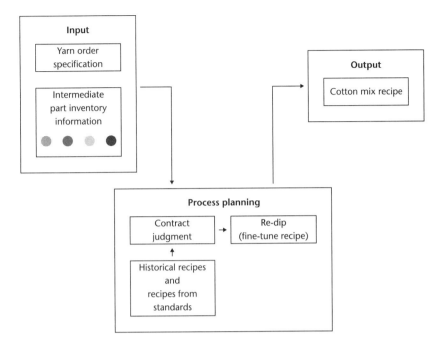

Figure 5.4   Consolidated process planning flow

cal engineers' use of historical data as recipes for initializing modification plans until an optimized plan for minimizing costs and better utilizing the available cottons is created.

Process Variations Between Heather Yarn and White Yarn

As noted, heather yarn is a mixture of dyed cottons whereas white yarn is a mixture of white cottons. The order size and requirements generate slight variations in the two yarn production processes: for heather yarn, color matching is critical; for white yarn, quality consistency is critical.

Figures 5.5 and 5.6 show the process planning flow for heather yarn and white yarn, respectively. Both processes include contract judgment, sample making, and buyer's approval, which leads to production. The flows differ in the sequences of these processes.

An order for heather yarn specifies a color code that triggers contract judgment, which suggests a preliminary plan, and then technical engineers check the availability of the dyed cotton in inventory. The fourteen hundred yarn color codes are mixed in combinations based on 140 cotton color codes. Once availability has been determined, samples are made until the customer is satisfied with the color. A white yarn order, conversely, is often much larger than an order for heather, so again, quality consistency is critical. As stated earlier, a lot weighs twenty tons. To meet quality consistency requirements, the conventional practice is to maximize the cotton lot usage. So, if an order is for less than twenty tons, the engineer finds one particular lot to fill the order. If it is greater than twenty tons, the primary concern is to utilize the minimum number of cotton lots. In addition, a cotton bale layout is essential to ensure the randomization of bales used. Otherwise, the two procedures are fairly similar.

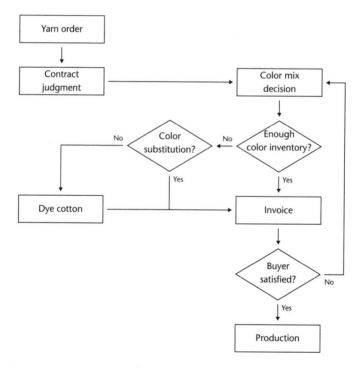

Figure 5.5   Heather grey yarn process planning flow

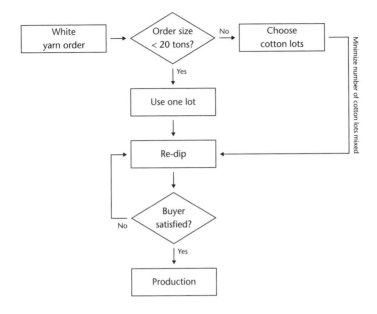

Figure 5.6   White yarn process planning flow

Opportunities for Planning Process Improvements

On the basis of Esquel's study of its current spinning practice, there are three opportunities for RFID to aid in production management practices: cotton usage classification, process planning of heather yarn, and process planning of white yarn.

Cotton Usage Classification

Cotton usage classification is a knowledge-based process. As mentioned earlier, after cotton lots arrive at the spinning mill, they undergo dyeability, three-fiber, and HVI-spectrometer quality testing. The results are then passed to technical engineers, who classify cotton usage on the basis of standards, historical data, and inventory level. To date, this has always been a manual process. But as more data are fed into the process, it becomes troublesome, and the burden falls into the lap of the engineers, who most likely will become incapable of processing the data manually.

Heather Yarn Process Planning

The process for planning heather yarn is based on experience, requiring the engineers, as described earlier, to make decisions about cotton mixing on the basis of availability of the raw material, cotton. As RFID data reduce the measurement unit to a bale, the number of cotton mix plans will increase dramatically. In fact, if the incoming data are properly manipulated, more optimized plans will be generated.

White Yarn Process Planning

As already noted, the white yarn planning process is similar to the heather yarn process in that both consider the correct mix of cotton to meet the order specifications. The two processes differ in how they meet order requirements. Whereas the heather yarn process focuses on color matching, the white yarn process focuses on yarn quality. Nevertheless, in order to manage and generate a systematic and automated plan, the two processes have been consolidated.

Generally speaking, these three RFID opportunities are similar in that they are based on experience. If in the near future all incoming bales are supplied with quality information on RFID tags, means to adapt to the changes brought by enriched data must be thoroughly planned. One suggestion is to redesign the management system using learning algorithms.

Planning Process Redesign

Two algorithmic systems for implementation are recommended: support vector machine learning and the nearest neighbor algorithm. These systems are applicable to the problems of cotton usage classification and yarn process planning, respectively.

The research team began this study by taking steps to understand the current situation in Esquel's spinning mills as well as the stages of RFID implementation in Esquel's supply chain. Through this process they concluded that the three areas of cotton usage—classification, heather yarn process planning, and white yarn process planning—had the most promise for RFID information integration. That is, it would be through integrating into these processes the information stored on RFID tags that Esquel's supply chain would benefit.

From that point, the team began to look into different algorithms that would fit the problems at hand. They consulted many textbooks and articles, as well as experts from both Hong Kong University of Science and Technology and Stanford University, on machine learning and supply chain management. In the data they gathered they were able to identify one solution for cotton usage classification and one solution for heather yarn process planning (which, again, can easily be adapted to white yarn process planning). The team's criteria for choosing solutions included proper fit to the problem at hand, ease of implementation, and sufficient available research and knowledge about the methods to justify suggesting them. They chose the methods that fit best, for which existing software packages exist, and on which there was a good deal of research suggesting both that the method is effective and that it is fully developed.

Support Vector Machines Learning

Support vector machines (SVMs) are learning systems that use a hypothesis space of linear functions in a high dimensional feature space, trained with a learning algorithm derived from optimization theory that implements a learning-bias-derived statistical learning theory. This learning strategy is a principled and very powerful method that in the few years since its introduction has already outperformed most other systems in a wide variety of applications. In simple, applied terms, this means that support vector machines provide a powerful way to classify cotton bales on the basis of known quality information. SVMs discover nontrivial relationships between the given inputs and outputs by using training data sets. They solve regression and classification problems by changing parameters that control how they learn as they cycle through training data. These parameters, usually called weights, influence how well the trained model performs.

In the simplest pattern recognition tasks, SVMs use a linear separating hyperplane to create a classifier with a maximal margin (minimal error). So that they may do that, the learning problem is cast as a constrained nonlinear optimization problem. In this setting, the objective function is quadratic and the constraints are linear, and a quadratic programming problem is to be solved.

Complex real-world applications, however, require more expressive hypothesis spaces than linear functions. A kernel function is used for this purpose. Kernel functions offer an alternative solution by projecting the data into a high dimensional feature space. By the use of kernels, all necessary computations are performed directly in input space and this greatly enhances the computational power of the learning machine. The kernel function $f(x)$ takes this difficult-to-separate input set and maps it to easily distinguishable sets. SVM modeling therefore requires the selection of a suitable kernel function for the problem at hand.[2]

Machine Learning Overview

Learning is making useful changes in our minds.

—Marvin Minsky

Learning denotes changes in a system that enable [it] to do the same task from the same population more efficiently and more effectively the next time.

—Herbert Simon

Machine learning (ML) is the study of computer algorithms that improve automatically through experience. There is a whole class of algorithms that are considered machine learning tools. These algorithms work to approximate a function of interest by looking at data that relate the inputs of the function to the outputs. In other words, ML algorithms treat problems as functions to approximate. They learn how to output the correct answer to past inputs by building an internal representation of the system.

Given the right amount of data, ML solutions can build robust, general problem solvers.

Because of ML's behavior, certain situations motivate its use:

- Too much knowledge is to be encoded—ML can allow the knowledge to be learned gradually.
- New knowledge needs to be prevented from rendering the system obsolete.
- There is the need to adjust to an unknown work environment.
- Correlations among data structures need to be discovered without human intervention.

Types of ML. There are two broad types of ML: speed-up and empirical. Speed-up ML algorithms focus on solving the same problems faster over time. For example, a novice, if given enough time to compute an optimal move, would play like the current world champion; however, if the time available is short, a novice plays like a novice. An expert has a large memory of game patterns plus appropriate strategies. The difference between the two is that experts make use of experience (or speed-up learning) to deduce a good move more quickly.

There are three kinds of empirical learning: supervised, reinforcement, and unsupervised. In all three, the system learns on the basis of experience over a set of data. The learning can occur in real time or as training, before the need to predict.

What Is Machine Learning Good For? Machine learning is suited for solving problems where information is incomplete or missing altogether. It is particularly useful when the relationship between variables and the solution is highly nonlinear, or, as in the spinning mill, when the relationships are obfuscated by the complexity of the problem and experiential nature of the solution. Basically, if you cannot write deterministic solutions or construct iterative approaches, ML will be very powerful. The greatest power of ML is its ability to generalize to new problems.

Method Justification. In method justification, the problem is first classified as a supervised learning problem. This means we need to learn from existing historical data and known classifications, both of which are given in the problem. There are two best-practice algorithms for such a problem: neural networks (NN) and SVM. SVM is better than NN for three major reasons. First, SVM provides insight from the solution into the problem; NN is notorious for offering no intuition from solutions. Second, SVM is based on a well-known optimization problem with existing tools to support implementation. Third, SVM provides the most flexibility in implementation, allowing for better real-world performance and greater accuracy. Beyond these academic reasons, the research team sought expert opinions from industry. SVM was recommended by Pieter Abbeel, a doctoral candidate in computer science at Stanford University concentrating in ML.

Although the use of SVM methods in applications has begun only recently, application developers have already reported state-of-the-art performances in a variety of applications in pattern recognition, regression estimation, and time series prediction. (The article "Support Vector Machines," by Hearst and colleagues, showcases an example comparing the performance of support vector learning with several other algorithms.) This algorithm lies at the intersection of learning theory and practice: it contains a large class of neural nets, radial basis function nets, and polynomial classifiers as special cases. Yet it is simple enough to be analyzed mathematically, because it can be shown to correspond to a linear method in a high-dimensional feature space nonlinearly related to input space.

In addition, readily available software packages for the SVM solution make this an implementable solution.

We make two assumptions here:

– Adequate-quality historical data are available for training, testing, and learning.
– The existing categorization framework is retained and considered appropriate in classifying the usage of the cotton.

Following are the main considerations for developing the SVM algorithm.

1. *Collecting historical data.* All the historical data to be used in training and testing the model should be clearly distinguished into certain categories based on the four major usage groups (that is, color dyeing cotton, fine cotton stripe, gray dyeing cotton, and raw cotton stripe) and further subcategories (for instance, gray dyeing cotton is further classified into dark coloring usage and light coloring usage).

2. *Defining the inputs and outputs.* The inputs into the models should be a vector of real numbers that contain the quality information obtained from the HVI testing, dyeability testing, and three-fiber testing of each cotton bale. To increase the efficiency of the computation and performance of the model, not all of the quality parameters in the HVI testing (especially those that have no influence in the classification process) should be included in the model. Selection of such parameters should be based on the judgment of the textile engineers and refined during the testing stage of the software.

Output from the SVM network should be an integer that classifies the type to which a certain cotton bale belongs.

3. *Algorithm variables.* Several variables have to be played with during the design process to optimize performance of the algorithms:

   - Kernel functions
   - Scaling of the data
   - Parameters in the objective function and kernel functions
   - Quality information included in the input set

4. *Training sets.* A minimum of one thousand sets of data are recommended for the algorithm learning process. Seventy percent of the data will be used for training the model, and the rest will be used for testing.

A handy and practical guide for implementing SVMs (with reference to the software LIBSVM) can be found at a Web site launched by Chih-Chung Chang and Chih-Jen Lin of the National Taiwan University: http://www.csie.ntu.edu.tw/~cjlin/libsvm. Free and commercial software packages are readily available to do the work. (See http://www.ece.umn .edu/groups/ece8591/software/svm.html#Background%20Information and http://www.csie.ntu.edu.tw/~cjlin/libsvm for free downloads of such packages.)

Nearest Neighbor Algorithm

The nearest neighbor method is a statistical classification model that can function primarily as a lookup, or search, tool. The advantage of using this method is its computational efficiency, which translates to speed in use. However, the key disadvantage of this method is that it relies on certain key assumptions; these will be discussed shortly.

The basic idea behind this method is that given a collection of past data, we can classify objects on the basis of objects that are similar to them historically. *The Algorithm Design Manual* provides a good example of this method.[3] Suppose we are given a collection of data about people (say age, height, weight, years of education, gender, and income level), each of whom has been labeled Democrat or Republican. We seek a classifier to decide which way a particular person is likely to vote. Each of the people in our data set is represented by a party-labeled point in D-dimensional space. A simple classifier can be built by assigning to the new point the party affiliation of its nearest neighbor.

For the problem of heather yarn process planning, we can use the method in a reverse manner from the preceding example. Here the processing of heather yarn orders is considered in depth. White yarn process planning presumably can be done in a similar fashion simply by removing the coloring element of the problem. Given a classification—in this case, the desired color—the system could determine the parameters, which would be the different cottons required to produce this color.

Historical data exist regarding heather yarn process planning. It is safe to assume that yarns of a particular color are typically produced in a similar fashion. Figure 5.7 illustrates this assumption in simplified form. In the example presented in the figure, there are only two types of intermediate parts in inventory ($x1$ and $x2$) to create yarn and only three colors are produced: red, yellow, and blue. The clusters of points signify historical mixtures of $x1$ and $x2$ that have resulted in the colors of the intermediate part. Because all red yarns, for instance, are produced in a similar manner, the points representing red yarn production are clustered together. The same holds true of yellow and blue yarn.

Each cluster or classification of data can be represented by a single point. The single point can be the center point in a cluster or the average of all points in the cluster, or it can be taken at random (which is the preferred approach). When a new order comes in for a particular color, the process planning reduces the order to a simple optimization problem to find a point the minimal distance away from the representative value given inventory levels. Using the case in which an order for red yarn comes in, the problem to solve is as follows:

$$\text{Min}(x_R - x)^T(x_R - x)$$
$$\text{s.t. } 0 \le x_i \le z_i \text{ for all } i$$

Here x is the output vector of cottons to use and z is the vector of cotton inventory levels.

Existing variations of this algorithm take into account more of the data. For example, a handful of points can be kept to represent each classification, and the single point used for comparison can be chosen at

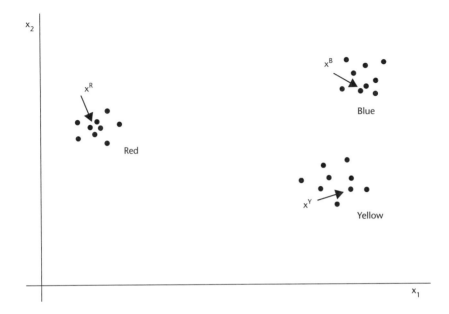

Figure 5.7   Example of nearest neighbor classification

random each time an order comes in. Using the same point repeatedly could deplete certain cotton stocks in inventory, and having multiple representative points would avoid this. The K-nearest neighbor algorithm, which is the same algorithm but takes into account the value of the K-nearest neighbors in the minimization problem rather than just one neighbor, is another variation. Also, error in the nearest neighbor algorithm can be limited by setting a maximum distance that the output can be from its neighbor. If the distance computed is too great, the algorithm does not return a solution.

The example presented here, which clusters historical data solely on the basis of color, is for illustrative purposes only. The actual situation for Esquel will have more than two inventory variables with quality information considered. For example, there may exist a high-quality red yarn cluster as well as medium- and low-quality red yarn clusters.

Nothing fits the problem better than this solution. Process planning is simply a mapping process based on historical data; this procedure takes Esquel's previous approach and fortifies it through automation. In addition, nearest neighbor is computationally inexpensive, running in fixed constant time, even as the complexity and number of order types grow. Hand in hand with this is the incredible scalability of the process. Handling new order types is as simple as defining a new cluster and providing several instances of order specifications.

Assumptions

One assumption on which this solution for yarn process planning rests is that different colors of yarn are created in nearly the same way. If there are very different ways of creating any particular color, the historical data will not cluster neatly. Figure 5.8 shows an example of a situation in which the algorithm would have trouble. Here there are two distinct clusters of red. In this situation, the color red could perhaps be divided into two subcategories so that the algorithm would work, but such a solution will not be possible in all situations.

Another assumption is that historical data on yarn process planning do exist and that for any given order the color ordered has been encountered before. If an entirely new color yarn is ordered, the nearest neighbor lookup will not work and the old manual means of process planning will have to be used. However, once the data surrounding this color are recorded, the system will remember how to create the color.

Implementation

Four steps are suggested for the implementation of the nearest neighbor algorithm in the heather yarn process planning problem. Before these steps are presented, however, one extremely important note must be made regarding implementation: for the algorithm to work correctly, everything must be entered and recorded for one unit. This means that past data will need to be scaled for one unit (such as 1 kilogram) and orders will need to be entered with one unit in mind. Inventory will also need to be scaled. A suitable way to do this is to divide all inventory quantities by the order quantity desired. After the algorithm processes the order and returns an output, the output can be rescaled to the original yarn quantity desired.

1. *Determine all relevant variables.* The suggested variables are as follows:

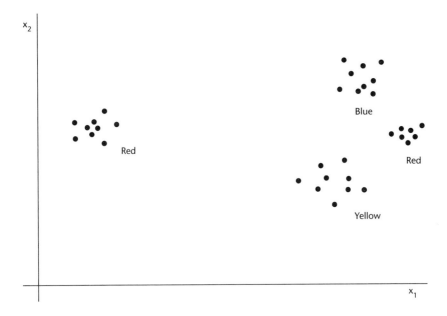

Figure 5.8   Potentially problematic nearest neighbor situation

- Inventory levels
- Desired color (this acts as the classifier)
- Amount of yarn desired, for scaling purposes

2. *Encode the algorithm input.* We propose that the input be encoded as follows:

   - N-vector of real numbers describing inventory levels, where N is the number of different types of dyed cotton in inventory. (This N-vector must be scaled for the one-unit representation.)
   - Encoded value for the desired color and quality (a unique integer value for each color and quality combination, for example).

3. *Collect data.* The historical data concerning yarn process planning is critical for the algorithm to fulfill its lookup functionality and reference old data. Historical data can be stored in the form of its encoded color value along with the N-vector of cottons used in the processing of the order scaled to one unit. If a particular

type of cotton, i, in inventory was not used at all, the i-value of the vector will be 0.

4. Develop the system and test. Several packages including tools for nearest neighbor analysis are available online and can be adapted for implementation. One of them is the MLC++ machine learning library. The advantage of using an existing package is that it saves implementation time and is already proven to work.

Alternatively, Esquel could build its own tool that solves the minimization problem. As an output, the tool would give an N-vector of the cottons in inventory to use (again with 0 indicating that a particular element in the vector is not used). An ideal tool would give several outputs, based on different neighbors used. As brand-new colors are ordered, these color points should be added to the data set for future use. Accuracy in general can be improved by adding data from new orders processed to the data set. This is especially true for orders in which the system returns an error; entering the correct data will force the system to avoid the same error in the future. The algorithm will likely need data management to ensure that incorrect points are not entered or that points that are throwing off the output as a whole are removed.

The last step of the algorithm is to rescale the output vector to reflect the size of the order, because the algorithm will be working on one-unit quantities. Another useful step here would be for the process planning system to send the amounts of inventory required to the inventory system for complete synchronization.

Clustering Through Neural Networks

Clustering

Clustering is a way of grouping data such that the data within a cluster are relatively homogeneous and the data among clusters are heterogeneous. Basically this means that clustering (or fuzzy clustering) is the segmenting of things into similar groups. Clustering does not require a priori information about the classes. The algorithm will learn from the data alone the appropriate number of clusters into which to segment the data set. If we use cluster analysis (widely known as unsupervised learning), the beauty is that we do not need to tell the computer what our outputs should be. We just let the model run through all our training data and identify how these data should be grouped together. This means that in the future the cotton may no longer be classified into four categories but into N categories, in which each type has its own distinguishing feature that may perhaps facilitate the cotton mix design process.

Mitchell Tseng, professor at Hong Kong University of Science and Technology, recommended that we give fuzzy clustering serious thought and research its applications. Indeed, there is good historical precedence for fuzzy clustering. Volterra, a U.K. consulting firm, has done several large-scale projects using fuzzy clustering, including segmenting U.K. geography by social and demographic characteristics to determine which locations are like other locations. They also applied a similar technique to segment universities in the United Kingdom.

We are making three assumptions here:

1. It is assumed that the cotton quality information is enough to classify the bales, yet there may be other factors that are visual or experiential.
2. Fuzzy clustering is considered new and cutting edge; another way to say this is that it has a short track record.
3. It is assumed that fuzzy clustering doesn't generalize to new types without retraining.

Several software packages are available to do the underlying work:

- MLC++ is a Stanford-made machine learning for C++ package.
- There are MatLab modules, such as Fuzzy Logic Toolbox and S-PLUS.

It is important that the clustering information be portable so that the definition of clusters from this part can be used to aid in the order classification problem.

Neural Networks

Artificial neural networks are massively parallel computing mechanisms modeled after the biological brain. They consist of nodes linked by weighted connections. Neural networks learn relationships between input and output vectors by iteratively changing interconnecting weight values until the outputs of the problem domain represent the desired relationship.

Neural networks are noted for their ability to perform with incomplete and noisy data, and for their ability to generalize their learned representations to handle new circumstances. This last quality makes neural networks an attractive tool for process planning in which each new product is likely to differ somewhat from past ones.

Feed-Forward, Back-Propagation Neural Network. The feed-forward, back-propagation neural network architecture was developed in the early 1970s by several independent sources (Werbor, Parker, Rumelhart, Hinton, and Williams). This independent co-development was the result of a proliferation of articles and talks at various conferences that stimulated the entire industry. Currently, this synergistically developed back-propagation architecture is the most popular, effective, and easy-to-learn model for complex, multilayered networks. It is used more than all other models combined and in many different types of applications. This architecture has spawned a large class of network types with many different topologies and training methods. Its greatest strength is in nonlinear solutions to ill-defined problems.

The typical back-propagation network has an input layer, an output layer, and at least one hidden layer. There is no theoretical limit to the number of hidden layers, but typically there is just one or two. Some work has been done that indicates that a minimum of four layers (three hidden layers plus an output layer) is required to solve problems of any complexity. Each layer is fully connected to the succeeding layer.

The in and out layers indicate the flow of information during recall. Recall is the process of putting input data into a trained network and receiving the answer. Back-propagation is not used during recall, but only when the network is learning a training set.

The number of layers and the number of processing elements per layer are important decisions. These parameters of a feed-forward, back-propagation topology are also its most ethereal elements. They are the art of the network designer. There is no quantifiable, best answer to the layout of the network for any particular application. There are only general rules that have been picked up over time and followed by most researchers and engineers applying this architecture to their problems.

How Neural Networks Differ from Traditional Computing and Expert Systems. Traditional computing methods work well for problems that can be well characterized. They can process data, track inventories, network results, and protect equipment. Balancing checkbooks, keeping ledgers, and keeping tabs on inventory are well-defined tasks and do not require the special characteristics of neural networks.

Expert systems are an extension of traditional computing and are sometimes called the fifth generation of computing. First-generation computing used switches and wires. The second generation occurred because of the development of the transistor. The third generation involved solid-state technology, the use of integrated circuits, and higher-level languages like COBOL, Fortran, and "C." End-user tools, or code generators, are known as the fourth generation. The fifth generation involves artificial intelligence.

Typically, an expert system consists of two parts, an inference engine and a knowledge base. The inference engine is generic. It handles the user interface, external files, program access, and scheduling. The knowledge base contains the information that is specific to a particular problem. This knowledge base allows an expert to define the rules that govern a process. The expert does not have to understand traditional programming. He simply has to understand both what he wants a computer to do and how the mechanism of the expert system shell works. It is this shell, part of the inference engine, that actually tells the computer how to implement the expert's desires. This implementation occurs by the expert system generating the computer's programming itself; it does that through programming of its own. This programming is needed to establish the rules for a particular application. This method of establishing rules is also complex and requires a detail-oriented person.

Efforts to make expert systems general have run into a number of problems. As the complexity of the system increases, the system simply demands too many computing resources and becomes too slow. Expert systems have been found to be feasible only when narrowly confined.

Artificial neural networks offer a completely different approach to problem solving and are sometimes called the sixth generation of computing. They try to provide a tool that both programs itself and learns on its own. Neural networks are structured to provide the capability to solve problems without the benefits of an expert and without the need of programming. They can seek patterns in data that no one knows are there.

Neural networks offer the opportunity of solving problems in an arena where traditional processors lack both the processing power and a step-by-step methodology.

Assumptions and Implementation of Neural Networks. We make the following assumptions:

- Neural networks do not lead to greater understanding of the underlying structure.
- They are computationally expensive as both nodes and input size grow.
- They use a data set that includes the information that can characterize the problem.
- The data set is adequately sized both to train and to test the network.
- Neural networks understand the basic nature of the problem to be solved so that basic first-cut decisions on creating the network can be made. These decisions include the activation and transfer functions and the learning methods.
- Neural networks have adequate processing power.

Designing a feed-forward neural network is more of an art than a science. You have to play around with the number of hidden layers and number of nodes in each hidden layer to optimize performance. Here some of the major implementation choices are explored.

There are several variables that will affect computation time:

- Number of hidden layers (HL)
- Number of nodes per HL
- Number of inputs

What the input and output should be is an important question without any one solution. There are several approaches. The one suggested for Esquel is to input the available number of bales (and associated information such as cost and quality) per cotton type and order size. The outputs should be the number of bales of each type required for the order.

The key is to divide and classify the cotton rigorously enough to have good performance. That may mean that more than the four existing classifications are needed. The number of such clusters, k, can be determined only by practice (see the previous discussion of clustering).

Training an Artificial Neural Network. Once a network has been structured for a particular application, it is ready to be trained. To start this process, the initial weights are chosen randomly. Then the training, or learning, begins.

There are two approaches to training—supervised and unsupervised. Supervised training involves a mechanism of providing the network with the desired output either by manually grading the network's performance or by providing the desired outputs with the inputs. Unsupervised training is where the network has to make sense of the inputs without outside help.

In supervised training, both the inputs and the outputs are provided. The network processes the inputs and compares its outputs against the desired outputs. Errors are then propagated back through the system, causing the system to adjust the weights that control the network. This process occurs as the weights are continually tweaked. The set of data that enables the training is called the training set. During the training of a network, the same set of data is processed many times as the connection weights are continually refined.

The current commercial network development packages provide tools to monitor how well an artificial neural network is converging on the ability to predict the right answer. These tools allow the training process to go on for days, stopping only when the system reaches some statistically desired point or level of accuracy. However, some networks never learn. This could be because the input data do not contain the specific information from which the desired output is derived. Networks also do not converge if there are not enough data to enable complete learning. Ideally there should be enough data so that part of the data can be held back as a test. Many layered networks with multiple nodes are capable of memorizing data. To monitor the network in order to determine if the system is simply memorizing its data in some insignificant way, supervised training needs to hold back a set of data to be used to test the system after it has undergone its training. (Note: memorization is avoided by not having too many processing elements.)

In unsupervised training, the network is provided with inputs but not with desired outputs. The system itself must then decide what features it will use to group the input data. This is often referred to as self-organization or adaptation. Unsupervised learning is recommended for the Esquel solution because it will provide the best generalization and incremental performance improvements with time.

Cost-Benefit Analysis of RFID Implementation

As mentioned before, the cotton quality information at Esquel's mill is currently at lot level, which is an average-based result obtained from sample testing. In the near future, cotton quality information will be embedded in an RFID tag in each cotton bale. With the help of RFID technology, Esquel can get more accurate and detailed cotton quality information in almost real time. This increased information visibility brings the production planning of spinning from the current lot level to bale level, which brings more benefits to the whole apparel manufacturing process. Two types of benefits, namely, cost savings and product quality improvements, are analyzed here, with the following hypothesis: With cotton information moving from lot level to bale level, production process planning (cotton mix decisions) can be improved by better utilizing the inventory of higher-quality cotton through improved cotton quality differentiation, so that material costs can be reduced and product quality improved.

To demonstrate the benefits quantitatively, two simulation models were built based on some reasonable assumptions and optimization models.

Assumptions

The two simulation models were built with different problem scales. However, they share some common assumptions:

- Because there are at least eleven quality attributes (such as neps, which are entangled pieces of immature fiber that do not dye properly; cotton fiber length; Micronaire, a quantification of fiber fineness or thickness; trash, including seeds and stems; and grade), to simplify the model only four major quality attributes—referred to in this discussion as A, B, C, and D—are considered here.
- The quality attribute values follow a normal distribution. The cotton quality is assumed to vary from lot to lot and also from bale to bale. The value of each quality attribute follows normal distribution. On the basis of practical experience, it is also assumed that the quality variation within one cotton lot (bale-to-bale variation) is smaller than the variation between lots.
- Cotton cost is positively proportional to its quality.

Table 5.3
Available cotton quality information used in simulation

Lot number	Quality attribute				Average Cost	Quantity (80)
	A	B	C	D		
Lot 1	$13.48	$13.76	$14.70	$13.94	$13.97	10
Lot 2	$5.39	$4.53	$4.86	$4.99	$4.94	10
Lot 3	$10.50	$11.73	$10.03	$11.97	$11.06	10
Lot 4	$7.81	$7.25	$6.84	$7.12	$7.26	10
Lot 5	$10.22	$10.79	$10.58	$10.57	$10.54	10
Lot 6	$2.93	$2.15	$4.11	$3.22	$3.10	10
Lot 7	$15.17	$13.97	$14.35	$13.00	$14.12	10
Lot 8	$6.87	$6.15	$7.17	$6.59	$6.70	10
Mean	$9.05	$8.79	$9.08	$8.93		
Std. deviation	$4.10	$4.40	$4.03	$3.97		

- Yarn order is specified in terms of the quantity and the cotton quality requirements (value of the four major cotton quality attributes).

Using these assumptions, two sets of data were randomly generated for use in simulation. One set of data, about the cotton quality information, contains information about eight lots of cotton. Each lot contains ten bales of cotton with one unit weight per bale. The data were generated by the following procedures: First, the costs of the cotton lots were randomly generated following normal distribution, with mean equal to $10 and standard deviation equal to 4. After that, within each lot the attribute values were generated following the normal distribution, with the mean equal to its lot cost and variance equal to 2. It was assumed that these attribute values had the same scale and were independent and identically distributed (i.i.d.) variables, that is, A, B, C, D Norm (μ = cost, σ = 2). Finally, the lot quality information is just the average values of its cotton bales. (See Table 5.3.)

Another data set is about the incoming orders and their specifications. As with the previous data set, the four quality attributes in an order are assumed to be i.i.d variables following uniform distribution. The order quantity is a random number following normal distribution. Detailed data are shown in Table 5.4.

Table 5.4
Order specifications used in the simulation

| Order | Quality attribute | | | | Quantity |
number	A	B	C	D	(23)
Order 1	$9.42	$8.20	$9.12	$6.40	3
Order 2	$6.06	$6.85	$9.13	$10.83	2
Order 3	$12.84	$6.34	$10.09	$12.38	3
Order 4	$10.56	$11.67	$13.05	$13.26	2
Order 5	$9.45	$10.51	$9.44	$8.42	2
Order 6	$6.58	$7.49	$6.44	$7.61	3
Order 7	$9.84	$12.28	$9.22	$12.38	2
Order 8	$4.43	$5.94	$3.71	$7.25	4
Order 9	$10.08	$6.74	$10.46	$10.38	2
Mean	$8.81	$8.45	$8.96	$9.88	
Std. deviation	$2.61	$2.41	$2.61	$2.53	

A Simple Model

In the first model, a simplified case is considered to demonstrate the general idea. Three cotton lots are considered as available cotton inventory, and three orders are considered as incoming orders. Two situations were considered. In the first situation, only cotton lot information was available (average value of the bale information); in the second situation, cotton bale information was considered. Attempts were made in both situations to determine the cotton mix recipe in order to fulfill the order specifications and compare the cost and quality that resulted in both situations.

In order to make optimal decisions on the cotton mix recipe, an optimization model was formulated to minimize the material usage cost with quality consideration.

$$\min \sum_j c^T X_j$$

$$\text{s.t. } I^T X_j = s_j \tag{1}$$

$$q_n^T X_j \mid s_j - q r_{jn} \geq \alpha \tag{2}$$

$$\sum_j X_j \leq Z \tag{3}$$

$$X_j \geq 0 \tag{4}$$

In the model, X_j is the decision variable, a vector specifying the cotton mix recipe for order j. The length of the vector depends on the number of lots or bales of cotton in the inventory. For example, one recipe in the lot situation could be $X_1 = (0.5, 0.8, 0, 0, 0, 0, 0, 0)$, which means that this is a recipe for order 1; there are a total of 8 lots in the inventory; and it mixes 0.5 units of cotton from lot 1, 0.8 units from lot 2, and the rest 0).

c is the material cost vector.

s_j is the order size of order j.

q_n is the quality attribute value of attribute n, $n = 1, 2, 3, 4$ (four quality attributes).

qr_{jn} is the required quality value of attribute n for order j.

Z is a vector specifying inventory status.

α is a quality consideration parameter.

Constraint 1 in the model ensures that the demand is fulfilled. Constraint 2 makes sure that the product quality is guaranteed. The left-hand side of the inequality is the difference between the planned quality attribute values and the order specified values. The right-hand side of the inequality is a quality consideration parameter, α. If $\alpha = 0$, this constraint will guarantee that the quality of the recipe found must be greater or equal to the quality requirements specified by the order. The higher the α value is set, the higher will be the guaranteed quality of the planning result. Constraint 3 simply means that the cotton used must not exceed the inventory capacity.

The results of adopting this optimization model for both the lot and bale situations are shown in Table 5.5. The table shows the trade-off between product quality and cost. When quality is similar ($\alpha = 0$), the bale

Table 5.5
Simulation result: Simple model

Lot	Bale	Cost Savings
$\alpha = 0$	$\alpha = 0$	20.9%
$\alpha = 0$	$\alpha = 1$	11.8%
$\alpha = 0$	$\alpha = 2.2$	0.3%

situation offers a 20 percent cost savings. When product quality is improved by setting $\alpha = 1$, which forces the quality of the product higher than the quality required, the cost savings is still nearly 12 percent. And when the tradeoff is examined by setting the cost of the bale situation equal to that of the lot situation, we get $\alpha = 2.2$, which is a high quality standard for the end product.

By comparing the cotton mix recipes generated by the model, we found out that cost savings and quality improvements come from better usage of some higher-quality cotton bales that belong to the cheaper lots. This proves the hypothesis that better information visibility will create chances of better utilization of high-quality cottons.

A Complex Model

A more reality-based and complex model is now considered. This model assumes three weeks of planning-time horizon. Each week, two lots of cotton will be delivered to the factory and three orders will arrive and be fulfilled. The planning is done iteratively. The inventory level at the end of the previous week serves as an input (starting inventory point) to the next planning horizon.

One important assumption is made in this model. In the bale situation it is assumed that half of the next week's cotton arrivals can be considered the inventory and be incorporated into the planning optimization model along with the current cotton inventory. This assumption is based on the fact that after RFID implementation, cotton quality information will be known even before actual arrival, and therefore some lots (if not all, depending on the delivery lead time) can be considered during the planning.

The same optimization model developed in the previous case was used and the planning was done iteratively until the three weeks of orders were fulfilled. Again, the α value is set to 0 for the lot situation and to 1 for the bale situation. The simulation results for two situations are shown and compared in Table 5.6.

The results show that the cost savings is changing along with the time and depends on the incoming orders and the qualities of raw materials. Still, a total of 8 percent cost savings can be achieved with higher quality guaranteed ($\alpha = 1$).

Table 5.6
Simulation result: Complex model

Week	Cost		Cost savings
	Lot ($\alpha = 0$)	Lot ($\alpha = 1$)	
Week 1	89.75	76.64	14.6%
Week 2	68.56	66.73	2.7%
Week 3	71.26	67.69	5.0%
Week 4	229.57	211.06	8.06%

The graphs in Figures 5.9, 5.10, and 5.11 show the meaning of "higher quality guaranteed." The graphs on the left in each figure show the difference between planned quality and required quality of the order with the constraint parameter, where $\alpha = 0$ (lot situation). Accordingly, the graphs on the right in each figure are the planned result in the bale situation, where $\alpha = 1$. The heights of the columns in the left-hand graphs are much more inconsistent than the ones on the right. This indicates that after changing bale level, the product quality is improved in terms of quality standards and quality consistency.

Discussion and Conclusion

The implementation of RFID at the spinning mill level benefits Esquel not only by improving that individual process, but also by setting the scene for additional RFID implementation throughout the company. RFID tracking provides application opportunities in inventory management, resource allocation, labor productivity, quality control, product tracking, and asset utilization. In each of these areas, RFID use holds the promise of reduced costs.

In summary, the integration of RFID technology into the spinning mills provides an opportunity to improve Esquel's current methods of cotton usage classification and yarn production process planning. This case has justified the use of the SVM and Nearest Neighbor algorithms for these two processes, respectively. The cost-benefit analysis shows that implementation of these two algorithms to improve the processes will result in a reduction in materials costs and an improvement in yarn quality.

However, as RFID helps to improve supply chain efficiency and gives

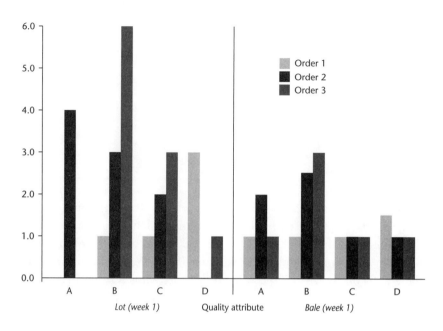

Figure 5.9   Week one quality fulfillment (lot vs. bale)

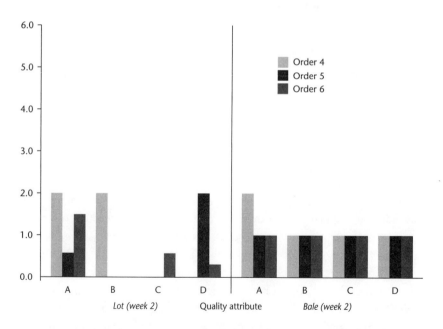

Figure 5.10   Week two quality fulfillment (lot vs. bale)

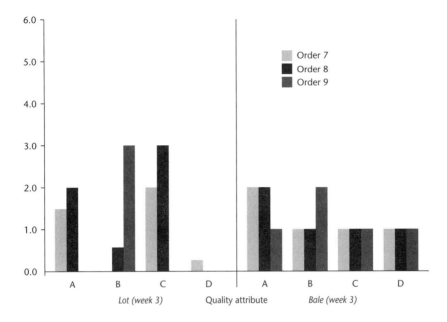

Figure 5.11   Week three quality fulfillment (lot vs. bale)

Esquel competitive advantages, RFID has also created a data deluge. Initially, cotton was tracked in terms of lot, but with RFID, cotton is tracked in terms of bale. Obviously, as more cotton information is captured, it will lead to a tradeoff: more labor-intensive data analysis will be demanded, which means that more experienced operators will be required for decision making. Further implementation will require Esquel to develop data management strategies that will integrate the data with Esquel's existing practice in a systematic and automated manner.

Case 2: The Esquel Group—Production Wastage Forecasting

Industry Overview

The worldwide garment industry is a US$226 billion industry that has seen tremendous growth through the years. With the exception of 2001, there has been growth in the world trade of clothing since 1980, and this growth is expected to continue into the future.[4] Hong Kong is a major player in the clothing industry, with US$23.15 billion of clothing exported in 2003 (second in the world only to China in terms of clothing exports).[5] In 2002, clothing and accessories represented 49.7 percent of Hong Kong's exports, the largest portion of manufacturing exports.[6] Table 5.7 details the HK$ (Hong Kong dollars) value and growth percentage of domestic exports and re-exports in Hong Kong for 2002, 2003, and January through September of 2004.

As a major sector in Hong Kong, the clothing industry is the largest employer for manufacturing jobs, with more than sixteen hundred companies employing more than thirty thousand people.[7]

Government Regulations

On January 1, 2005, the World Trade Organization (WTO) finally terminated the Agreement on Textiles and Clothing (ATC). ATC replaced the Multifibre Arrangement (MFA) in January 1995 and set out a transitional process for the ultimate elimination of the quota system described by the MFA. The Multifibre Arrangement is a piece of U.S. legislation established in 1974 mainly to protect the United States' feeble garment industry. It limits the amount of garments each textile-manufacturing country can export. Developing nations, including China and India, whose competitive advantages are cost and abundance of labor, found that the MFA significantly affected the growth of their garment industry. Hence, they demanded removal of the quotas. An agreement was made in 1994 that called for the incremental phaseout of the quota system and its final termination in 2005.

Unexpectedly, since it came into force the quota system had also encouraged other developing countries to start their own garment industries, because other, stronger players were also working under imposed

Table 5.7
Hong Kong clothing exports 2002 through September 2004

	2002		2003		Jan.–Sept. 2004	
	Value HK$ billion	Growth %	Value HK$ billion	Growth %	Value HK$ billion	Growth %
Domestic Exports	65.04	–10	63.88	–2	45.50	–3
Re-exports of Chinese	109.91	–1	116.48	+6	96.83	+12
mainland origin	*98.53*	*–3*	*103.80*	*+5*	*87.19*	*+13*
Total Exports	174.95	–4	180.36	+3	142.33	+6

quotas. In a quota-free market, these countries and their budding garment industries would find it very difficult to compete in huge, profitable markets like Europe, Japan, and the United States.

With the quota system in place, purchasers including large retailers like Wal-Mart, J.Crew, the Gap, and JCPenney were compelled to buy ready-made garments and textiles from a long list of countries rather than just a few. This definitely helped boost the initial growth of garment industries in developing countries.

The quota cancellation signifies productivity liberation for major textile-manufacturing countries, including China. With its 1.3 billion population and some of the lowest wages in the world, China is forecasted to dominate the market. WTO predicts that China's share of the U.S. apparel market will grow by 30 percent.

Elimination of the quota system has brought great opportunity to China's textile industry, particularly in exports. The limits on its productivity are relaxed and have resulted in a rapid expansion of potential markets for Chinese manufacturers. Because of the MFA, Chinese textile manufacturers had been operating at undercapacity and their advantages in cost and quality had been limited. However, export of Chinese textiles and ready-made garments has been increasing along with the incremental phaseout of the quota system.

In addition, China is now in the spotlight. More and more overseas capital and advanced technology are attracted to China. This encourages Chinese textiles and garment enterprises to cooperate with overseas companies, which in turn enhances the development of the Chinese textile and garment industry in technology, quality, brand, and management.

However, the benefit for China brought about by the quota cancellation is not as big as expected. In reality, there are more complex challenges and barriers facing Chinese textile and garment export.

First, world garment production is overmuch. Excessive competition is unavoidable, especially during periods of quota cancellation and slow growth in the world economy. Second, many countries are introducing alternative protective measures to protect their own garment industries against China. In the meantime, limits are still imposed on Chinese textile and garment exports. China has agreed to restrict the export growth of relative products to 7.5 percent (of wool products to 6 percent) until December 31, 2008, upon the request of a number of countries. The Especial Product Transitional Guarantee System described in the sixteenth article of "China Enter WTO" stipulates that an importing country can set limits to Chinese products until 2013 if Chinese exports create threats in the importing country.[8] In particular, the U.S. textile industry has pressured the Bush administration to consider setting up strict limits on a dozen categories of imports from China. This could result in a reimposition of the quota system on China. Like their counterparts in the United States, Mexico's textile manufacturers are compelling the Mexican government to start a multination lawsuit against China at the WTO. An even stronger defense has been set up by the Dominican Republic and five countries in Central America. A preliminary Central American Free Trade Agreement (CAFTA) has been signed by these nations and the United States. The United States is considering increasing the number of imported textiles and garments for which tariffs have been eliminated from 16 percent to 36 percent if yarn or cloth from the United States or locally made fabric is used. These imports would have an edge over garments subjected to tariffs. Meanwhile, these countries are waiting for CAFTA to be approved by the United States.

Last but not least, international trade barriers are alternative ways for developed nations to protect their own garment industries and control garment imports from China. Tariff barriers, among other trade obstacles, will be the major trade protection measure utilized by developed countries. Other methods include technological barriers, antidumping laws, green barriers, and anti-allowance measures.

According to Edward Leung, chief economist of the Trade Development Council of Hong Kong, the termination of the MFA is having a strong spillover impact on Hong Kong textile and garment manufacturers who possess production facilities in China.

Hong Kong is in an excellent position to tap the growing domestic market since China's accession to the WTO and the subsequent liberation of China's retail, wholesale, and import-export trade. China's WTO reforms have generated and will continue to generate a sizeable class of affluent consumers. This, together with the wide acceptance and popularity of Hong Kong–branded apparel targeting the medium to high end of the China market, presents numerous opportunities for Hong Kong garment manufacturers.

To further leverage the existing strongholds, Hong Kong garment manufacturers should consider regions other than the Pearl River Delta for setting up their production facilities. Zhejiang, Jiangsu, Shanghai, Liaoning, and Shandong are good candidates due to their proximity to the burgeoning markets along the coast. In addition, Hong Kong enterprises should also consider partnering with local companies to better understand the needs of Chinese customers and the local distribution system.

As for capturing a larger share of the overseas market, is strongly recommended that Hong Kong manufacturers expand their production bases in China to take full advantage of the high cost efficiency. Furthermore, the reduction in Chinese tariff rates enables Hong Kong companies to achieve additional cost savings by importing fabrics for manufacturing in China.

Hong Kong manufacturers should strive to improve cost effectiveness, creativity, quality of delivery, and customer service, and to differentiate themselves from their competitors in China.[9]

The Esquel Group

The Esquel Group, introduced in the previous case, was established in 1978 and is one of the world's largest and leading producers of premium cotton shirts. The Group currently employs more than forty-three hundred people worldwide and has production facilities in China, Malaysia, Vietnam, Mauritius, and Sri Lanka, and a network of branches servicing key markets worldwide. It produces shirts with total sales up to US$500 million per year.

The degree of vertical integration adopted by Esquel makes it unusual in the industry. The production process at Esquel is fully integrated in that its operations encompass everything from cotton farming, spinning, dyeing, weaving, knitting, cutting, sewing, washing garments, producing accessories, and finishing and packaging its products and distributing them to customers.

Being a full-service provider or a one-stop-shop vertical supply chain gives Esquel direct control over the lead time and the quality of its products and enables it to react to customer needs more efficiently. This makes Esquel unique among its competitors. In addition, Esquel sources certain raw materials, accessories, labels, and packaging from a large number of suppliers.

Through its vertical integration, Esquel is able to provide better service to its customers. Customers' time and money are saved because they no longer need to be involved in the procurement of component parts or finished products. Esquel is their one source for everything.[10]

Since Esquel is a vertically integrated company, its competitors are both fabric and garment manufacturers. As with Esquel, many of these competitors operate across many nations. Table 5.8 lists some of the major competitors and describes them.

Esquel's products are sold around the world. Their main markets are the United States, Europe, and Japan. Esquel has built an impressive customer profile, including some of the world's best-known fashion names, such as Hugo Boss and Abercrombie & Fitch. See Table 5.9 for more of Esquel's customers from around the world.

Esquel's unique vertically integrated supply chain structure ensures the highest quality in every step of the apparel manufacturing process. Esquel controls every step of the supply chain from the production of cotton to finished garments. It has its own cotton field in Xinjiang Province to supply the raw material and its own factories around the world to do spinning, weaving, dyeing, manufacturing, and packaging. Esquel also has its own brand for retailing.

In addition, Esquel pays a lot of attention to technology. It has been investing heavily in technology and applying state-of-the-art technology to improve its manufacturing. It also has its own research and development center to create unique garments with wrinkle-free and nanotechnology performance qualities that consistently put Esquel on the cutting edge in the apparel industry.

Table 5.8
Esquel's competitors

Type	Company	Description
Garment	TAL Apparel Ltd. (Hong Kong)	TAL Apparel owns its main garment supply factories with production located in Hong Kong, Taiwan, Thailand, Malaysia, Indonesia, and China. The company also has a garment factory in Mexico and a spinning and weaving mill in North Carolina. TAL deals with external suppliers that provide such items as fabric, thread, garment pieces, buttons, and zippers. TAL's buyers are mainly in the United States, to which 80 percent of production is exported.
	Luen Tai Garment Co. Ltd. (Hong Kong)	Luen Tai is one of the biggest distributors of polyurethane raw material and also a leading manufacturer specializing in polyurethane products.
	Tristate Holdings Ltd. (Hong Kong)	Tristate's principal activities are manufacturing and trading of garments and textiles. Operations are carried out in Hong Kong, the Philippines, the United States, the People's Republic of China, Taiwan, Thailand, and Union of Myanmar.
	Texwinca Holdings Ltd. (Hong Kong)	Texwinca's principal activities are the production, dyeing, and sale of knitted fabric and yarn; and the retail and distribution of raw fabrics, casual apparel, and accessories. Its production processes are fully vertically integrated with various working functions to offer its customers the choice of a variety of raw fabrics and finished knitted fabrics according to customers' requirements.
	Youngor (China)	Youngor has an integrated framework of textiles and fabrics, ready-to-wears, and retail chains in the field of fabrics and garments.
	Fountain Set (Holdings) Ltd. (Hong Kong)	Fountain Set's principal activities are the production and sale of knitted fabrics, dyed fabrics, and sewing threads and yarns. Other activities include production and sale of garments, cotton spinning, and the provision of knitting, dyeing, printing, and finishing services. It has operation facilities in the People's Republic of China, Sri Lanka, and Indonesia. The group markets its products in Hong Kong, Taiwan, the United States, the People's Republic of China, and the rest of Asia.
Fabric	Lu Thai Textile Co. Ltd. (China)	Lu Thai is the biggest yarn-dyed fabric producer in the world. The group is a textile enterprise of complicated vertical production capacity, including cotton planting, spinning, discharge, weaving, disposal, and clothes making, and is the top shirt yarn-dyed fabric facing material manufacturer with the largest output in the world.

Table 5.9
Esquel's customers

Region	Company	Description
USA	Abercrombie & Fitch	Casual clothing and accesssories for men and women.
	Banana Republic	Casual professional clothing for men and women.
	Brooks Brothers	Business and casual clothing for men and women.
	Eddie Bauer	Outdoor-themed casual wear and accessories for men and women.
	Hugo Boss	Known by the fashion-conscious; designs and licenses clothes, accessories, and fragrances.
	J.Crew	Leading retailer of men's and women's apparel, shoes and accessories.
	Lands' End	Casual clothing for men, women, and children, accessories, footwear, home products and soft luggage.
	Nike	The world's number one shoemaker. Also sells clothes and a line of athletic apparel and equipment.
	Nordstrom	Upscale apparel, shoes, and accessories.
	Tommy Hilfiger	Men's and women's sportswear, children's wear and accessories.
Europe	Marks & Spencer	Based in the U.K. Mid-priced clothing, food, and household items.
Japan	Muji	Focuses on natural and simple design for apparel, accessories, and household items.

Problem Definition and Methodology

A noted problem within Esquel's current manufacturing process is wastage. Wastage is inevitable for several operations due to scrap and fabric quality, for example, and it needs to be taken into consideration in production planning. To do this, a certain amount of extra materials are assigned to the operations to buffer against wastage. The current approach within Esquel for allocating the extra amount of material is experience-based and independent of specific operational situations. The extra amount of fabric is determined by adding a certain percentage of the nominal required amount. Such a uniform approach tends to be too rough and results in unnecessary wastage.

According to information from Esquel, half of its investment goes to material such as fabric and thread. Since fabric contributes to a large amount of material investment, decrease in the wastage of fabric results in an increase in profit. The objective of the research team's project was to find a systematic way to define the driving factors of the wastage level and to develop a wastage standard model for each process. By using a better wastage model, the unnecessary wastage can be reduced. First, a clearer picture of Esquel's current wastage level needed to be obtained.

- *Scope:* Three operations at Esquel's Gaoming garment factory were examined: cutting, sewing, and washing processes. The desired deliverables were as follows:

  1. A list of identified factors and their characterization
  2. Wastage models for each process (cutting, sewing, washing, and additional wastage standard model)
  3. Financial benefits analysis in terms of cost savings
  4. A methodology for application extension

An array of methods was used for the project, including interviews, field study, data collection, and analysis.

- *Interviews*: Staff at Esquel (project manager, production managers, and workers) were interviewed to obtain their requirements and concerns for the project. The interviews provided insights and a solid background on the project so that the project objective could be clearly defined.
- *Field study*: At the start of the project, the current practices of Esquel's garment factory were examined by visiting the garment factory in Gaoming. The manufacturing process within the factory was closely observed. A clear understanding of the manufacturing process was helpful in identifying the driving factors for wastage. Also, data were collected for further analysis.
- *Data analysis*: Data analysis was the core aspect of the project. The general methodology for data analysis was to use statistical methods to identify clusters or patterns within the data based on which wastage drivers could be identified. With the wastage drivers identified, regression methods were used for model construction. The specific techniques used included the following:

  1. *Cause-and-effect analysis.* Cause-and-effect analysis based on Fishbone diagrams was used to list all possible driving factors

for wastage. The diagram gave a well-structured overall picture of the factors in the three processes under consideration.

2. *Process stability and capability analysis.* The process stability and capability analysis was used to determine if the problem was in data or in the process.

3. *Correlation analysis.*

4. *Hypothesis testing.* Because the current wastage standards in the manufacturing process were known, hypothesis testing was utilized to check whether they were aligned with the actual numbers.

5. *ANOVA and regression model.* ANOVA was used to find the significant factors. The linear model resulted from ANOVA analysis, and other regression model analyses were compared with the linear model. In the final model, these were combined.

Analysis

The data set used for analysis consisted of five months of data from the Gaoming factory. These data were collected by the Manufacturing Unit department for each order at various stages of the garment manufacturing process to track a relevant performance matrix. For orders processed during this period, the data contained fields such as order size, fabrication type, fabric allocated, and the wastage amounts in each stage of the process.

The company receives orders from customers. Once the garment type and fabric information are confirmed, the sales department notifies the garment factory to buy fabric for the order. One critical step is determining the right amount of fabric needed. Excessive fabric leads to leftovers and increases costs. Not having enough fabric, on the other hand, leads to unfulfilled customer orders and therefore results in penalty cost, loss of customer goodwill, and reduction in revenue. An accurate forecasting of fabric demand for each order is crucial in the planning phase.

The account (A/C) holder passes order information to the marker room. The marker room adds in cutting and sewing wastage standard numbers and sends a piecegoods purchase order (PPO) and marker yard per dozen (YPD) to the A/C holder. After further consideration of wash-

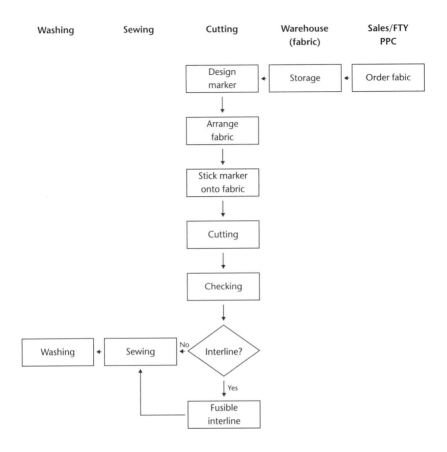

Figure 5.12   Manufacturing process flowchart

ing and additional wastage, the A/C holder calculates a final figure for the fabric order.

In the planning procedure, two kinds of wastage are taken into account: one is cutting and sewing wastage, the other is washing and additional wastage. Cutting and sewing wastage results in wasted fabric, while additional and washing wastage results in the loss of a whole garment.

The process for manufacturing a garment is shown in Figure 5.12 and the major sources of wastage are depicted in Figures 5.13 and 5.14.

Cutting and sewing wastage includes wastage caused by defective fabric and end loss of rolls as well as splice loss when changing rolls in spreading. All these kinds of wastage are influenced by a variety of fac-

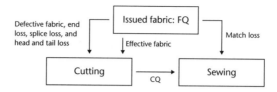

Figure 5.13   Fabric utilization and wastage generation in cutting and sewing department

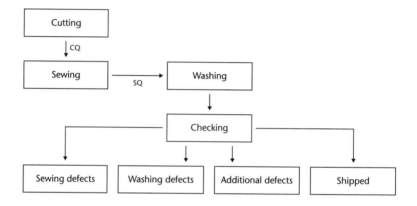

Figure 5.14   Handling of garment in sewing, washing, and checking departments

tors, and the degree to which they are influenced varies from job to job. Sewing and washing wastage includes wastage due to garments with defects such as holes, dirt, or other issues. A quality control process prevents defective garments from being shipped to the customer.

Cutting and sewing wastage is denoted as $c\%$, washing and additional wastage as $w\%$. The fabric purchase order is calculated on the basis of the following equation:

Fabric Order Quantity = ORDER SIZE x Net YPD / $(1 - c\%)$ / $(1 - w\%)$(1)

where ORDER SIZE is the amount (in dozens) ordered by the customer and Net YPD measures the theoretical amount of fabric (in yards) needed to produce one dozen garments.

As can be seen, the two most important parameters in planning fabric order quantity are the wastage levels. As the factory continues to update its manufacturing line to improve efficiency, it is crucial to verify these archaic standards with current factory manufacturing capability and calibrate it to fit the real situation.

Cause-and-Effect Analysis

The first step of the analysis stage is the cause-and-effect analysis. This step allows for the creation of a visual organization of causal relationships in complex ideas or events. Based on observations and an understanding of the operations in the Gaoming factory, a cause-and-effect diagram was constructed to list systematically the possible causes that were attributed to the wastage level, to accumulate existing knowledge about the causal system surrounding the problem, and to group causes.

Five major categories of causes were defined: manpower, measurement, method, material, and management.

Manpower

- *PPC:* The department responsible for ordering fabric

- *Manufacturing department*: The department that produces garments

- *Customer's requirements:* The customer's requirements as to the washing and sewing method and overship or undership allowances

Management

- *Communication between mill and PPC:* Communication between the PPC, which orders the fabric, and the fabric mill, which produces the fabric, is important in the prevention of excessive buffer.

- *Communication between each department and PPC:* Communication between each department and the PPC is critical because each department is responsible for an independent part of the production process. More cooperation between them can improve the accuracy of wastage prediction.

Method

- *Process capability:* Comparison between the output of a stable process and the process specifications and how well the process meets specification.

– *Washing method:* Some washing methods affect the level of washing wastage.

– *Order quantity:* Some wastage results from the trial stage for a specific sewing and washing method. Wastage level varies with order quantity.

Material

– *Fabrication:* Knit and woven. Wastage varies with properties of fabrications.

– *Fabric type:* Checks, solids, and stripes. Workers in the factory employ different methods in handling different fabric types. As a result, wastage levels differ.

– *Fabric color:* Particular care must be taken with white fabric because it gets dirty easily and also turns yellow. If it is not under special care throughout the manufacturing process, wastage level becomes high.

– *Fabric quality:* Fabric quality dominates the variations in fabric defect and garment defect levels. If the fabric quality is poor, wastage will be high.

Measurement

– *Material utilization department:* The department that measures wastage level for each customer order. The method used to measure the wastage level in the manufacturing process is critical for future wastage prediction.

Cause-and-effect (fishbone) diagrams can be found in Figure 5.15 (all wastage level), Figure 5.16 (cutting wastage level), Figure 5.17 (sewing wastage level), and Figure 5.18 (washing wastage level).

The list of potential causes was then used to perform ANOVA analysis on data collected from the previous five months to derive the relationship between driving factors and current problems in wastage prediction.

Process Stability Analysis

Process stability analysis was conducted at the beginning of the analysis process. This analysis served to ensure that there were no trends in

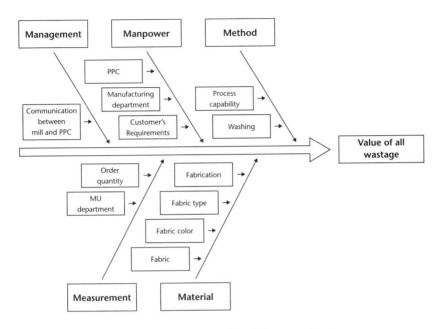

Figure 5.15   The cause-and-effect analysis: Value of all wastage level

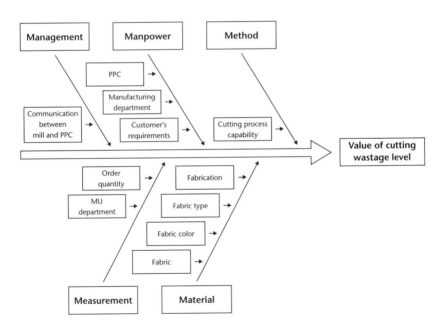

Figure 5.16   The cause-and-effect analysis: Value of cutting wastage level

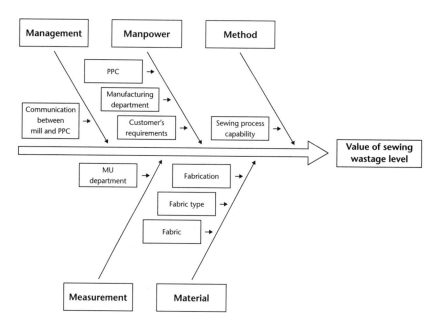

Figure 5.17   The cause-and-effect analysis: Value of sewing wastage level

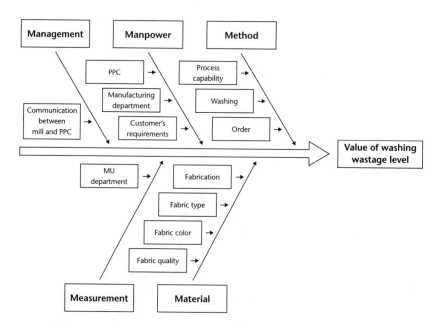

Figure 5.18   The cause-and-effect analysis: Value of washing wastage level

Table 5.10
Analysis of defect combinations

Measured Variables	All	Knit	Woven
Cutting wastage vs. sewing wastage	x	x	x
Cutting wastage vs. washing wastage	x	x	x
Washing wastage vs. sewing wastage	x	x	x
Cutting defect fabric vs. cutting match loss	x	x	x
Cutting defect fabric vs. cutting end loss	x		
Cutting defect fabric vs. cutting splice loss	x		
Cutting match loss vs. cutting end loss	x		
Cutting match loss vs. cutting splice loss	x		
Cutting end loss vs. cutting splice loss	x		

the data over time that would have an effect on the analysis, and that the process was behaving in a predictable manner. By creating a run chart of the wastage levels over time for each order in the data set, it was possible to see that there were no trends despite the variation of the data.

Correlation Analysis

The purpose of this analysis was to identify correlation relationships among all kinds of wastage. Scatter diagrams were rendered to determine if a change in one of the measured variables was associated with a change in another variable. Table 5.10 lists all the combinations analyzed.

The results of scatter diagrams gave a broad understanding of the correlation of the variables. No patterns were observed, which indicated that there was no correlation between any two variables.

Hypothesis Testing

Current wastage standards used in calculation of fabric order quantity can be found in Table 5.11. The objective of the hypothesis testing was to check the validity of using those standards.

For this study,

- H0: optimal wastage level = current standard
- H1: optimal wastage level ≠ current standard

Table 5.11
Current wastage standards

Garment type	Fabric or washing type	Wastage (%)
Cutting and sewing wastage		
Woven	Solid	2.5
Woven	Check	3.0
Woven	Stripe	3.0
Knit	Solid	4.0
Knit	Check	6.0
Knit	Stripe	6.0
Washing and additional wastage		
Woven	Normal garment wash	0.0
Woven	Heavy garment wash	0.5
Woven	Sand wash	1.0
Woven	Bleach wash	3.0
Woven	Stone and bleach wash	3.0
Woven	Chemical wash	3.0
Woven	Chemical stone wash	3.0
Woven	Enzyme wash	1.0
Woven	Destroy wash	3.0
Woven	Wrinkle free	3.0
Woven	Garment dyed	3.0
Woven	Pigment dyed (pigment wash)	5.0
Knit	Normal garment wash	0.5
Knit	Heavy garment wash	1.0
Knit	Sand wash	2.0
Knit	Bleach wash	3.0
Knit	Stone and bleach wash	4.0
Knit	Chemical wash	3.0
Knit	Chemical stone wash	4.0
Knit	Enzyme wash	1.0
Knit	Destroy wash	4.0
Knit	Wrinkle free	—
Knit	Garment dyed	5.0
Knit	Pigment dyed (pigment wash)	5.0

- Confidence level or interval (CI) = 95 percent
- As a common practice, the threshold was set to 5 percent, that is, H0 was rejected for $p < 0.05$ and H0 was not rejected otherwise. (For an explanation of terms used in hypothesis tests, see Table 5.12.)

Hypothesis tests were applied to both cutting and sewing wastage standards and to washing and additional wastage standards. The results of these tests are summarized in Table 5.13.

Due to lack of data, hypothesis tests could not be run for certain washing types. Furthermore, the limited sample size for some data leads to high probability of error in the test results. However, based on the available data, it was found that a significant number of the current standards used may not be optimal (as indicated by the lower p-value); they are either too high or too low. Thus it will be beneficial for Esquel to revise the current standards.

Table 5.12
Explanation of terms for statistical hypothesis tests

Null hypothesis (H0): In hypothesis testing, the null hypothesis (H0) is a theory that has been put forward either because it is believed to be true or because it is to be used as a basis for argument. For our purpose, H0 is the statement "optimal wastage level = current standard."

Alternative hypothesis (H1): The alternative hypothesis, H1, is a statement of what a statistical hypothesis test is set up to establish. In our case, H1 is simply "not H0," that is, "optimal wastage level ≠ current standard."

Probability value (*p*-value): The probability value (*p*-value) of a statistical hypothesis test is the probability of wrongly rejecting the null hypothesis if it is in fact true.

Small *p*-values suggest that the null hypothesis is unlikely to be true. The smaller it is, the more convincing is the rejection of the null hypothesis. It indicates the strength of evidence for, say, rejecting the null hypothesis, H0, rather than simply concluding "reject H0" or "do not reject H0."

Conclusion: The final conclusion of a hypothesis test is often given in terms of the null hypothesis. We either "reject H0 in favor of H1" or "do not reject H0." If the conclusion "do not reject H0" is reached, it does not necessarily indicate that the null hypothesis is true (in our case, the current standard is optimal); it only suggests that there is not sufficient evidence against H0 in favor of H1. If the null hypothesis is rejected, however, it suggests that the alternative hypothesis may be true (current standard may not be optimal).

Source: http://www.cas.lancs.ac.uk/

Table 5.13
Detailed analysis of wastage

Garment type	Fabric or washing type	Current standard (%)	No. of samples	Mean (%)	95% CI (%)	p-value	Conclusion
Cutting and sewing wastage							
Woven	Solid	2.5	111	3.4059	3.1567, 3.6551	0.000	Reject H0
Woven	Check	3.0	123	2.5648	2.3889, 2.7408	0.000	Reject H0
Woven	Stripe	3.0	82	3.0699	2.8440, 3.2958	0.540	No reject H0
Knit	Solid	4	311	4.7555	4.6057, 4.9054	0.000	Reject H0
Knit	Check	6	12	4.6158	3.6731, 5.5585	0.008	Reject H0
Knit	Stripe	6	90	4.9469	4.663, 5.2308	0.000	Reject H0
Washing and additional wastage							
Woven	Chemical stone wash	3.0	—	—	—	—	—
Woven	Garment dyed wash	2.5	4	1.0417	0.7935, 1.2899	0.000	Reject H0
Woven	Normal garment wash	0.0	30	0.4297	0.2624, 0.5970	0.000	Reject H0
Woven	Heavy garment wash	2.0	4	0.4715	0.0442, 0.8988	0.001	Reject H0
Woven	Light garment wash	0.0	2	0.4018	0.0614, 0.7421	0.042	Reject H0
Woven	No wash	0.0	150	0.6916	0.5725, 0.8106	0.000	Reject H0
Knit	Chemical stone wash	4.0	3	0.3918	−0.0714, 0.8549	0.001	Reject H0
Knit	Garment dyed wash	5.0	5	9.3179	−2.8551, 21.4910	0.380	No reject H0
Knit	Normal garment wash	0.5	85	1.9806	0.8373, 3.1239	0.012	Reject H0
Knit	Heavy garment wash	1.0	17	1.2865	−0.2533, 2.8263	0.698	No reject H0
Knit	Sand wash	2.0	—	—	—	—	—

ANOVA and Regression Analysis

Fabric Wastage Regression Model Development

Fabric wastage is generated in cutting and sewing processes. In particular, five distinct types of wastage are identified: defective fabric, match loss, splice loss, end loss, and head and tail loss. In the cutting process, rolled fabric is first spread on a long table. The head and tail of each roll are usually discarded due to distortion of edges. This loss is then counted as head and tail loss. Because more than one fabric roll is needed for each order, it is necessary to overlap a new roll with the previous one. The corresponding loss is treated as splice loss. Split of roll due to defects in fabric may cause splice loss as well. On the basis of the size of the marker, each layer has one or more inches of cutting margin.

This type of wastage is referred to as end loss. After the fabric is cut to produce the various components of a garment, the cutting department checks each piece carefully; any defective piece is discarded and counted as defective fabric wastage. The outputs of the cutting department are components of garments. All the pieces are transferred to the sewing department for further operation. The sewing department does another check for defects. If a defective piece is spotted in the sewing department, it will be replaced by a new piece, which is counted as match loss.

Because each type of wastage comes from a different source, models were developed for each type. They were then combined to predict total fabric wastage level. However, the amount of end loss is not recorded, Because it is relatively consistent for each order. Hence, due to a lack of actual data, the model for end loss was not recorded. Overall, four models were developed.

1. *Defective fabric wastage model.* As mentioned earlier, defective fabric wastage is due mainly to defective fabric pieces in the cutting department. Four driving factors were identified. They were then included in the model.

   a. *Fabric categories.* There are two categories of fabric: knit and woven. Knit and woven fabrics are quite different from each other. Therefore, each order is classified on the basis of the fabric used.

   b. *Fabric type.* Fabric type is another major factor that influences wastage. There are three types: solid, striped, and checked. Customers specify the fabric type when they place their orders.

   c. *Fabrication.* Fabrication (such as fleece, jersey, or pique) indicates the look and feel of a garment. This is specified by customers when orders are placed.

   d. *Order size.* There is a learning curve in setup, and factory workers become more adept as time progresses. Therefore, order size is considered in the regression analysis.

Among the four factors, the first three are categorical, while the last one, order size, is not. In order to incorporate all factors into one model, the generalized linear modeling method is used. The response variable of the model is the defective fabric wastage level. The covariates include fabric type, fabrication, and order size. Two separate models were developed for knit and woven; therefore, the fabric type is not an explicit variable in the model.

Table 5.14
ANOVA analysis for knit defect fabric wastage

General linear model: knit defective fabric percentage versus fabrication

Factor	Type	Levels	Values
Fabrication	fixed	10	FLEECE, FRENCH TERRY, INTERLOCK, JACQUARD, JERSEY, LACOSTE, PIQUE, RIB, TWILL, unknown

Analysis of variance for defective fabric percentage, using adjusted sum of squares (SS) for tests

Source	Degrees of freedom	Seq SS	Adj SS	Adj MS	f-value	p-value
LogT Garment Order	1	0.0031963	0.0012493	0.0012493	6.91	0.009
Fabrication	9	0.0042863	0.0042863	0.0004763	2.63	0.006
Error	402	0.0726629	0.0726629	0.0001808		
Total	412	0.0801455				

$S = 0.0134445$; $R^2 = 9.34\%$; $R^2(\text{adj}) = 7.08\%$

Term	Coefficient	Standard error coefficient	t-value	p-value
Constant	0.032366	0.004248	7.62	0.000
LogT Garment	−0.003281	0.001248	−2.63	0.009
Fabrication				
FLEECE	−0.005315	0.003998	−1.33	0.184
FRENCH TERRY	−0.006854	0.002340	−2.93	0.004
INTERLOCK	−0.005139	0.003286	−1.56	0.119
JACQUARD	0.003387	0.003345	1.01	0.312
JERSEY	−0.001799	0.001855	−0.97	0.333
LACOSTE	0.011111	0.004882	2.28	0.023
PIQUE	−0.006556	0.002387	−2.75	0.006
RIB	−0.003250	0.002438	−1.33	0.183
TWILL	0.01992	0.01215	1.64	0.102

The model developed for knits is shown in Table 5.14.

Only order size and fabrication are found to be significant factors. All other factors are removed from the model. The final model for knit defective fabric wastage is

Knit defective fabric wastage =   (2)

    0.032366 − 0.003281 x log(ORDER SIZE)

    − 0.005315 x FLEECE − 0.006854 x FRENCH TERRY

    − 0.005139 x INTERLOCK + 0.003387 x JACQUARD

    − 0.001799 x JERSEY + 0.011111 x LACOSTE

    − 0.006556 x PIQUE − 0.003250 x RIB + 0.01992 x TWILL

When the fabrication of an order is fleece, then the value of *fleece* is set to one while all other fabrication values (*french terry, interlock, jacquard, jersey, lacoste, pique,* and *twill*) are set to zero. In this way, wastage level can be predicted for all possible settings.

By a similar method, the woven defective fabric wastage model is developed:

Woven defective fabric wastage =   (3)

    0.011596 − 0.003576 x CHECK + 0.004559 x SOLID

It was found that only fabric type is significant in the prediction of woven defective fabric wastage level.

2. *Combined model for fabric wastage.* To develop models for match loss wastage, splice loss wastage, and head and tail wastage, the same set of factors is chosen. Separate models are developed. Because the total fabric wastage is the sum of all kinds of wastage, a final fabric wastage model is obtained by combining all types of wastage.

3. *Model for total knit fabric wastage:*

Knit fabric wastage =   (4)

    0.094995 − 0.013211 x log(GARMENT ORDER SIZE)

    − 0.002346 x CHECK + 0.000181 x SOLID

    − 0.011489 x FLEECE − 0.011296 x FRENCH TERRY

    − 0.010256 x INTERLOCK − 0.000592 x JACQUARD

    − 0.003848 x JERSEY + 0.020077 x LACOSTE

    − 0.008642 x PIQUE − 0.008 x RIB + 0.038097 x TWILL

(See Table 5.15.)

4. *Model for total woven fabric wastage:*

Woven fabric wastage =   (5)

0.020777 − 0.004258 × log(GARMENT ORDER)

+ 0.001270 × CHECK × 0.000192 × SOLID

− 0.002396 × FLEECE − 0.003082 × FRENCH TERRY

− 0.001360 × INTERLOCK − 0.003062 × JACQUARD

− 0.000150 × JERSEY − 0.000707 × LACOSTE

− 0.001333 × PIQUE − 0.000224 × RIB + 0.013946 × TWILL

(See Table 5.16.)

Table 5.15
Model for knit fabric wastage

	Solid	Check	Stripe
Fleece	0.08369	0.08116	0.08351
French terry	0.08388	0.08135	0.08370
Interlock	0.08492	0.08239	0.08474
Jacquard	0.09458	0.09206	0.09440
Jersey	0.09133	0.08880	0.09115
Lacoste	0.11525	0.11273	0.11507
Pique	0.08653	0.08401	0.08635
Rib	0.08718	0.08465	0.08700
Twill	0.13327	0.13075	0.13309
Unknown	0.09518	0.09265	0.09500

Note: For each cell subtract 0.013211 × log(GARMENT ORDER)

Table 5.16
Model for woven fabric wastage

	Solid	Check	Stripe
Dobby	0.05510	0.04498	0.04943
Oxford	0.04938	0.03926	0.04371
Pinpoint	0.05056	0.04044	0.04489
Poplin	0.05060	0.04047	0.04492
Twill	0.04952	0.03939	0.04385
Unknown	0.05109	0.04097	0.04542

Note: For each cell subtract 0.005668 × log(GARMENT ORDER)

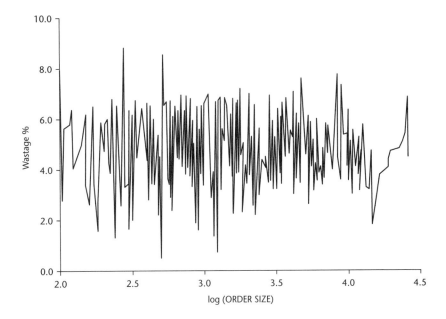

Figure 5.19   Variation of knit wastage

Variation Analysis of Fabric Wastage

After analyzing the data, it was found that the variation in wastage level is quite large. A plot of knit wastage versus order size is shown in Figure 5.19.

As shown in the graph, the wastage level varies from 2 percent to 7 percent. The 5 percent difference is considered large. Therefore, further analysis is conducted to identify practical reasons for the difference.

Because the whole process includes cutting, sewing, and washing processes, the variation in each process is identified. Pareto chart analysis shows that fabric wastage contributes significantly to this variation and, hence, fabric wastage is further exploited.

The decomposition of fabric wastage variation in Figure 5.20 indicates that, first, the variation of knit is higher than that of woven. Interviews with the factory operators revealed that knit fabric is elastic and unstable and therefore results in large variation. This in turn leads to large variations in defective fabric and head and tail wastage because they are directly influenced by fabric quality as well.

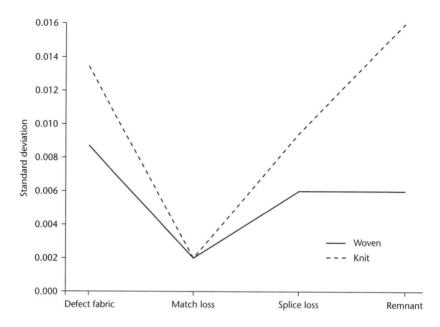

Figure 5.20   Decomposition of variation of fabric wastage

Garment Wastage Regression Model Development

In addition to fabric wastage, garment wastage is another important component that contributes to the overall wastage level. Garment wastage is generated as fabric is sewn into a garment. Its sources include sewing, washing, and defective fabric. Sewing and washing defects are those caused by each process, respectively. These three garment defects are counted in pieces.

Because the three types of garment defects are independent from each other and are counted separately, a wastage model for each type of garment wastage can be developed.

Sewing Wastage

Sewing defects are all the defects produced by the sewing process. The sewing wastage percentage is calculated to act as a response variable. Fabric type, order size, and fabrication are the explanatory variables. After analysis using ANOVA, it was found that the critical driving factors of the sewing wastage model for woven and knit fabrics are different. Factors that were found to be insignificant were not considered.

Sewing wastage model for woven =
$0.000251 + 0.000113 \times$ CHECK $- 0.000076 \times$ SOLID

Sewing wastage model for knit =
$0.0007489 - 0.00018414 \times \log(\text{ORDER SIZE})$

Washing Wastage

The washing process gives special effects to garments by washing them with chemicals. Customers indicate the specific washing methods to be used, and depending on the customer's requirements, garments may or may not go through washing.

Currently, washing is carried out in a batch mode because garment washers measure production in pounds of dry garments and each garment washer has a certain production minimum. Different washing methods correspond to the particular composition of the chemicals to be used, which is the major factor that determines the success or failure of the washing process. Inaccurate composition of washing chemicals will result in the wastage of a whole batch of garments. Hence, washing method is a critical factor for wastage levels in washing.

For example, among 309 orders that went through washing, 96 orders had washing defects. For 420 orders without washing, 11 orders had washing defects (see Table 5.17). The inconsistency results from quality assurance (QA) workers' miscategorization of defects, because QA workers categorize defects according to their experience. This analysis focuses on the orders that went through washing.

Within the database provided by Esquel there are fourteen types of

Table 5.17
Orders with and without washing defects

	Washing (309)	No washing (420)
With defects	96	11
Without defects	213	409

washing methods. Because the data display in a binary mode (with or without defects), the assumption of normal distribution is not valid. Therefore, instead of using regression techniques to develop a prediction model, the frequency of defects caused and the actual wastage level in washing were recorded and compared to the current standard of setting wastage levels (see Table 5.18).

After analysis, it was determined that most of the current standards for washing wastage are set higher than actual wastage levels. In addition, mature methods tended to have lower wastage levels, an intuitive result. However, it was also found that washing defects seem to be random. In the available data there are some outliers without obvious causing factors. This is due mainly to the difficulty of matching the particular washing effects with an accurate composition of washing chemicals. The order size is suspected to be another driving factor for washing wastage. However, this could not be verified due to the limited available data.

Although current standards tend to be conservative, on the basis of this study actual wastage is random and displays a binary mode. Due to the limitation of the data, the analysis of washing wastage is not conclusive. Based on the field study of the washing room in the factory, it is clear that there is no systematic way to collect data or do related analysis. So, in the washing stage the following measures are recommended to better characterize and reduce wastage:

1. Institute a procedure to record data on the difference between the effects due to customer requirements and those due to the washing method actually used, particularly the composition of chemicals.

2. Devise a detailed categorization of defects resulting from washing.

3. Develop a tracking mechanism for washed garments so that defects found by QA can be traced back to the actual washing method used and the composition of chemicals.

Fabric Defect Wastage

Some garment defects are caused by defective fabric. These defective garments are counted and analyzed separately. Using the percentage of garment wastage caused by defective fabric as a response variable, and

Table 5.18
Frequency of defects and wastage level in washing

Washing type	Actual (%)	Frequency (%)	Standard (%)
Knit wastage			
Chemical stone wash	0	0/3	0
Chalky wash	0	0/8	0
Crinkle wash	N/A	N/A	N/A
Enzyme stone	N/A	N/A	N/A
Garment dyed	0.02	1/5	0
Normal garment wash	0	0/85	0
Heavy garment wash	N/A	0/17	0
Heavy stone	0	0/5	0
Light garment wash	0	0/11	0
Na wrinkle free	N/A	N/A	0
Sand wash	0	0/1	0
Silicon wash	N/A	N/A	N/A
Tie dyed	0.004	2/8	0
Wrinkle free	N/A	N/A	N/A
Woven wastage			
Chemical stone wash	0	0/1	0.03
Chalky wash	N/A	N/A	0
Crinkle wash	0.01	2/7	0–0.01
Enzyme stone	0	0/2	0.03
Garment dyed	0.0001	1/4	0–0.05
Normal garment wash	0.002	2/30	0.005–0.03
Heavy garment wash	0	0/4	0.01–0.03
Heavy stone	N/A	N/A	N/A
Light garment wash	0	0/2	0.01–0.03
Na wrinkle free	0.02	2/2	0.03–0.05
Sand wash	N/A	N/A	1–2
Silicon wash	0.001	1/1	0.03
Tie dyed	N/A	N/A	N/A
Wrinkle free	0.004, 0.005	85/113	0.02–0.05

fabric type, fabrication, and order size as explanatory variables, a prediction model was developed:

Knit garment wastage caused by defective fabric =   (6)
$\qquad$ 0.020777 − 0.004258 x log(ORDER SIZE)
$\qquad$ + 0.001270 x CHECK + 0.000192 x SOLID
$\qquad$ − 0.002396 x FLEECE − 0.003082 x FRENCH TERRY
$\qquad$ − 0.001360 x INTERLOCK − 0.003062 x JACQUARD
$\qquad$ − 0.000150 x JERSEY − 0.000707 x LACOSTE
$\qquad$ − 0.001333 x PIQUE − 0.000224 x RIB + 0.013946 x TWILL

and

Woven garment wastage caused by defective fabric =   (7)
$\qquad$ 0.008702 − 0.001022 x log(ORDER SIZE)
$\qquad$ − 0.001232 x CHECK + 0.001582 x SOLID
$\qquad$ − 0.000818 x DOBBY + 0.003018 x OXFORD
$\qquad$ + 0.000069 x PINPOINT − 0.000852 x POPLIN
$\qquad$ − 0.000936 x TWILL

Data for models (6) and (7) can be found in Table 5.19 and Table 5.20, respectively.

Additional Wastage

Additional wastage can be caused by the following factors:

- Dyeing defects on finished garments
- Fluorescent garments
- Printing defects on finished garments
- Embroidery defects
- Wrong size (out of the acceptable range)
- Absence of marker
- Other defects

Other defects cannot be categorized as cutting, sewing, or washing process defects, although they can be caused by the washing or sewing process, because they are not identified until the checking procedure, which

Table 5.19
Model for knit garment caused by defective fabric

	Solid	Check	Stripe
Fleece	0.01857	0.01965	0.01838
French terry	0.01789	0.01897	0.01770
Interlock	0.01961	0.02069	0.01942
Jacquard	0.01791	0.01899	0.01772
Jersey	0.02082	0.02190	0.02063
Lacoste	0.02026	0.02134	0.02007
Pique	0.01964	0.02071	0.01944
Rib	0.02075	0.02182	0.02055
Twill	0.03492	0.03599	0.03472
unknown	0.02097	0.02205	0.02078

Note: For each cell subtract 0.004258 x log(GARMENT ORDER)

Table 5.20
Model for woven garment caused by defective fabric

	Solid	Check	Stripe
Dobby	0.009466	0.006652	0.007884
Oxford	0.013302	0.010488	0.01172
Pinpoint	0.010353	0.007539	0.008771
Poplin	0.009432	0.006618	0.00785
Twill	0.009348	0.006534	0.007766
Unknown	0.010284	0.00747	0.008702

Note: For each cell subtract 0.001022 x log(GARMENT ORDER)

occurs at the end of the overall manufacturing process rather than after each subprocess.

Originally, the potential driving factors were order size, fabrication, and fabric type. However, after the regression analysis was performed, fabric type and order size were excluded. The most important factor was found to be fabrication.

According to regression analysis,

Knit additional wastage =

$0.00199 + 0.002540 \times \text{CHECK} - 0.000848 \times \text{SOLID} + 0 \times \text{STRIPE}$

Table 5.21
Model for knit additional wastage

	Solid	Check	Stripe
Additional wastage: knit	0.014%	0.453%	0.199%

Table 5.22
Model for woven additional wastage

	Solid	Check	Stripe
Additional wastage: woven	0.0101%	0.023%	0.0133%

Woven additional wastage =

0.000133 + 0.000097 x CHECK − 0.000032 x SOLID + 0 x STRIPE

Data for these models can be found Tables 5.21 and 5.22.

Cost Analysis

After the new wastage model was developed, the derived cost savings were determined. To calculate these savings, two metrics were considered: fabric quantity ordered and ship-to-order ratio. These metrics were chosen because costs would be saved with less fabric ordered, but a lower ship-to-order ratio would result in fewer garments being shipped and have a negative impact on profits. These savings were calculated on the sample data set, utilizing several assumptions. By applying the new model, savings of US$XX were realized over the five months, which would translate to annual savings of US$XX at the Gaoming factory. If equivalent savings could be applied in the other XX factories, Esquel could observe savings of $USXX per year.

Recommendations

Process Capability

Within the data there is significant variation, which was an obstacle to analysis. The cause of the large variation comes from instability of fabric quality and a communication problem between different departments.

These two factors affect the wastage level, the number of defective garments, and the leftovers.

1. *Improve the stability of fabric quality.* To reduce the variation in the number of finished garments, the stability of fabric quality must be improved. From the data, for a similar order size the wastage in fabric defects and remnants (which depend mainly on fabric quality) varies significantly. On the basis of observation and information from the factory staff, it was determined that it is impossible for the production process to cause those defects. The most likely reason is unstable fabric quality.

2. *Improve communication.* The problem of leftover garments and fabric results in large inventory costs. These costs can be avoided, especially when they are related to the communication problem. The PPC sometimes does not have enough information from the sales department or from the customer when they place an order. If this is the case, it becomes hard for the PPC to make the order accurate. Communication between each department and the PPC is essential because there might be a need to recalibrate certain wastage standards as time progresses.

On the basis of the given data, several key wastage drivers were identified in each stage of garment production. A regression model based on these drivers was then developed using statistical techniques. The model can estimate the actual wastage level more accurately than the current standard. A more accurate estimate of the actual wastage level can help PPC allocate fabric more accurately, and hence reduce the amount of fabric wasted.

This reduction of wastage is from an aggregate level and without changing the actual production process. In other words, the model estimates the actual wastage more accurately than the current standards, but it does not reduce the wastage directly. To reduce the wastage incurred in each stage of the production process, improvement or reengineering is needed, which is beyond the scope of this case. Several recommendations, however, can be made on the basis of the findings.

First, the model identified the major contributors to the overall wastage, which could serve as pointers to focus wastage reduction efforts. (See the analysis results for the major wastage contributors discussed previously.) With such pointers, the wastage reduction efforts could be more targeted and effective.

Second, a certain amount of variation that cannot by explained with the model was found. Communications with the factory staff suggested that there were several potential wastage drivers that were important but unquantifiable. These potential drivers include the following:

1. *Fabric quality.* This contributes a lot to the wastage identified in the production process, but so far there is only a very rough categorization of fabric quality.

2. *Human factors.* Some workers are good at a particular set of jobs and not as good at others. If the right workers can be assigned to the right jobs, efficiency will increase and wastage will decrease.

3. *Garment complexity.* The number of components within a garment could affect the cutting and sewing wastage.

4. *Machines.* Different machines incur different levels of wastage. Better machines tend to have lower wastage.

Accordingly, the following measures are recommended to reduce wastage:

1. Fabric
   a. Enhance the quality of the fabric (this is the responsibility of the fabric mill).
   b. Classify and record fabric quality and attributes in a detailed and systematic fashion.
   c. Link the quality and attributes of the fabric to the requirements from customer orders to ensure that the right fabric is used for each customer order.

2. Human factors
   a. Set up a communication channel between PPC and the shop floor's production planning and control so that when an order is finalized the information can be transferred to the shop floor and optimal worker assignment can be achieved with enough time.
   b. Set up incentives for waste reduction. Shop floor workers know the most about specific processes, and rewarding workers who

find innovative ways to reduce cost can encourage innovation and enhance morale.

3. Garment complexity
   a. Characterize garment complexity by considering the number of components in each garment, the fabric type, garment size, and so on.
   b. Test the hypothesis that garment complexity correlates with wastage.

4. Machines
   a. Buy new machines with more advanced technology to reduce wastage.
   b. Record the performance of different machines. Given the improbability of renovating the whole factory, the coexistence of new and old machines is inevitable. A detailed recording of the performance of different machines can help to control the wastage.

There is still considerable opportunity for improvement in data definition, collection, analysis, and sharing about wastage, particularly in the fabric quality and garment washing processes. It is recommended that Esquel be more systematic about wastage information and that it provide the right incentives for managers as well as workers in order to gain their support in such a continuous improvement process.

Methodology

Although the new wastage model performs better than the old one, there is still room for further improvement. To better meet customers' order quantity requirements and reduce variation in the garments produced, continuous improvement must be implemented in the future.

Continuous improvement can be done in three steps:

1. Reduce process variation.
2. Reduce wastage level.
3. Refine wastage model.

The first step in continuous improvement is to reduce the process variation. Variation is an important factor in the overall wastage level because variation will propagate along the production line. Therefore, large varia-tion in each subprocess will result in amplification of wastage levels across the overall production process. A reduction in variation can improve the wastage level significantly by reducing the effect of amplification.

The next step is to reduce the wastage level. After process variation has been reduced, there will be a clearer picture of the difference between the new model with actual data and the old model. Therefore, the wast-age level of the new model can be lowered.

The final step is to refine the wastage model. After the first two steps have been taken, there will be a better estimation of tyhe wastage level. However, as both the process variation and the average wastage level of the model are changed, the wastage model must be refined with the new data.

Case 3: Sterling—Global Supply Chain and Production Management

Sterling Products, Ltd., is an apparel manufacturer and trader based in Hong Kong with worldwide manufacturing operations in Mainland China, Malaysia, Sri Lanka, the Philippines, and El Salvador. Sterling partner Mamiye Brothers is located in the fashion capital of the world, New York City. Both companies work together strategically to compete in the children's wear market. Mamiye's responsibilities include assessing market research, concept generation, customer support, marketing, sales, and design. It encompasses six strategic business units (SBUs), including brand names such as Mickey & Company and Jet Set. Sterling is responsible for manufacturing and production, including production and materials planning, production coordination and execution, delivery, and so on.

Both companies have historically operated in a disjointed fashion: Sterling's business is a production-driven process whereas Mamiye's is market driven. Because Mamiye representatives are more closely tied to the market in the United States, they are very sensitive to the needs of U.S. customers and thus respond when necessary. Sterling, conversely, as a group of manufacturing companies, strives to meet production and delivery schedules and to provide high-quality products to customers.

Because of the global nature of Sterling and Mamiye operations, the business process is highly complex. Information and materials must flow between different countries, which introduces significant communication barriers. Operating in such an environment can be very complex and difficult. Currently, Sterling is seeking simpler and more efficient modes of communication and information transfer.

Project Scope

The complexity of operations has led to a breakdown in communication and a lack of common goals (see Figure 5.21), which in turn have contributed to the current prototype production lead time of six weeks. Because the prototype developed by Sterling is used as a sample for Mamiye's customer, both companies depend on shorter development time. Prototype development time is the period between concept genera-

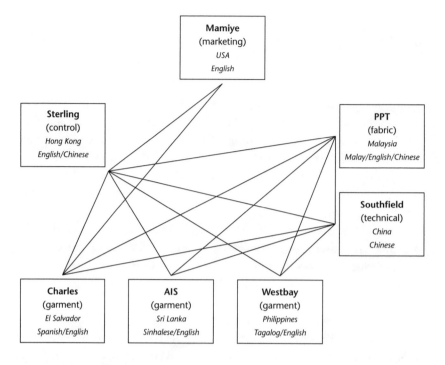

Figure 5.21   Sterling worldwide operations

tion, done by Mamiye, and the delivery of a finished prototype, done by Sterling, and prototype production lead time is defined as the length of time between Sterling's receipt of the inquiry from Mamiye and the delivery of the prototype. Also, the prototype in this case refers to samples presented by salesmen to buyers for order taking.

From both Sterling's and Mamiye's perspectives, there are three principal areas of potential growth: quality, profits, and prototype development time. All three of these are critical drivers in company success. By expanding these capabilities, Sterling and Mamiye have the potential to increase long-term return on investment.

To achieve effective use of the limited time (eight weeks) for the research project, the scope and objectives were defined. The project's scope was limited to the prototype development cycle, which includes Mamiye's operations and some of Sterling's operations involving the merchandising department, materials planning department, art-processing department (art room), and pattern-making department. Southfield, Sterling's technical center located in Mainland China, is also involved in the cycle. To focus the project, the ACC SBU was selected for the investigation.

The agreed-upon project objectives were as follows:

1. To shorten the prototype production lead time from six weeks, which is currently standard, to two weeks
2. To improve communication between Sterling and Mamiye

Deliverables

The project deliverables included a presentation and a written report that document the findings from the analysis and the recommendations made to achieve the objectives. A comprehensive discussion was also to be included in the written report.

As noted, the project scope first adopted was to reduce the prototype development time from six weeks to two or three weeks. In conducting a thorough analysis using the data from Sterling and Mamiye, a serious misalignment of goals was found, beginning at the top level and trickling down through the organization. The fundamental objective of the project was to assist Sterling and Mamiye in winning their markets, to provide the highest-quality children's wear to the population, and to provide higher value to their customers. The misalignment of goals and priorities is a strategy issue; thus, in order to create changes and win market share, the organizations must begin from the top. Both Sterling's and Mamiye's business strategies are constrained within the parameters defined by the market. To maximize the gains subject to these parameters, both companies need to build a relationship founded on trust (see Figure 5.22). Furthermore, they must be transparent to one another regarding costs and prices.

To help Sterling and Mamiye verify the validity and accuracy of their business strategy, the model suggests that the next level is measurement. It is vital for management to agree on the key measurements of success. It is management's responsibility to determine these vertices, such as market share, meeting production schedules, and quality design.

The level below measurement is structure. Both the structure and measurement ought to reflect the business strategy; that is, whatever structure is adopted or whichever measurements are taken, they must all be consis-

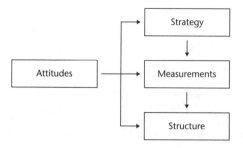

Figure 5.22   Building a relationship founded on trust

tent with the overall strategy of winning the market. The recommendations provided by the project deal with the structural issues, but the road map given suggests the need to transplant these structural issues to a higher level of business strategy. The model provides a way for the Sterling and Mamiye management teams to work jointly in order to align their goals and, ultimately, increase market share.

Methodology

The methodology used for the project consisted of the following steps:

1. Understanding the current practice
2. Analyzing the current practice
3. Reviewing process and system design
4. Validating the design

Understanding the Current Practice. Several interviews were conducted with the management and operations staffs of Sterling and Mamiye. In the fact-finding stage, functional requirements and constraints of the business as well as the current business processes were identified. The models and descriptions of the current operations are documented in the chapter's appendix.

Analyzing the Current Practice. To diagnose the prototype development processes, tables of non-value-added activities and information requirement and information flow lists were made. The highlights of the analysis results are presented in the next section.

Reviewing Process and System Design. Recommendations on system and process design and redesign were made according to the findings from the analysis and the functional requirements of the business. Several areas such as information and material flow, organization structure, and teamwork of the two organizations were addressed. A later section is devoted to discussion of these recommendations.

Validating the Design. The recommendations were discussed and validated with the management and the operations staff of Sterling and Mamiye to ensure their feasibility. Additionally, computer simulation technology was employed to validate the recommendations.

Results of the Analysis

Prototype Production Lead Time

The analysis verified that it currently takes about six weeks to deliver finished prototypes to the United States. The main reasons for this long lead time include incomplete inquiries issued from Mamiye, lack of information to order sample yardage or special trims, and lack of immediate action by Sterling.

Long Lead Time Items

At the time an inquiry is received from Mamiye, either the fabric, accessory, embroidery, or design is incomplete. Consequently, not all materials and information are available to begin prototyping. Especially when the fabric and some special trims (which require a long lead time to order) have not been ordered previously, an additional four to eight weeks are needed to ready the materials for production.

Release Pattern of Design Specifications

Currently, a batch of ten or more inquiries is released at one time. This large number of inquiries received by Sterling causes delays in prototype production. Particularly, the prototype at the end of the queue of inquiries will experience a long delay. Moreover, the design drawings are released in a batch mode that causes even longer delays. This is because some complex designs take a long time to be processed in order to produce the films for screen printing. Conversely, if it is found that the images on the garment do not fit into the actual garment size, the image sizes need to be adjusted, which can take a long time when approval from the design office is needed. The current release pattern amplifies the delay.

Design Changes

In many cases, production costs per unit specified by Sterling do not meet the target price demanded by the SBU manager at Mamiye. (Again, this price is driven by the market.) Thus, design changes are necessary in order to meet production costs, thereby increasing prototype development time. Currently it takes about three days to compute the cost figures, and the economical feasibility of the design can be affirmed thereafter.

Conflict of Priority Between Prototype Production and Order Production

The same resources (especially human resources) are used for both order production and prototype development at Sterling, so the merchandisers and materials planners have to prioritize the work coming in to manufacturing.

The profit and loss from the order production are tangible benefits and costs, respectively. The contracts for these orders are very formal and specify strict target dates, so the merchandisers feel the pressure to meet these dates. Conversely, the due date for prototypes is not as critical (at least from the perspective of the merchandisers), so there is a tendency to push the prototype production back when necessary. Furthermore, the costs of not meeting target dates for prototypes are not as tangible because these orders are more informal and less strict.

Serial Operations

Currently, the prototype development process is a series of steps. Product design, sample fabric preparation, cost evaluation, preparation of other materials, and production and delivery are done in sequence. It is understood that some activities have to be started first and followed by others; however, this does not mean they cannot occur concurrently, at least in some stages. Also, when a process is finished it is sometimes too late and too costly to discover that there are faults or that modifications are needed.

Working Relationship Between Sterling and Mamiye

Although Sterling and Mamiye have a long-term partner relationship, at the operational level they act as independent buyer and supplier. In other words, they have their own priorities and work for their own interests. More seriously, the lack of trust between Sterling and Mamiye can lead to serious communication breakdowns. More and more barriers may be produced and only suboptimizations of one or more parts of the organization will be achieved instead of partnership. Furthermore, as with the relationship between the companies, relationships between departments at Sterling experience the same problems.

Insights from the Analysis

Originally it was expected that some opportunities for improvement or reengineering would be identified from the analysis. However, instead of business processes, the working relationship between the two companies seems to be the more critical issue affecting the performance of prototype development. The traditional process flow seems to be the cause of the virtual wall between Sterling and Mamiye, but lack of trust may be the real factor.

Discussion and Recommendations

General Discussion

As has already been noted, the fundamental objective of the project was to help Sterling and Mamiye win their markets and to provide the highest-quality children's wear to the population and higher value to their customers. It was first thought that this could be done by reducing the prototype production lead time from six weeks to two or three weeks, but the project's analysis found a serious misalignment of goals across the organization and consequently determined that investing in technology and rationalizing the operations alone would not ensure the desired performance. The model discussed and presented earlier in Figure 5.22 was formulated.

Strategy

Strategy will provide direction for both Sterling and Mamiye. It is management's responsibility to formulate the strategy for both organizations. The strategy of reduction of prototype development time has to be affirmed by Sterling and Mamiye because the two organizations need the commitment to put forth effort and invest resources to realize the desired gains. This aligned mission needs to be understood by both companies. Without a well-defined strategy, the measurement for evaluating the achievement can never be determined. However, shortening the prototype development time is not sufficient as a direction for the company. Therefore, this tactical strategy needs to be linked with a higher-level goal in order to ensure that the business mission is served.

Measurement

Time, cost, and quality are always the performance measures for a business. The project's original objective was to address only one dimension of these measures, time, by shortening prototype development time. This focus alone would not have enabled a higher-level goal to be achieved. The other factors—quality and cost—are critical as well. A measurement for the higher-level goal is required to evaluate how the shortened prototype development time contributes to the business. The measurement could be the success rate of adopting new styles for the prototypes. The next question to ask would then be how the higher adoption rate contributes to the increase of market share. Is the higher adoption rate sufficient to explain the increase in market share? How do all these improve the profit margin? And how can both Sterling and Mamiye derive benefits from these?

Measurements should be determined with the formulation of a strategy. A tree of business strategies needs to be constructed and then the corresponding measurements can be defined for evaluation.

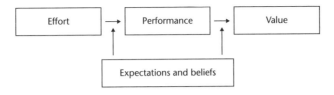

Figure 5.23   Relationship between attitude and behavior

Attitude: The Missing Link

Figure 5.23 illustrates the relationship between attitude and behavior. Without a positive attitude, people will not strive for change. The model in the figure highlights the importance of an individual's expectations and beliefs. Without positive expectations and beliefs, people will not link their efforts with their performance, and unless the target performance means something valuable to people, no one will care about it. In the context of this project, this means that the staff of both companies will work hard only when they believe and expect that good performance can be achieved or that something will really change by putting forth greater efforts. Furthermore, unless achieving certain performance or change brings them something valuable, staff will not care about the performance or the changes. It is obvious that expectations and beliefs affect behavior; hence, it is very important to tune the attitude of the staff of both companies to be positive. One way to achieve this is through training that examines employees' perceptions and helps them communicate with other team members and learn to trust them. Training is especially important for designers and production staff because they are always subject to others' stereotypes, and this perception becomes a barrier to communication and trust. It is recommended that some programs be offered to help the staff of both organizations develop their positive thinking and their relationships with others.

Structure

The analysis identifies the following four approaches to achieving the strategy:

1. Organization restructure
2. Teamwork enhancement

3. Concurrent engineering

4. Flow time reduction

These four approaches address and solve the problems and issues identified in the analysis. They are not mutually exclusive and ought to be seen as an integrated whole. They support one another and contribute to a reduction in the prototype development time. Together with the aim of aligning goals, the four areas of recommendation can be classified into three dimensions:

1. Managerial

2. Organizational

3. Operational

Again, these three dimensions are not independent but support one another and contribute to adopting a common business strategy.

Managerial. Relationships and trust will help the management teams of both organizations to be transparent. The parameters of customer values, manufacturing cost structure, and selling price parameters should be shared. The companies' visions and missions need to be aligned so that their mutual goals and objectives can be derived accordingly.

Organizational. Within the organizational dimension recommendations include creating either a global product development team or seasonal merchandisers and promoting teamwork.

The global product development team should be cross-organizational and cross-departmental and include all of the Mamiye SBUs and all of the ACC merchandisers, materials planners, art room technicians, and pattern makers from Sterling. These teams will help define accountability, break down organizational and departmental walls that restrict effective teamwork, improve direct communication among team members throughout the entire process, and involve more people at an earlier stage of development. Thus a larger number of key people will be involved in the prototype development from the beginning to the end.

An alternative is to change the scope of the merchandisers at the Sterling manufacturing site from product focus to seasonal focus. Currently, the merchandisers work exclusively with a particular product line, such as clothing for young boys or for adolescent girls, and so forth. However, the organization permits one merchandiser to be working on two or three seasons at any particular time. Consequently, the merchandiser who is pressured by the demands of order production for one season may not be available to assist a designer in the early stages of design for a different season. Seasonal merchandising solves this inconsistency. The benefits derived from implementing seasonal merchandisers make clear the importance of the two companies having similar goals and incentives. One of the potential difficulties, however, is that the merchandisers who work for more than one product line need to become familiar with other products and have extensive technical skills.

Alignment of goals can be achieved by promoting teamwork both within and between the companies. First of all, there must be a clear link between the product development team and Sterling and Mamiye. The team must strive to accomplish the same goals as the companies. An incentive scheme can be an option to promote teamwork. A nonfinancial incentive especially can create team spirit and help drive the team toward its goal. This along with the programs suggested in the previous section on attitude can help a real working team form.

Also, real teamwork requires more than just a working relationship. Sterling and Mamiye have to see themselves as standing on the same side rather than on opposite sides of the wall. When one of them profits, the other ought to profit as well. The rewards and benefits from a shorter prototype development time should be shared by both companies.

Operational. To facilitate communication between the team members regarding the tasks they perform, advanced computing technology should be applied. The design task and cost management should be addressed to reduce the prototype development time, especially for the tasks performed by Mamiye. A design support and cost management system can facilitate designers' use of the old modules with minimum modifications, and thus not only save time but also enable estimation of fabric consumption using existing data. Using the figures for fabric and accessory costs, embroidery and screen-print costs, and cut-and-make costs obtained from different databases, the preliminary garment cost can be estimated. This can save the time and cost of redesign efforts due to incompatibility of manufacturing cost and target selling price. Moreover, the standard module that the designer has selected can be a reference for the pattern maker to create new patterns for the prototype.

Information Flow

As already noted, information flow between Sterling and Mamiye operations gets caught in bottlenecks throughout the prototype development process. If communication begins when Sterling receives an inquiry, it is too late. Information should be shared earlier during the design process. Because changes cannot be made instantaneously, it is important to share information and obtain feedback about design, materials, and accessories before a formal inquiry is completed. Scheduled milestone discussions and unscheduled daily communication can convey and clarify the information required by both the design and the manufacturing partners.

Other information flow issues pertain to modes of communication. Both companies should utilize the available technology. Through video-conferencing, teleconferencing, and electronic mail, Sterling and Mamiye can share information and data in real time. Practically speaking, this can prevent many headaches and reduce housekeeping chores. The reduction in faxes and paper documents makes information organization much simpler. In addition, a better workflow system is required. Information completeness plays a key role in shortening prototype development time; both companies need to know at all times who possesses the required information. Using the available workflow technology, these information communication issues can be significantly improved.

Material Flow

Although the constraint of China's government policy does exist, it is still worthwhile to work out the direct material transfer. This would not only reduce the time by about two days, but would also save on overhead costs for receiving, storing, and dispatching the material in Hong Kong.

Work Shift

Once screen-print films are prepared in SFT, a pitch sheet can be sent directly from Mamiye by either air or e-mail. The whole process of screen printing can be done in SFT, and the batch size, and thus the cycle time, can be significantly reduced. Furthermore, because of the steady demand for embroidery, it is recommended that the embroidery section

located in SFT be expended with to save cost and time as well as to reduce the uncertainty of contractors' capacity.

Validation

Computer simulation has been applied to validate the recommendation and a reduction of 57 percent in prototype production time has been
realized in that simulation. It takes 16.3 days on average to deliver design prototypes to the market after the design specifications are finalized.
Development time can be further reduced by releasing the design information in smaller batches and by instituting a more efficient design practice at Mamiye.

Conclusion

The benefits of understanding the new model and of working toward
alignment of goals and priorities are clear. Not only will Sterling and
Mamiye win a larger share of the children's wear market, but they will
also achieve increased satisfaction and fulfillment by doing so. By having
a common strategy and understanding, these companies can carry out
policies and implement the necessary structure to achieve these gains.

A joint investment of resources between Sterling and Mamiye is a
must. By pouring investment into policies that create greater understanding, they will commit themselves to these policies. This is a long-term
strategy. Sterling and Mamiye are not independent of one another; they
need each other to succeed. Thus the burden rests on management to invest both financial and human resources.

Significant improvements and great long-term benefits are expected.
Serious consideration of the recommendations made in this chapter is
needed in order to realize the gains. The recommendations provide a
conceptual model to link the business mission with resources (both human and technological) and suggest in detail the use of management, engineering, and information technology to achieve the objective.

Appendix: Processes at Sterling and Southfield

Process at Sterling

When Sterling received the color standard from Mamiye, the merchandisers in Sterling would send a copy of the color standard to Southfield for reference. Then the material department would send the color standard to PPT. The time for these two processes would be about three days. PPT would then do the lab dip. About 20 percent of the lab dips took two weeks and 80 percent took twelve days. PPT would then send one copy of the lab dip to Mamiye for approval and another copy to Sterling. The material department in Sterling would receive an acknowledgment of the approval status from Mamiye. The lab dips would then be sent to PPT, where normally about 60 percent were approved for the first time. The time required was approximately ten days and 40 percent needed approval a second time, which required seven more days. When the lab dip was approved by Mamiye, the art room staff would keep one at the library and send one to the merchandisers.

After receiving the preseasonal sample yardage, the merchandiser at Sterling would need about one day to issue the sample fabric order (SFO). According to the information in the print fabric artwork in the SFO, the material department would do the sourcing and get the allocation decision. About 30 percent of these decisions were made in one and a half weeks and 70 percent NIL. Next, the material department would refer to the allocation decision and the SFO and issue a purchase order (PO) to PPT or the fabric supplier. About 5 percent of these orders were issued in one day and 90 percent NIL. For 10 percent of the orders it normally took ten days for the fabric (mostly from local fabric suppliers) to be ready in Sterling. For about 85 percent of the orders the fabric came from PPT and it took two to three weeks plus five days of transportation time. And for about 5 percent of the orders, the fabric came mostly from Taiwan and took twenty days. After Sterling got the fabric, the merchandiser referred to the inquiry and detailed line plan and issued a sample fabric requisition to Southfield (SF). The material department received the fabric and sent it to SF, which usually required one and a half days for transportation.

After receiving an inquiry or sample requisition form (SRF) from

Mamiye, the merchandiser needed about two days to issue the sample accessory order (SAO). The material department would then do sourcing according to the SAO and get the allocation decision. The material department would then issue the PO according to the allocation decision. About 70 percent of the trims were ready in about two weeks, and 30 percent were ready in one month. The material department would then arrange for transportation to send the trim to SF, which normally took one and a half to three days. Conversely, the merchandiser in Sterling would need about one day to issue the SFO. According to the information in the print fabric artwork, the material department would do the sourcing and get the allocation decision. About 30 percent of the decisions took one and a half weeks and 70 percent NIL. Referring to the allocation decision and the SFO, the material department would then issue a PO to PPT or the fabric supplier. About 5 percent of the POs were issued in one day and 90 percent NIL. The time it took for the fabric to arrive in Sterling was normally ten days for 10 percent of the orders, which mostly included those from local fabric suppliers; two to three weeks plus transportation time of five days for about 85 percent of the orders, which came from PPT; and twenty days for about 5 percent of the orders, which mostly came from Taiwan. After Sterling got the fabric, the merchandiser would refer to the inquiry or detailed line plan and issue the sample fabric requisition to SF. The material department would receive the fabric and send it to SF, which generally required one and a half days for transportation.

Once the SRF was received from Mamiye, the merchandiser issued the sample sheet to SF. After receiving the artwork from Mamiye, three parties would work simultaneously: the art room would plot the film for those fabrics needing screen printing, usually handling about three inquiries per day; the merchandiser would check the actual size of the artwork and adjust when necessary, then supply the information for embroidery (EMB) to SF; and the paper pattern makers would make the suitable size and style paper patterns or give the instructions to SF. About 80 percent of the paper patterns were made at Sterling (STG), and the remaining 20 percent were made at SF with the instructions given by STG.

After finishing all the preparation for SF, the merchandisers performed all the costing according to the cost of fabric and trims, cut and make, screen printing or EMB or both, and garment wash.

Process at Southfield

After receiving an inquiry, FR, AR, and a sample sheet from STG, the order control group at SF and Ms Tai would spend about three hours planning and scheduling, working out the salesmen sample loading, and translating the inquiry, AR, and FR into Chinese. All processes at SF followed the schedule listed on the salesmen sample loading.

As noted, about 80 percent of the paper patterns were sent to SF from STG. The other 20 percent were made at SF according to the instructions provided by STG. The patterns received would be recorded and then sent to the cutting room. The paper pattern makers made about two and a half patterns per day (needing about three hours for one paper pattern).

The workers in the cutting room would start to cut the fabric when it was available at SF. The time for cutting knits was normally one hour, or one and one-half hours maximum, per worker per inquiry. For woven fabric or jeans, the cutting time was one to two hours per worker per inquiry. Roughly 60 percent of the patterns were cut from knit and 40 percent from woven fabric. The cut fabric would then be divided into two groups: one group required no artwork, just sewing; the other group needed artwork.

About 70 percent of the sales personnel samples needed EMB. For EMB, if the hardcopy of the artwork, the pitch sheet, and the color combos were ready at SF, the order control group would distribute the artwork to the subsidiary factories to make the disk for the EMB path and contact the factories. The time for this process was around a half hour. The factories would then go to SF to collect the artwork. In most cases, this took about four hours (or half a day), and the factories normally needed one day to make the disk for the EMB path. The factories would send the disk back to SF for approval. The order control group would take about a half hour to check the disk and approve or disapprove it. If the disk was approved, it would be returned to the factory along with the fabric to make the EMB. The time for making the EMB was about six hours.

For screen printing, the workers in the print shop would make the screen frame first and then add a layer of coating after getting the film from Hong Kong. The workers would then develop the artwork on the screen for printing. The time for the whole preparation was about four hours. Next, the artwork was printed on the appropriate fabric according to the color standard, lab dip, and the translated FR. Normally the time for printing the artwork (assuming six colors) was two hours per inquiry per worker and three hours for drying.

While the artwork was being manufactured, the workers in the sewing department were sewing together parts that had no artwork and could be sewn together before adding the fabric with artwork. When the fabric with artwork was ready, the workers in the sewing department would sew together almost the whole salesmen sample, without the parts for SMO. Sewing time was normally about one day. The salesmen sample would then be taken to the other factory to undergo garment wash or prewash. Normally it would take about one day to finish the garment wash. Next, the salesmen sample would undergo the SO, an operation that needed to be done after washing. The time needed for SO was about four hours. Finally, the salesmen sample needed to be packed and ironed before being sent to the United States. Normally the wait time for sending the salesmen sample was one to two days, and after it was sent, it would be received in the United States after four days.

Notes

Chapter 1

1. http://www.lifung.com
2. http://www.flextronics.com/Design/intellectualproperty.asp
3. By request, the company's real name and identity have been changed.
4. *Standard & Poor's Industry Surveys*, Vol. 2, M–Z (New York: Standard & Poor's, July 1996).
5. Philip Mattera, *Inside U.S. Business* (New York: Irwin, 1994).
6. Unless otherwise noted, the source for this section is Standard and Poor's.
7. Ronald H. Brown and Jeffrey E. Garten, *U.S. Industrial Outlook* (Lanham, MD: Bernan Press, January 1994).
8. Keri Davies, "Foreign Investment in the Retail Sector of the People's Republic of China," *Columbia Journal of World Business*, 1994, 29(2), 56–69.
9. *Columbia Journal of World Business*, Fall 1994, p. 61.
10. The following sections on quantitative and qualitative analysis focus on Hong Kong competitors because little information about Chinese competitors was available.
11. Lou Cohen, *Quality Function Deployment: How to Make QFD Work for You* (Boston, MA: Addison-Wesley, 1995), pp. 36–39.

Chapter 3

1. By request, the company's real name and identity have been changed.
2. Stuart Chirls, "Cotton Summit: Big Surge for Mexico," *Women's Wear Daily*, September 22, 1998.

3. See http://www.ustr.gov/Document_Library/Press_Releases/2001/December/US_Trade_Representative_Submits_Report_to_Congress_on_the_Caribbean_Basin_Initiative.html?ht=

4. David Murphy, "Succeeding in China: PCH International—Up Close and Personal," *Far Eastern Economic Review,* July–August 2006.

5. Murphy, "Succeeding in China."

6. Supply Chain Management, SearchCIO.techtarget.com

7. Arthur Clennam, *Riding That Chain, CFO Asia,* June 2003.

8. Clennam, *Riding That Chain.*

9. From www.pchintl.com

10. From www.pchintl.com

11. Murphy, "Succeeding in China."

12. Clennam, *Riding That Chain.*

13. "Exel and the House of Fraser: RFID on Trial," *Datamonitor CommentWire,* February 20, 2004.

14. Mark Roberti, "Exel and Energizer Partner on RFID," *RFID Journal,* October 21, 2005.

15. George Day and Liam Fahey, "Valuing Market Strategies," *Journal of Marketing,* 1988, 52(3), 45.

16. For a detailed discussion on CAPM and beta, refer to Stephen A. Ross, Randolph W. Westerfield, and Jeffrey Jaffe, *Corporate Finance,* 7th ed. (New York: McGraw-Hill/Irwin, 2004).

17. Ross, Westerfield, and Jaffe, *Corporate Finance.*

Chapter 4

1. The client has asked not to be mentioned directly and has suggested using GTP instead. The names of the individuals mentioned are also fictional.

2. American Textile Manufacturers Institute (http://www.atmi.org), 2003.

3. Plunkett Research on Apparel and Textile Industries, 2003.

4. "Wal-Mart and Sweatshops," United Food and Commercial Workers, http://www.ufcw.org/press_room/fact_sheets_and_backgrounder/walmart/sweat_shops.cfm

5. Todd Furniss, "China: The Next Big Wave in Offshore Outsourcing," Everest Outsourcing Center, June 2003, http://www.outsourcing-asia.com/china.html

6. Wayne Forrest, "Analyzing the Pros and Cons of Outsourcing to China," *Purchasing,* February 3, 2005.

7. Forrest, "Analyzing the Pros and Cons."

8. Joint study by Lazard Freres (investment banker) and BG Strategic Advisors (logistics consulting firm).

9. Diana Farrell, "Beyond Offshoring: Assess Your Company's Global Potential," *Harvard Business Review*, December 2004.

10. Peter Weill and Jeanne Ross, "A Matrixed Approach to Designing IT Governance," *MIT Sloan Management Review*, 2005, 46(2), 26–34.

11. The client has asked not to be mentioned directly and to use ABC instead.

12. Boston Consulting Group, *Aim High, Act Fast: The China Sourcing Imperative*, March 2003, http://www.bcg.com/publications/files/Aim_High_Act_Fast_OfA_Mar03.pdf

13. Boston Consulting Group, *Aim High, Act Fast*.

14. "International Sourcing Spells Infinite Opportunities for Chinese Products," July 1, 2003, http://www.tdctrade.com/alert/cba-e0307h.htm

15. Boston Consulting Group, *Aim High, Act Fast*.

16. Harry E. Hough, *Purchasing for Manufacturing* (New York: Industrial Press, 1996).

17. For further information, refer to http://www.alibaba.com

18. *China Financial Reporting Update* (Hong Kong: Deloitte Touche Tohmatsu, 2003).

19. Alan West, *Managing Distribution and Change: The Total Distribution Concept* (Chichester, UK: Wiley, 1989).

20. Senior manager of global sourcing at Ford.

21. http://www.ponton-consulting.de/en/products/xe.html

22. Boston Consulting Group, *Aim High, Act Fast*.

23. Neal M. Goldsmith, *Outsourcing Trends*, Report no. R-1332-03-RR (New York: The Conference Board, July 2003).

24. Geoffrey A. Moore, *Crossing the Chasm: Marketing and Selling High-Tech Products to Mainstream Customers* (New York: Harper Business, 2002).

25. Bruce D. Temkin, "Outsourced Manufacturing: An OEM's Guide" (Cambridge, MA: Forrester Research, April 2002).

26. Temkin, "Outsourced Manufacturing."

27. Goldsmith, "Outsourcing Trends."

28. Theodore Levitt, *The Marketing Imagination* (New York: Free Press, 1993).

29. Paul Wiefels, *The Chasm Companion* (New York: Harper Business, 2002).

30. Tom Kosnik, partner matrix and strategies presented in Global Entrepreneurial Marketing class, Stanford University, Winter 2004.

31. "PSA Peugeot Citroen and Dong Feng Motors Expand Their Cooperation to Produce and Market New Citroen and Peugeot Vehicles in China," *Datamonitor News & Comments*, November 15, 2001.

32. Interview with Richard Dasher.

33. Interview with Liam Casey.

34. Interview with Jonah Houston.

35. "Alibaba Refining Chinese Business Culture," *Wall Street Journal,* January 13, 2004.

36. Interview with Jonah Houston.

37. Open Sesame! www.computertimes.com, July 10, 2002.

38. www.alibaba.com

39. Interview with Richard Dasher.

Chapter 5

1. For more information, refer to http://www.esquel.com

2. For further information on the concepts, theory, and applications of SVMs, see John Shawe-Taylor and Nello Cristianini, *Introduction to Support Vector Machines* (New York: Cambridge University Press, 2000). An article by Marti A. Hearst, Susan T. Dumais, Edgar Osman, John Platt, and Bernard Scholkopf, "Support Vector Machines," *IEEE Intelligent Systems,* 1998, *13*(4), 18–28, also provides a nice introductory overview on this algorithm and its applications in text categorization and face detection problems.

3. Steven S. Skiena, *The Algorithm Design Manual* (New York: Springer-Verlag, 1998).

4. WTO, "World Trade in Clothing," Table IV.54 (Geneva, Switzerland: WTO, 2003).

5. WTO, "Leading Exporters and Importers of Clothing," Table IV.69 (Geneva, Switzerland: WTO, 2003).

6. Country Briefings, Hong Kong, http://www.economist.com/countries/HongKong, accessed February 22, 2005; updated January 26, 2004 from Economist Intelligence Unit, http://store.eiu.com/index.asp?layout=country_home_page&country_id=HK&ref=country_list

7. "Profiles of Hong Kong Major Manufacturing Industries: Hong Kong's Clothing Industry" (November 23, 2004), http://www.tdctrade.com/main/industries/ipclot.htm, accessed February 22, 2005.

8. "The Opportunity and Challenge in Post Quota Time of Textile Industry," *CISMA News* (October 11, 2003), http://www.cisma.com.cn/media/enews04101101_e.htm

9. World Trade Organization, http://wto.org; Hong Kong Trade Development Council, www.tdctrade.com

10. T. S. Chan, "The Use of Channel Integration as a Strategic Option: A

Study of Hong Kong Clothing Manufacturers"; Staci Bonner, "Convergence: One-Stop Shopping in the Apparel Supply Chain," *Apparel Industry Magazine,* 1997, *58*(9), 82–93; Julia Gilkes and Kylie Uebergang, *Measuring Sustainability—A "SnapShot" of a Hong Kong Company: The Esquel Group* (Hong Kong: Civic Exchange, Ltd., June 2002).

Index

About the Authors

BEHNAM TABRIZI is Consulting Professor in the Department of Management Science and Engineering at Stanford University. His article in *Administrative Science Quarterly*, coauthored with Kathy Eisenhardt, won the 2001 Award for Scholarly Contribution for a paper that had the greatest influence on subsequent theory and research in the field of management. He has also published articles in *Harvard Business Review*. As a frequent traveler to China in recent years, Tabrizi has worked with more than 300 CEOs of the largest private and public Chinese companies on their corporate transformation. He has been featured in *China Daily* and on BBC and C-SPAN.

MITCHELL M. TSENG is Professor in the Department of Industrial Engineering and Engineering Management at Hong Kong University of Science and Technology (HKUST) and Director of the Advanced Manufacturing Institute. He coedited (with Frank T. Piller) *The Customer Centric Enterprise: Advances in Mass Customization and Personalization* (2003). Tseng has held senior management positions at Xerox and Digital Equipment Corporation and faculty positions at University of Illinois at Urbana-Champaign and Massachusetts Institute of Technology.